P9-DFV-371

THE
GREAT
BOOK
OF
QUESTIONS & ANSWERS

THE GREAT BOOK OF QUESTIONS & ANSWERS

HAMLYN

Published in 1991 by
Hamlyn Children's Books
part of Reed International Books,
Michelin House, 81 Fulham Road,
London SW3 6RB

ISBN 0 600 56125 9

Printed in Portugal

CONTENTS

Is the Earth really round?

The Earth is like a big round ball but it is not completely spherical. Because it rotates on its axis, it bulges slightly at the "waist" – its Equator. The polar regions are therefore correspondingly flatter. The Earth's diameter at the Equator is 12,756 km, while at the poles it is 12,713 km. The bulge was first discovered from differences in measurements of the Earth's gravity. Gravity is less at the Equator than at the poles because the surface is farther away from the centre of the Earth. Observations of satellites orbiting the planet have indicated that the Earth is in fact slightly pear-shaped.

Above: A cross section of volcanic rock showing the various strata

What is the Earth made of?

The Earth has a layered structure of crust, mantle and core. The Earth's crust is made up of masses of rocks and these are classified into three groups: "igneous" rocks, such as gabbro, are formed from molten materials at very high temperatures; "sedimentary" rocks, including shale, slate and limestone, are formed from layers of sand and mud turned to stone; "metamorphic" rocks are those altered by heat, pressure or chemical action, and include marble, quartzite and schist. The Earth's mantle is hot rock which slowly moves. The core is made of metals and may be liquid.

How much of the Earth is water?

The surface area of the Earth is more than half a billion sq km – 510,100,000 to be exact. Of this total, seawater covers 360,700,000 sq km, while land occupies only 149,400,000. Thus, 70.9 per cent of the area is ocean, 29.1 per cent land.

It should be remembered that while water has by far the greater surface area, things are quite different where volume is concerned. It has been estimated that of the more than 1,000 billion cu km which make up the volume of our planet, water occupies no more than $1\frac{1}{2}$ billion cu km, and this includes underground waters as well as rivers, lakes, seas, oceans, glaciers and the polar icecaps. All this water could be contained in a sphere of around 1,100 km in diameter (one-third the size of the Moon) – a mere bucketful by comparison with the 13,000 km diameter of the Earth. Only 3 per cent of this is freshwater, the rest salt.

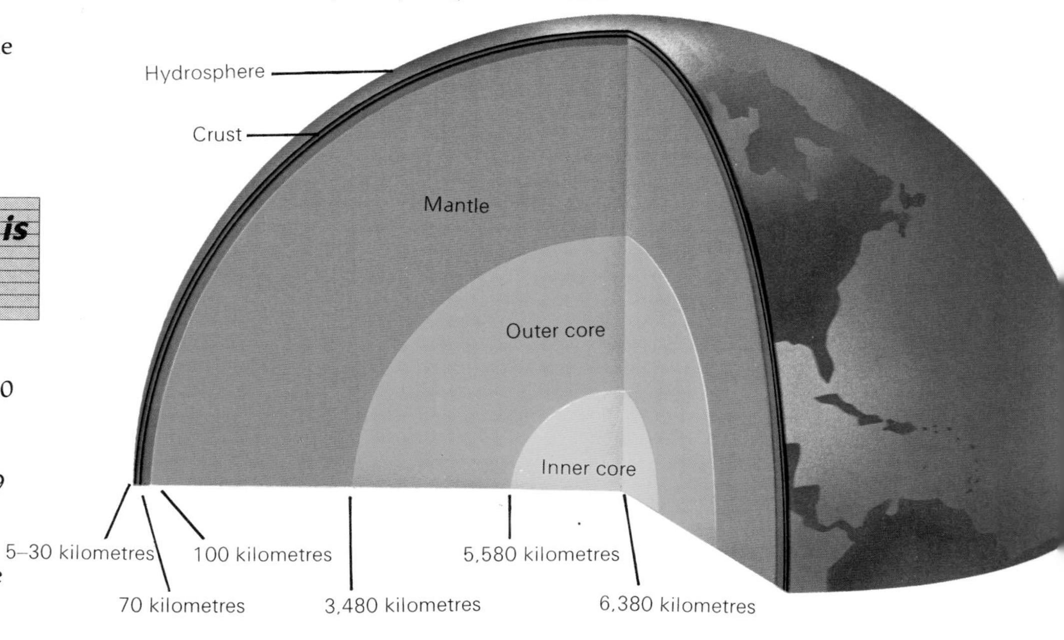

Bottom: A cross section of the Earth, its layered structure of crust, mantle and core clearly visible.

How old is the Earth?

Possibly the most definite (if not the most accurate) answer to this question was published by James Usher (1581–1656), Archbishop of Armagh, who wrote that the beginning of time fell upon the night before the twenty-third day of October in the year 4004 BC. However, geological evidence has demonstrated that the Earth is certainly much older than this.

The modern figures for the age of the Earth are based on the dating of rocks by radioactivity. The constant decay of radioactive substances into non-radioactive substances is the basis of this method. The radioactive element Uranium 238 is known to have a "half-life" of 4,500 million years, which means that a given quantity of the material will be reduced by one half over that period of time. Therefore, the age of rocks which contain Uranium 238 can be determined directly by measuring the amount of Uranium 238 and the amount of the non-radioactive substance into which it decays.

Promising results have also been obtained by other methods, and some rocks have been dated as 3,500 million years old. The Earth itself is probably some 4,600 million years old.

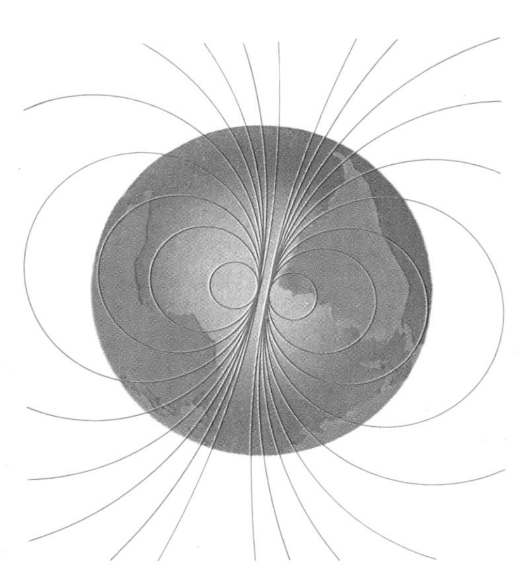

Above: The lines of force (shown in red) of the Earth's magnetic field

Why is the Earth magnetic?

The Earth behaves as though there were a gigantic magnet inside it. It has two "magnetic poles", which, at the moment, are about 1,000 km away from the corresponding geographical poles. They are found in north-east Canada and Antarctica respectively. The magnetic poles are not stationary: they move in small circles over a period of about 500 years.

The origin of the Earth's magnetic field has not yet been completely explained. One theory assumes that because of the Earth's rotation, the currents of molten material inside the planet act like gigantic dynamos, capable of producing the electric currents required to maintain the Earth's magnetic field. Another suggests that the planet's heavy core is made of magnetic material.

Below: Fossil of a vertebrate of the Permian period

Where are fossils found?

Almost all fossil remains of plants and animals have been enclosed in sedimentary rocks, which have been formed over millions of years by means of small particles piling up and consolidating to form uniform horizontal layers or "strata". The lower down a stratum of rock lies, the older it is (except where the layers have been overturned and their order has been changed). So normally, the fossils found in the deepest strata of rock are older than those in the surface strata.

In the deeper parts of sedimentary rocks, fish fossils are found; a little higher up are the remains of reptiles. Finally, at the top of this "geological column", are the fossils of birds and mammals. This arrangement makes it clear that living organisms did not all appear on the Earth at the same time, but that they followed at different times and only appeared after a long period of evolution.

What is seismology?

"Seismology" (from the Greek word *seismos* meaning a shaking) is the study of earthquakes. The shock waves produced by them are recorded on a special apparatus called a seismograph.

There are many centres throughout the world recording and studying earthquakes. The instruments used are able to detect even the smallest Earth tremors. Such waves prove that our Earth is not the solid and unmoving mass we might imagine. Seismologists can study them and use them to build up a picture of the Earth's interior.

Earth tremors can occur anywhere, but severe earthquakes, during which whole cities or towns may be shaken to pieces and thousands of people killed, are almost all limited to certain regions. These regions correspond to the major mountain ranges, volcanoes, and deep sea trenches. There, land is still being built up and subterranean (underground) activity is, therefore, most frequent.

How are earthquakes measured?

In 1935, thanks to the American seismologist Charles Francis Richter, the "magnitude" scale for measuring the violence of earthquakes was adopted. Instruments can reveal how much energy is released at an earthquake's focus. This scale is expressed in units (and fractions of units) from 0 to over 8. The energy of an earthquake of magnitude 3, for example, is the equivalent of that released by an explosion of about 20 t of TNT; one of magnitude 5 releases energy comparable to that of a 20 kt atomic bomb (the same as the bombs dropped on Hiroshima and Nagasaki in Japan in 1945). The strongest earthquakes have reached 8.6 degrees of magnitude, developing an energy 400,000 times stronger than one of magnitude 5.

Are all volcanoes the same?

The shape of a volcano depends on the type of eruption it produces. An "explosive" volcano rises very steeply while a "shield" volcano slopes gently downwards. Explosive volcanoes can be of considerable size. Examples include Fuji in Japan (3,776 m), Etna (at 3,263 m the highest active volcano in Europe), and Vesuvius in Italy (1,277 m).

These volcanoes are built up by a succession of layers composed of "pyroclasts" (volcano fragments) and cooled lava. This is caused by the initial explosive activity, followed by an effusion of lava. After every explosion–effusion cycle, there is a period of inactivity which can last for many years. During this time the viscous lava cools and blocks the vent of the volcano. Pressure builds up under the blocked vent of the volcano until there is a violent explosion.

Shield volcanoes, on the other hand, erupt quietly. Their lava is very runny and can flow for long distances before solidifying. This makes them broad but not very tall. The most famous shield volcanoes are in Hawaii and Iceland.

Facing page.
Top: The city of San Francisco, USA after an earthquake in 1906
Inset: A seismograph used to record the intensity of earthquakes

Below: A geyser in the Yellowstone area of the USA

Bottom: An Icelandic volcano erupting

Where do volcanoes occur?

There are around 600 active volcanoes in the world, including some which are dormant today, but which have shown signs of life within human memory. Dead volcanoes have shown no sign of activity within human memory.

Volcanoes are concentrated in three belts. The best-known goes round the Pacific Ocean and is known as the "ring of fire". Another belt runs from east to west through Indonesia and the Mediterranean. A third crosses the Atlantic Ocean from north to south.

How do volcanoes form mountain ranges?

When a volcano erupts, lava (molten magma from the Earth's mantle) flows out of the crater and runs down the volcano's sides, where it cools and solidifies. If the volcano remains active for a long time, different layers of lava will pile on top of each other or spread out. In this way a volcano erupting at the bottom of the sea can eventually grow tall enough to reach the surface. If there are a number of volcanoes close together, in time they will link up to form a chain or range of mountains.

What are geysers?

Hot springs, geysers or fumaroles are a sign that volcanic activity is dying out. Hot springs are found in New Zealand, Japan, Iceland and the USA. The minerals in the water are often deposited around the springs, causing terraces to form. Geysers are distinct from hot springs in that they send up enormous columns of hot water, sometimes at regular intervals: Old Faithful in Yellowstone National Park in the USA is probably the most famous. Fumaroles are holes in a volcano through which gases escape.

Above: A butte in Monument Valley

Facing page.
Top left: A crystal of sulphur
Bottom left: Stalactites and stalagmites in a cave in Italy
Right: Two varieties of opal

Why is Monument Valley famous?

Arizona's Monument Valley in the USA is one of the country's main tourist attractions and has been the scene for many Westerns. The familiar buttes (flat-top rocks) rise in some cases to over 150 m in height. These dramatic natural monuments are carved by wind and water as part of the process of erosion which has lowered the desert floor over a long period of possibly millions of years.

What are rocks made of?

The Earth is made up of rocks, and rocks are made up of minerals. A mineral has a definite chemical make-up, and is classified according to this. It is also inorganic, which means that it is not like an animal or a plant and is found naturally in the Earth's crust.

Each mineral has a particular set of properties, such as hardness, crystal shape, weight, etc., which are used to identify it. The form of a mineral is often expressed in terms which are self-explanatory – for example, columnar (shaped like a column). Coloration is a less reliable clue, since the same mineral can occur in any of several colours. However, colour can be used as a starting point for identification.

Where is the world's biggest cavern?

The cavern (or cave) reputed to be the biggest in the world is the Big Room in the Carlsbad Caverns in New Mexico in the USA. It was hollowed out by an underground river on three different levels, the lowest of which is over 400 m from the surface. This cavern is 1,250 m long, 200 m wide and at certain points reaches a height of 100 m. Just as famous are the Mammoth Caves in Kentucky, also in the USA, which are 290 km long and the Pierre-Saint-Martin caves on the border between France and Spain. These go down to 1,332 m below ground level.

What are stalactites and stalagmites?

Stalactites and stalagmites are formed in limestone caves. As water slowly drips through the roof of a cave, it dissolves the mineral calcium carbonate and re-deposits it on the ceiling, the walls and the floor, slowly building up structures called stalactites and stalagmites. Stalactites hang downwards from the roof of a cave while stalagmites rise up from the floor.

Sometimes, over the course of the years, a stalactite joins up with the stalagmite beneath it, thus creating proper "columns" (this is the technical term) which gradually grow thicker and become adorned with precious "lace". The white calcium carbonate is often accompanied by other minerals which add pale colours of many shades.

What is crystallography?

The crystal structure of a mineral is one of the most useful aids to its identification, and the science of crystallography (the study of the structure, form and properties of crystals) is most important.

There are six major crystal systems and their names describe their shapes – these are cubic, tetragonal, hexagonal, orthorhombic, monoclinic and triclinic.

Which is the hardest mineral?

The resistance a mineral offers to being scratched is called its "hardness". Hardness is measured against a scale known as Mohs' Scale, named after the German mineralogist Friedrich Mohs (1773–1839).

The relative hardness of minerals can be tested by scratching one against another, using the following set of minerals as standards. They range from the softest – talc, to the hardest – diamond: **1** talc; **2** gypsum; **3** calcite; **4** fluorite; **5** apatite; **6** orthoclase; **7** quartz; **8** topaz; **9** corundum; and **10** diamond. As a very rough guide, a fingernail will scratch up to hardness **2**, a penknife to hardness **6**.

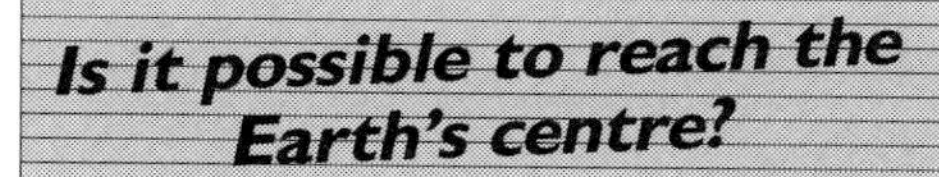

Is it possible to reach the Earth's centre?

There is a definite boundary line between the Earth's crust and the mantle. It is called the Mohorovicic Discontinuity, after the Yugoslav scientist Andrija Mohorovicic who first identified it in 1909.

American scientists once had the idea of drilling to the mantle to find out what it was composed of. This project was called Mohole (from the Mohorovicic Discontinuity). The scientists decided the best place to drill would be at sea at a point where the crust of the Earth was fairly thin. The technical difficulties of drilling at sea, and lack of funds, caused the project to be abandoned. The greatest depth reached so far is 9.7 km on the Kola Peninsula in the USSR.

What are gemstones?

Gemstones are minerals which have a good lustre or brilliance, are capable of being cut and are reasonably rare. Gemstones have been valued by people for centuries. Diamond (the hardest mineral) is the most valued gem.

With the advance of modern science it has been possible to produce a number of gemstones artificially, and manufactured "diamonds" are of great value to industry.

The collecting together of several substances makes up a mineral deposit. There may be only one mineral present but almost always there are several. Like other minerals, gemstones may occur either as veins within ordinary rock or as very big lumps.

Above: Mt Auzangate in the Andes of Peru, one of the world's highest mountain ranges

Where are the world's highest mountains?

The highest mountain range in the world is the Himalayas in Asia. It extends for 2,800 km from east to west and includes more than a hundred peaks over 7,000 m high. The highest peak, Mount Everest, is 8,848 m.

Despite the 4,000 m high passes, the Himalayas have always been inhabited. Buddhist holy men went there to meditate and settlements grew up around the monasteries and along the pilgrim routes. Over the course of centuries people have patiently built a perfect farming environment on the slopes that are exposed to the Sun, building terraces and making use of the thawing snow water. The invaluable mammal of the region is the yak, which is bred for meat, wool and milk, and is also a beast of burden.

Next to the Himalayas in grandeur are the Andes in South America and the Rocky Mountains in North America.

What is a river delta?

As a river runs its course, it picks up large quantities of earth, sand and gravel (known as "alluvial" material) and carries them towards the sea. Once it nears its mouth, the river's speed of flow slows down and it begins to deposit its alluvial material. If the difference between high and low tide is not very great at the river's mouth, the alluvial material will not be carried out to sea. The subsequent build-up of earth, sand and gravel forces the river to divide into rivulets to overcome this obstacle. At this point, the river forms the shape of the Greek capital letter *delta* (Δ) – hence the name of this formation.

If the tides are sufficiently strong to carry this alluvial material out to sea, it is then dispersed by ocean currents. However, the mass of water pumped into, and then withdrawn from, the river by the tides, widens the river at its mouth and forms an "estuary".

How are sea cliffs shaped?

If a coastline is made up of the same type of rock throughout, the motion of waves will erode it uniformly, to form a steep or even vertical coastline which can rise to great heights. The highest cliffs in the northern hemisphere are found in the Faroe Islands, but there are also imposing cliffs in Iceland and northwestern France. Cape St. Vincent at the southwestern tip of Portugal is a good example of the way cliffs can rise vertically from the sea.

If cliffs are made of rock which is not particularly hard, they cannot withstand the motion of the waves. The cliff base is especially vulnerable and in a relatively short space of time, the sea hollows out caves. Some can be of a considerable size. The layer of rock above the cave finally collapses, and debris from the landslide is broken up by the action of waves. Heavy winter seas hurl these small rocks and pebbles against the

Above: Limestone cliffs on the Normandy coast of France. These cliffs are a good example of how the continuous motion of the waves can erode a coastline composed of this type of soft rock.

newly-exposed cave wall and the erosion cycle begins again.

Cliffs can develop slowly over hundreds of years, but this is not always so, and in some cases they are worn away much more quickly. In certain places along the eastern coast of Britain, erosion can reach several metres per year – the lost village of Dunwich in East Anglia is a famous casualty of this coastal erosion.

Can wind erode rocks?

The Earth is subject to continuous change. Rain, rivers, waves, ocean currents, glaciers and wind are all wearing away its surface by their slow yet effective action. This action has been called erosion.

The force of wind alone is not sufficient in itself to wear rocks away. It can only do so by blowing sand and rock fragments against the rock faces. Wind-eroded rocks can vary enormously in appearance. They can look like enormous statues, piles of cushions or even animals but the wind can also erode the base of an isolated rock to form strange umbrella shapes called "wind mushrooms".

Below: Aladdin's lamp in Argentina, a rock form caused by erosion

Which are the coldest and hottest places in the world?

In the hearts of continents, far from the moderating influence of the oceans, climates tend to be extreme. Intense heating of the land in summer results in hot days, unrelieved by cool sea breezes, while temperatures often drop sharply at night. Cooling in winter in the middle latitudes can lead to the development of large, cold high pressure air masses, which are responsible for prolonged spells of freezing weather.

There are four main types of air masses. The "polar continental" air masses are cold and dry in winter and warm in summer. They contrast with "polar maritime" air masses which are moist and relatively warm. Similarly, "tropical continental" air masses, like that over the Sahara, are warm and dry, compared with "tropical maritime" air masses which are warm and moist.

The lowest temperature ever recorded (−88°C) was at a Soviet research base in Antarctica. Eastern Ethiopia has the highest average annual temperature in the world (34.4°C).

How does the sea affect climate?

The sea has a moderating influence on the climate of coastlands. This is because water heats more slowly than land, but retains heat far longer. By day, therefore, the land in coastal regions heats up swiftly and the lower layers of air are warmed. The warm air rises, creating a temporary low pressure into which cool air from the sea is drawn. At night, the land cools quickly and cold air flows from the land towards the sea, because the pressure gradient – the difference between high and low pressure – has been reversed.

Water also transports heat, and so warm ocean currents flowing towards the North Pole from the tropics temper the winter cold of some coastlands. In the same way, cold currents from polar regions chill subtropical and tropical coastlands in summer. For example, the Gulf Stream is a warm current which flows from the Caribbean Sea across the North Atlantic Ocean. Its extension, called the North Atlantic Drift, brings mild conditions to the British Isles and even to northern Norway. This is why London in England enjoys milder winters than New York on the east coast of the USA.

Below: Scorching deserts and the snows of Siberia illustrate the extremes of the world's climate.

What is the greenhouse effect?

Industrial development in the last hundred years or so has been largely fuelled by oil and coal. These fossil fuels have released their energy through combustion. Carbon dioxide is one of the many residues of combustion. 600 million years ago, in the Cambrian period, there was a high percentage of carbon dioxide in the atmosphere and very little free oxygen. If this situation were to be repeated, modern animals would not be able to breathe.

A high percentage of carbon dioxide would have another worrying effect. Carbon dioxide lets radiation from the Sun pass through it to the Earth's surface, but it reflects the Earth's radiation back in on itself. If the carbon dioxide concentration in the atmosphere were to exceed a certain level, the resulting "greenhouse effect" would cause the Sun's energy to be trapped in the atmosphere, and the air temperature would increase. This could lead to the polar icecaps melting, and the levels of the oceans would be raised.

What causes the seasons?

The Earth's seasons are due to the planet being tilted on its axis at an angle of $23\frac{1}{2}°$ with respect to the path it follows round the Sun. This means that the northern and southern hemispheres receive varying amounts of sunlight, and therefore heat, depending on whether they are tilted towards (summer) or away (winter) from the Sun.

Because of this tilt the Sun appears to be low in the sky in winter and high in the sky in summer. In the northern hemisphere it reaches its highest point on about 21 June. This is called the "summer solstice". It reaches its lowest point on 21 December, the "winter solstice". The summer solstice is the longest period of daylight, the winter solstice the shortest. In the southern hemisphere the dates are reversed.

Far left: Waste gases from a refinery being burnt off

Below: A diagram showing how different parts of the Earth receive varying amounts of sunshine through the year

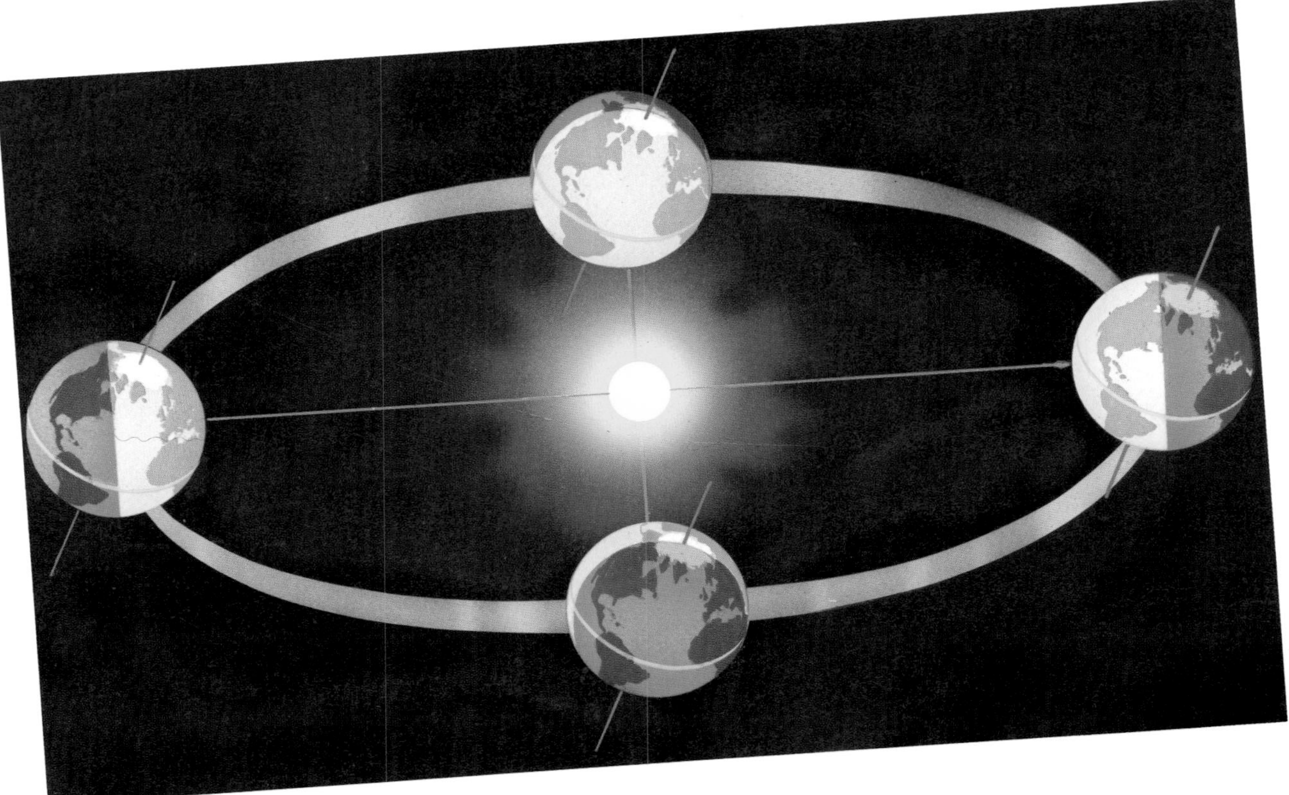

What is snow?

Snow is water vapour which turns to crystals of ice at low temperatures. Each crystal is hexagonal (six-sided), but there are thousands of different shapes.

A snowflake is formed from many snow crystals which stick together when the air is around 0°C. At lower temperatures, the snow crystals tend to separate, so that large, fluffy flakes are replaced by a "mist" of tiny snow specks. The crystals reflect and refract sunlight, giving snow its whiteness.

Below: Four hexagonal snow crystals

What are warm and cold fronts?

A warm front is the boundary between an area of warm air and the cold air *above* it, formed when the warm air flows into the cold. The warm air and the cold air move in the same direction, with the less dense warm air rising above the cold air at an average slope of 800 m in 160 km.

A cold front is the boundary between an area of warm air and the cold air *below* it, formed when the cold air flows into the warm air. The advancing cold air forces the less dense warm air to rise ahead of it. This rapid rising of warm air leads to quick cooling and cumulus-type clouds are formed.

Why do fogs occur?

On very cool, clear nights the air in contact with the ground may become cool, forming droplets of water which are left on the ground as dew. Mists and "valley fogs" are caused in the same way, especially when the process of cooling extends upwards from ground level or, for instance, up the sides of a valley. If the air contains a large number of specks of dirt and dust, fog will be the result. Fog also happens where warm air passes over cool surfaces, for example off the coast of Newfoundland where warm air from the Gulf Stream passes over the cold Labrador current.

Right: The atmosphere is divided into layers and each layer has particular characteristics. The first layer is the troposphere, whose height varies from 11–16 km. It is the layer where normal weather occurs.

The next layer is called the stratosphere, which extends from 17–63 km above the Earth. It is where the ozone layer, which shields our planet from ultra-violet radiation, occurs.

The outer layers of the atmosphere, 64–640 km above the Earth, are called the ionosphere. This contains layers capable of reflecting radio waves. Beyond the ionosphere, the exosphere extends for about 8,000 km.

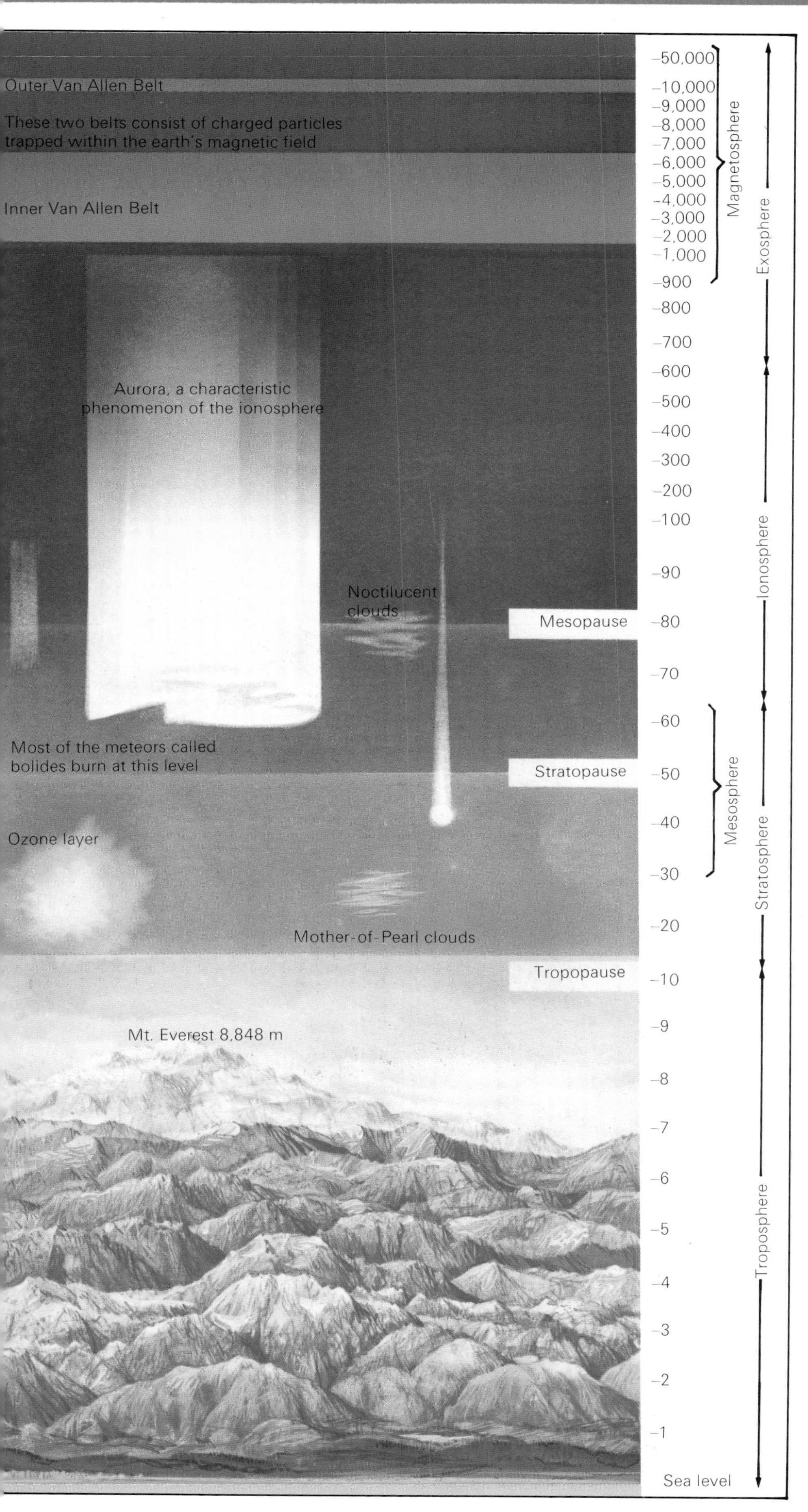

What keeps the atmosphere in place?

Gravity holds down everything on Earth and makes everything have a natural tendency to fall towards the ground. Particularly important is that it presses down towards Earth the "atmosphere" of oxygen and other gases which are necessary for life. If the Earth were much less massive, gravity would not be strong enough to retain an atmosphere, and the Earth would be a dead world.

The atmosphere not only provides oxygen for living, it also forms an insulating "blanket" around the Earth which prevents everything from scorching in the sunlight and freezing in the dark, as well as offering protection from other dangerous particles and radiation coming from space.

What makes it rain?

Water evaporates into the atmosphere from the sea and from the land. Warm air is able to pick up a great deal of moisture from large areas of water – for example, as it passes over the Atlantic Ocean. On reaching coastal areas, the air is forced by mountains to rise and hence to cool. As the air cools so the vapour condenses and turns into water again, to fall either as rain or snow, according to how cold it becomes. "Cloudbursts" are no more than heavy downpours of rain.

How fast can raindrops fall?

Large drops of rain fall on the Earth's surface at a speed of around 30 km/h. At this speed, raindrops can remove the top layer of soil to a depth which is dependent on the amount of resistance offered. The type of plant cover is important – leafy plants greatly slow down the impact of the rain so that it cannot erode the soil.

What is the difference between weather and climate?

While weather is the condition of the air at a particular moment or over a short period of time, climate is the average or usual weather of a place. Any description of climate is based, therefore, on statistics acquired over a long period, usually several decades. In classifying climates, climatologists are concerned not only with absolute values of weather features, such as temperatures and rainfall amounts, but also with the reliability of such features.

Climate is obviously related to latitude, because the Sun's heating is most intense in the tropics and least effective near the poles. This difference between the cold and dense air of the polar regions and the warm, light air of the tropics is responsible for the general circulation of the atmosphere, with a heat exchange between the tropics and the poles. Winds are the chief mechanism whereby the heat exchange occurs as they blow the air.

How are clouds formed?

There are many different kinds of clouds to be found in the troposphere (the lowest layer of the atmosphere which extends to a height varying between 11 and 16 km), but they are all formed in essentially the same way. Warm air can hold more moisture than cold air. If a mass of warm air is forced upwards and is cooled, the temperature falls to the point where some of the water vapour must condense out. At a height of 6,000 m or above, it takes the form of ice crystals – snow; at lower levels it condenses into water droplets – rain.

All our normal clouds and weather patterns occur in the troposphere. The only clouds which appear above this are the rare mother-of-pearl clouds in the stratosphere and the noctilucent (shining at night) clouds of the ionosphere.

Cirrocumulus

Cumulostratus

Cirrus

Cumulonimbus

How are gales measured?

The terms force 4, force 9, etc. mentioned in weather forecasts are of particular use to sailors who need to have advance warning of sea conditions. The terms do not, however, refer to the sea. They indicate wind strength and so, indirectly, the effects of wind strength on wave motion.

The English admiral Francis Beaufort compiled a scale in 1805 to show the various strengths of the wind. At Force 0 the wind is non-existent, and there is a calm. The sea is as smooth as oil, without the slightest ripple. At Force 5 the wind becomes brisk. The foaming waves become higher and there is some spray. The height of the waves is roughly 2 m. By Force 10 the gale is in full storm. The waves greatly hamper visibility. Height is 7 to 10 m. Few people, fortunately, experience Force 12. The wind is at hurricane force. The sea is wholly white, the air is full of foam and spray and visibility is reduced to practically nothing. Enormous waves swamp the coast and great damage is caused.

What are hurricanes?

A "hurricane" is the name given to a tropical depression – a region of low air pressure – that results in a violent storm caused by strong winds spiralling into the low pressure at the centre. Hurricanes are found mainly in the Caribbean and on the south coasts of the USA from June to October. A lot of research has been done into how to spot hurricanes in advance and so give enough warning to those likely to be affected.

In the Far East and the western Pacific Ocean, hurricanes are often called "typhoons", whereas in the area of the Indian Ocean they are known as "cyclones".

"Tornadoes" are violent whirlwinds which vary in their width from a few metres to 400 m. They move at speeds of 15 to 50 km/h. A water spout occurs when a typhoon passes over water and draws it up into the air , sometimes to a height of 1,500 m.

Above: A typical tornado cloud

What causes winds?

Winds are caused by differences in air pressure. Where the pressure is high, the atmosphere will tend to flow outward across the Earth's surface producing a wind. These winds tend to flow towards areas of low pressure, but the directions of the major winds are affected by the rotation of the Earth (the "Coriolis effect"). The winds blowing towards the Equator are north-easterly in the northern hemisphere, but south-easterly in the southern hemisphere. For the same reason, the movement of air round a centre of low pressure (a depression) is clockwise in the southern hemisphere and anti-clockwise in the northern hemisphere.

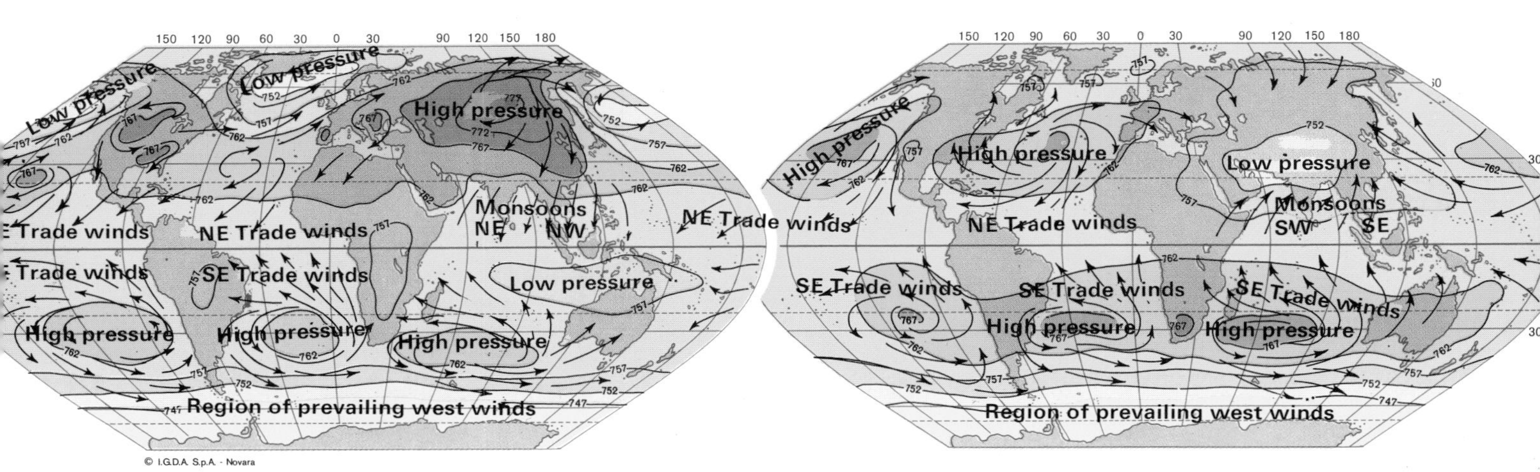

Below: Maps showing winds in January (left) and July (right). The numbered lines are isobars, connecting places of equal barometric pressure.

Above: A view of the Norwegian tundra

What is tundra?

In the strict sense of the word, "tundra" means vegetation consisting of mosses and lichens, typical of the areas surrounding the Arctic Ocean. In common usage, however, the word tundra refers to all the areas that have this particular type of vegetation.

The tundra extends from west to east, from Alaska across to the Kamchatka Peninsula at the extreme northeastern tip of Asia, forming a circle which is more than 9,000 km long inside the Arctic Circle. The largest area of tundra is to be found in the USSR, in the northern part of Siberia.

The tundra is usually divided into three zones: "wooded" tundra towards the south, bordering on the Scandinavian forests, where dwarf trees grow (birch, pine and willow); "grassy" tundra, an unbroken expanse of mosses, lichens and herbaceous plants which extends northwards to the permanent ice line; and "desert" or "Arctic" tundra, consisting of little areas scattered in the polar desert.

What is a glacier?

A glacier is a mass of ice that moves like a river, but more slowly. Glaciers are found in polar regions and the highest mountain ranges. There are glaciers near the Equator, but you have to climb 4,400 m up the Ruwenzori to find them. You only have to climb 2,500 m in the Alps and 1,500 m further north in Norway. Glaciers are found at sea level on the coasts of Greenland and Antarctica.

Special conditions are needed for the formation of glaciers. More snow has to fall than can melt and evaporate normally. This means that every year a new layer of snow forms on the old. Temperature and air pressure changes are the most important factors in the processes which now take place. The snow is first transformed into granular ice and then, as the layers sink deeper and deeper into the glacier, into highly compacted ice crystals.

Above: A magnificent iceberg moves slowly across the ocean

As the compacted ice crystals accumulate to a depth of 50 m, the surface layers begin to expand, extending their mass to occupy the largest possible surface area. This causes the glacier to move. "Mountain" glaciers slowly descend the mountainside, eroding the rocks beneath, and "continental" glaciers slowly expand from their centre.

Below: A large glacier surrounded by moraines (ridges of debris)

Why do icebergs float?

Water is liquid at temperatures between 0° and 100°C. At 0°C it freezes and becomes ice. At 100°C, it boils and becomes steam.

These limits may vary if the water is not pure. Salt water – sea water, for instance – does not freeze at 0°C. It has to be even colder, and to boil, salt water requires a higher temperature than ordinary water.

Unlike other substances, which usually contract in volume and become denser as the temperature drops, water expands and becomes lighter when it freezes. This is why ice floats and why, amazingly, icebergs sail through the seas – and why, of course, a gigantic floating mass of ice covers the Arctic Ocean around the North Pole.

Why do lakes never freeze solid?

Unlike most liquids, which become more dense the colder they get, water reaches its maximum density at 4°C. This means that at 4°C, a cubic centimetre of water weighs more than it does at any other temperature; therefore, it will tend to sink towards the bottom of a lake. As a result, when the water at the surface is colder than 4°C, it cannot sink downwards, because it is lighter than the less cold water below it.

If the air temperature falls below zero, the ice crust which forms at once is yet another protection, since ice is a good insulator and prevents the water's heat from escaping. So as a general rule, below a certain depth, lake water is kept at a constant temperature of 4°C – that is above freezing point.

Why is the North Pole warmer than the South Pole?

Polar regions are the coldest environments on Earth. Summers are short, and winters are long. The North Pole is warmer than the South Pole because it is mostly sea, and ocean currents are free to circulate with waters from warmer regions. The land at the South Pole, called Antarctica, is so cold that hardly anything can live there. There is also little available water because, although there is a lot of ice covering Antarctica, it is frozen so hard that no plant or animal can use it. Polar life is, therefore, nearly all in the sea. Since cold water holds more oxygen than warm water, there is a great deal of life in it.

Can trees grow on high mountains?

Height exerts a strong control on the type and abundance of trees. In highland rainforests the trees are widely spaced, rather like an English parkland, while in lowland rainforests they are thick and impenetrable. The highest that trees can grow is about 5,800 m. This is the tree line in the Himalayas, which, visually, is a very distinct line separating the trees from rocks and sparse vegetation. The tree line is much lower in the Alps due to their more northerly position.

Firs, pines and larches can survive in mountains because the trees have a conical shape, which allows snow to fall off without breaking their branches. They also have leaves reduced to fine needles and are rich in frost-proof resin.

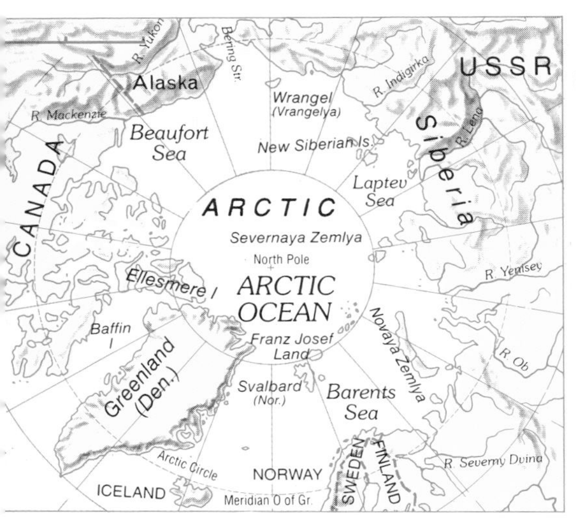

Above: An Eskimo igloo built from blocks of ice

Left: Maps of the Arctic and Antarctic

Below: A sno-cat attempts to bridge a crevasse

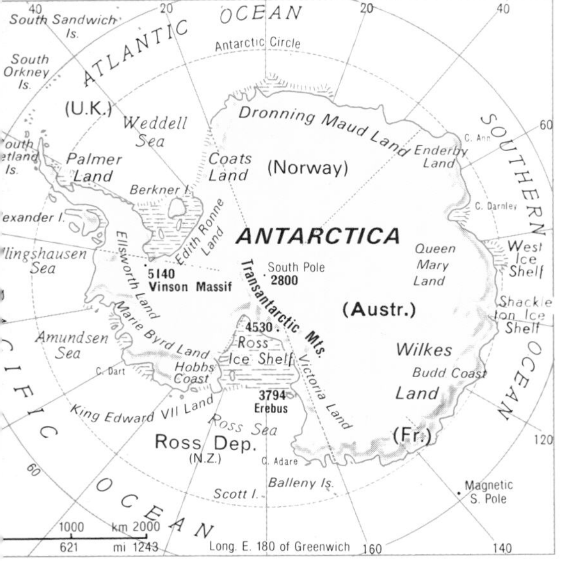

What is prairie?

"Prairie" is generally divided into two basic types: "real" prairie, of the temperate and continental regions, which is a huge expanse of rather tall grass (known as prairie in North America, "puszta" in Hungary and "pampas" in South America); and "steppe", which we find in the more arid regions, consisting of short grasses that do not cover the ground completely but leave large areas barren (like the steppe-lands of the USSR, for example, or the South African "veldt"). In the tropical zones, we find "savannah", where grasses taller than a man grow together with the occasional bush or tree.

The prairies have a vegetation consisting of herbaceous plants, the most dominant among them being grasses. However, in modern times, a great deal of prairie has been used for wheat crops and stock-rearing.

Left: An Alpine scene

Below: Horses grazing on the Oregon prairie, USA

How cold are mountain tops?

The range of environments found when climbing a mountain is very similar to that encountered between the Poles and the Equator. Starting at the bottom, where the temperature is the same as that of the surrounding region, every 300 m up the mountain the temperature falls by nearly 2°C. The temperature at the top depends on how high it is and on the climate at the base. The nature of life on the mountain will be defined by a combination of temperature, how steep the slope is, and how windy or exposed the site is.

How deep are the world's oceans?

The average depth of the oceans is 3,600 m, compared with an average land height of 760 m. The Swiss scientists Auguste Piccard and his son Jacques designed the bathyscaphe *Trieste* to explore the sea-bed. The occupants of the bathyscaphe rode in the sphere at the bottom of the craft. In 1960, Jacques Piccard descended in it to a depth of some 11,000 m in the Challenger Depth in the Pacific Ocean – the deepest point. Life existed even at this depth in the dark and near-freezing water.

Facing page, left: A diagram showing the relative size of the world's oceans

Below: Underwater exploration has led to a greater knowledge of the immense variety of marine life.

Which is the largest ocean?

The Pacific is the largest ocean of all, with a surface area of some 180 million sq km (162 million sq km excluding all its seas such as the Yellow Sea and the Coral Sea), an overall length of more than 16,000 km and overall breadth of about 17,000 km.

Indian Ocean
Atlantic Ocean
Pacific Ocean

Christened the South Sea by Vasco Núñez de Balboa, who saw it for the first time in 1513 from the hills overlooking Panama, the Pacific was also called the "Great Ocean" and the "Southern Ocean". But these names were all outweighed by the name Pacific, given by Magellan in 1520 because he was much struck by the calm of its waters, then almost entirely unexplored.

The average depth of the Pacific is over 4,000 m, and its waters contain the largest number of "deep-sea trenches" – the deepest is the Marianas Trench, at 11,033 m, followed by at least six others more than 10,000 m deep.

What is on the ocean floor?

The bottom of the ocean, or "abyssal plain", is covered with extremely fine mineral sediment or ooze, made up of volcanic dust or the remains of marine organisms. The deepest parts of the abyss are the ocean "trenches", which reach a maximum depth of 11,033 m in the Marianas Trench in the Pacific. These trenches are zones of crustal instability, being associated with much earthquake activity.

Many volcanic mountains rise from the abyss and some of them surface as islands (as in Hawaii). But the most impressive mountains are the long ocean ridges, extending from about 1,000 m deep to about 4,000 m, with occasional peaks (as in Iceland), emerging above the surface of the ocean.

Below: These two photographs show high and low tides in the harbour of St Mary's in the Scilly Isles.

What causes tides?

The tides are caused by the gravitational pull of the Moon and to a lesser extent the Sun. The Earth's gravitational pull is overpowered by the Moon's and the water is literally pulled towards it. The pull of the Moon also makes the Earth swing slightly and this movement throws out another mass of water on the side away from the Moon. As the Earth turns within these two "bulges" of water, each place experiences two high and two low tides every twenty-four hours. The incoming tide is known as the "flood" tide and the outgoing one as the "ebb".

The range between high and low tides varies from place to place according to differences in the shape of the land – for example, the depth of the sea bed or the width of a bay. The greatest range (over 16 m) is in the Bay of Fundy in Canada, while in the Gulf of Mexico it is only a few centimetres.

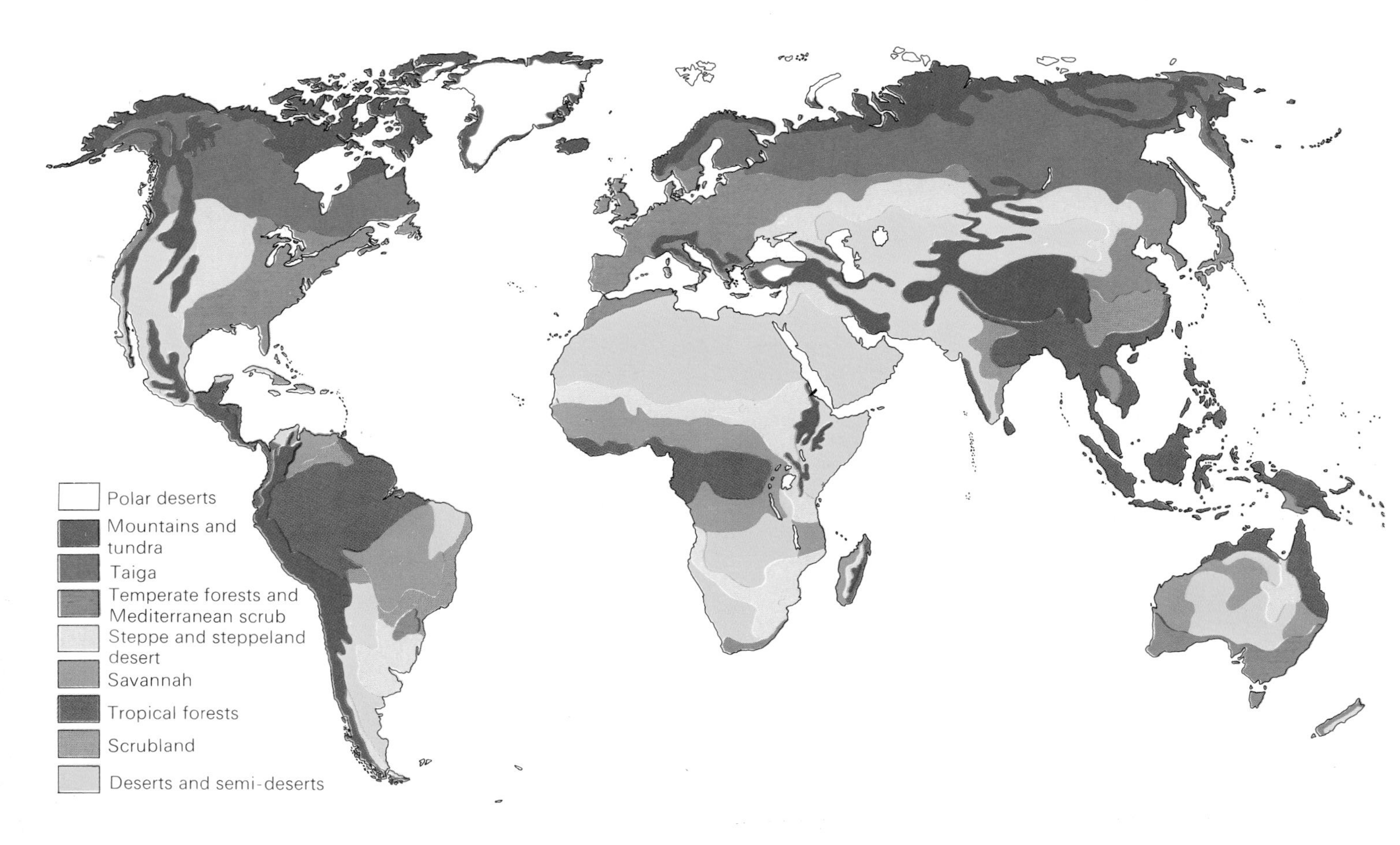

Above: A map showing the different types of vegetation found in different regions of the world. Deserts are marked yellow.

Where are deserts found?

The colours of some maps show the types of vegetation found in different regions of the world, and deserts are usually shown in yellow. The largest deserts are found in a zone between the fifteenth and thirty-fifth parallels, corresponding to the belt of permanent high pressure which surrounds our planet.

Chains of high mountains can also be the cause of very low rainfall, and, thus, of the creation of deserts. If a region is located in the lee of a mountain system, it only receives rain in exceptional circumstances, as the banks of clouds discharge their rain on the opposite side. These are the natural causes of deserts, but humans can cause them too by over-grazing and tree felling.

Does every continent have a desert?

There are deserts in every continent of the world except Europe. In South Africa, the Kalahari Desert is known for its red sands and extensive marshes. In Asia, virtually forming an extension of the Sahara, are the Arabian and Iranian deserts and the Turkestan, a great plateau furrowed by rugged mountain chains. Further to the east are the Chinese deserts of Takla Makan and the Gobi, with their dunes sometimes over 90 m high.

In America there is a vast desert area, covering the southwestern states and northern Mexico, flanked by mountains whose rugged slopes of bare rock divide to form winding valleys and deep canyons. The Atacama Desert in Chile is an extensive plateau reaching a height of 4,000 m with very cold winters and stormy summers. Finally, in Australia, almost the whole of the centre of the continent is made up of desert regions, with some vegetation.

Where is the world's largest desert?

The Sahara, the largest desert in the world (*sahra* means desert in Arabic), covers 9 million sq km with very fine sand, gravel and rock – a limitless expanse, dotted with dried-up bushes. The nights are cold in the desert, and the days blazingly hot. In the Sahara, the thermometer can hover around zero at night and reach 35°C during the day. In summer, the air temperature can reach an amazing 58°C. Survival can really become a problem, especially when the heat is coupled with sandstorms.

Are all deserts hot and sandy?

The cold polar areas of the Arctic and Antarctic are, in fact, deserts. They cover an area twice the size of Europe. All the water is locked in ice, and the little that is available is only released in the short summer. But as the ice layer never completely melts, it is not possible for vegetation to develop.

The Arctic desert, consisting of those regions of Asia and North America extending beyond the Arctic Circle, is covered with a layer of ice 2–3 m thick. This is a mere skin compared to the Antarctic, a continent of over 13 million sq km, buried under an icecap up to 2,000 m thick.

What is desertification?

Extensive farming or, conversely, its abandonment, can contribute to "desertification" – the creation of a desert in a region which already has a delicately balanced natural environment. Over-grazing and the felling of trees for firewood or to create new pasture can turn once-fertile regions into near-deserts. This is a very real danger and it is estimated that there are 20 million sq km of land at risk, an area twice the size of Europe. The United Nations has set aside special funds to help economically deprived countries, particularly in the Sahel belt, south of the Sahara in Africa, to fight against the onward advance of deserts.

What is an oasis?

An oasis is a fertile area surrounded by desert, where the presence of water enables vegetation to grow naturally. So a scattering of bushes and a lone tree beside a little spring is an oasis, just as a little wood around a pool or a short watercourse which surfaces for a few hundred metres before being swallowed up again in the desert is an oasis. The wide spreads of fertile land where human habitation is possible are also technically oases.

The typical oasis – with very varied vegetation of the herbaceous type and different kinds of trees, from date palms to fig trees and pomegranates – is to be found in the Sahara and the deserts of Arabia, Iran and central Asia.

The size of an oasis is determined by the amount of water present. These "islands of green" usually form in depressions which allow underground watercourses to surface, but they may also form in places where the watercourse is deflected by the composition of the rock and comes to the surface for that reason.

Below: An oasis on the banks of the River Nile

Below: Sand dunes in the Algerian Sahara

How are stars formed?

A star is formed from a whirling cloud of hydrogen gas and dust called a "nebula". Vast, cool pockets or globules of gas condense out of the nebula just as droplets of water condense out of a cloud of steam. Gravitational attraction gradually draws the gas globule into a denser, more compact, mass. As the globule contracts, its temperature rises. Eventually its core is hot enough to allow nuclear reactions to take place which change hydrogen into helium. Then the star begins to shine. It glows red, orange and yellow in turn as its surface temperature increases.

What is a red giant?

There comes a time, after millions and millions of years, when most of the hydrogen in a star is used up. Some very large stars may then explode dramatically as "supernovas", leaving behind very dense neutron stars. More often, such stars suddenly swell up to a gigantic size and become what are called "red giants". They are much cooler than before, but more luminous because their diameter is 200–300 times bigger.

Eventually, in a few thousand million years' time, the Sun will expand into a red giant. In so doing it will engulf the solar system up to and beyond the Earth's orbit. Earth and the inner planets will disappear in the hot, luminous gaseous outer layers. Then the Sun will contract and become a "white dwarf".

What is a white dwarf?

The core of a red giant is so hot that nuclear processes take place in it in which helium is converted into heavier elements until it is all exhausted. Gravity then causes the star to collapse. Eventually it shrinks to only a few thousand kilometres across. Its surface is very hot and it gives out a white light. Such a star is called a "white dwarf".

The matter inside a white dwarf is incredibly dense. One white dwarf, called Kuiper's Star after a famous American astronomer, is much smaller than the Earth, with a diameter of only about 6,500 km, yet its mass is equal to that of the Sun! It is so dense that a teaspoonful would weigh up to 10 t.

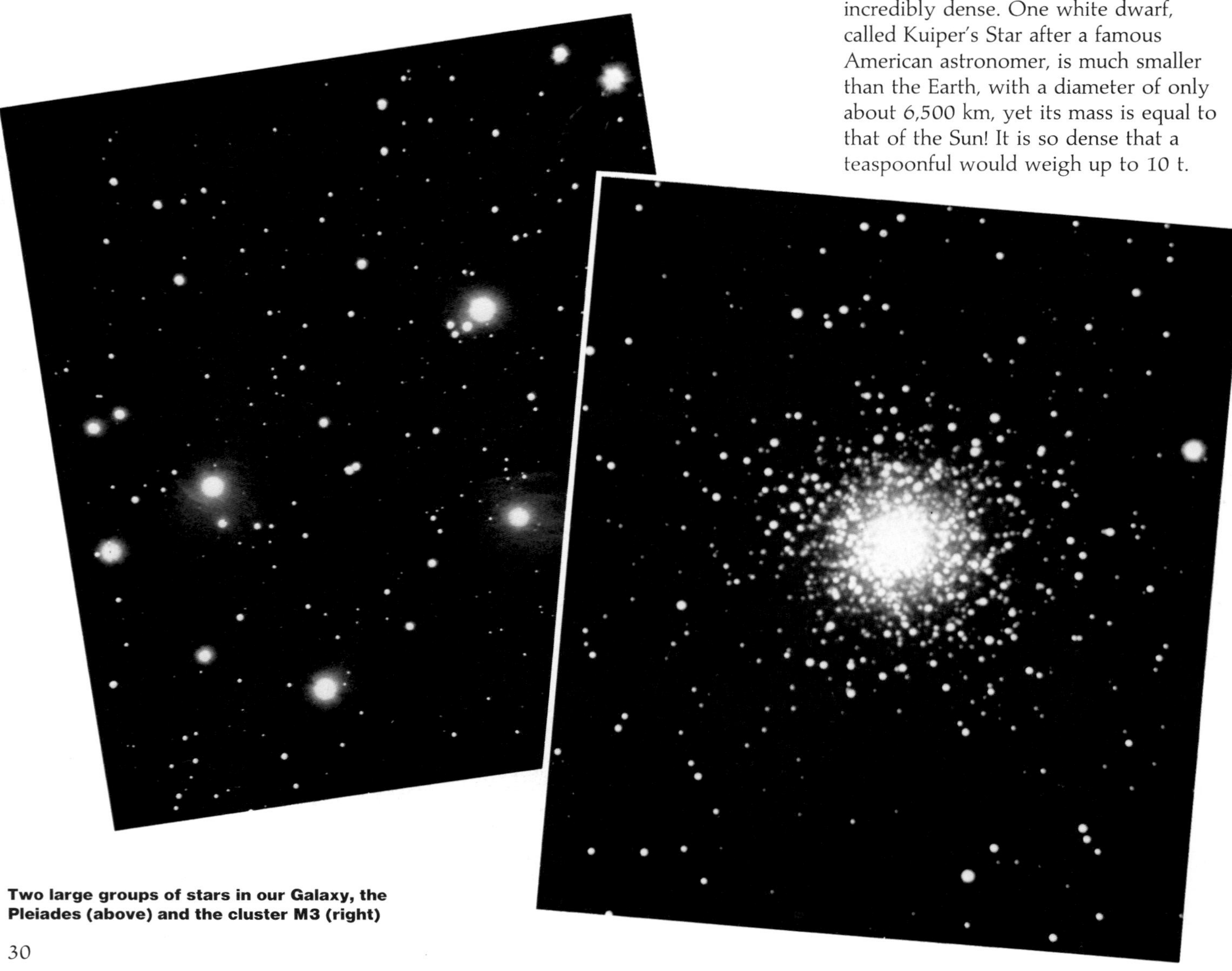

Two large groups of stars in our Galaxy, the Pleiades (above) and the cluster M3 (right)

How are black holes formed?

Stars which have a mass at least one-and-a-half times larger than that of the Sun usually have a much shorter life. They expand until all the fuel they contain has been burnt up and then explode. In this way they become extremely bright "supernovas". The cores of such stars then collapse rapidly in on themselves, reaching a density of hundreds of millions of tonnes per cubic centimetre and a diameter of little more than 10 km. These very dense objects are called "neutron stars".

If the original mass of the star is more than about three times that of the sun, the collapse continues and its density increases so much that a black hole forms. A black hole's gravity is so strong that it generates a cosmic trap from which not even light can escape, and where everything vanishes without trace.

What are quasars?

Towards the end of the 1950s, astronomers began to use powerful radio telescopes with which they could study distant radio sources in space. These mostly proved to be galaxies or clouds of gas. However, some radio sources seemed to come from luminous star-like bodies. So strange were their characteristics that astronomers were reluctant to admit that they were stars and therefore called them quasi-stellar radio sources or "quasars".

Quasars are millions of light years away from us and are the most distant cosmic objects known. To be visible at such distances, they must emit a huge quantity of light, more than 100 times greater than that of a galaxy – even though the quasar is hundreds of thousands of times smaller. If an explanation is found of this phenomenon we may be able to understand much more of the mysterious creation of the Universe.

Right: Some scientists believe that quasars are masses expelled by galaxies at a speed close to that of light.

Below: Other scientists think that quasars are very distant objects that can be seen because their light is focused by black holes (shown in blue) or galaxies.

Bottom: The "core" of the quasar contains electrons and protons which are trapped in a magnetic field (shown in red) and emit radio waves and light waves (shown in yellow).

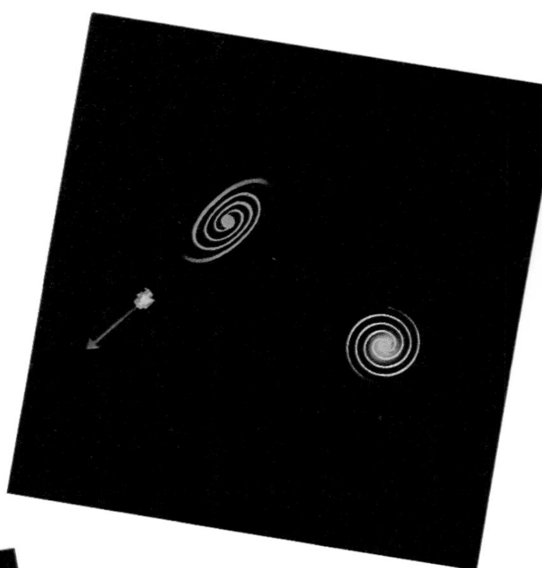

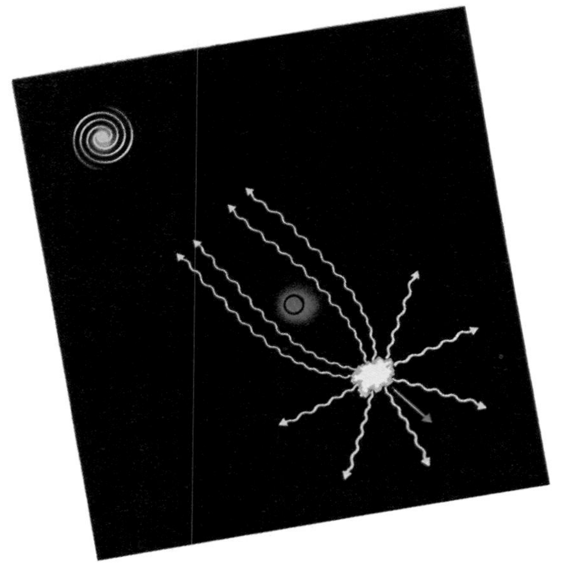

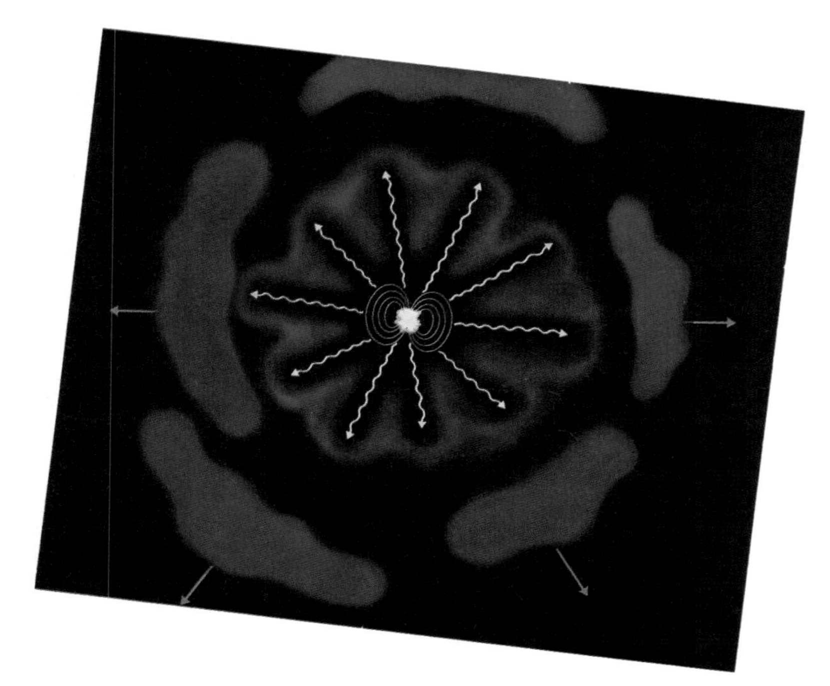

Left: How our Galaxy would appear to us if we could see it from above.

Bottom: A typical spiral galaxy. The blue colour of the arms is caused by the presence of young stars with a high metal content.

What does our Galaxy look like?

The stars we see in the sky belong to the galaxy or star system of which our Sun is a part, namely the Milky Way galaxy, or simply the Galaxy.

The Galaxy is believed to be a vast, flat, rotating disc with spiral arms, somewhat like an enormous Catherine Wheel. At the centre of the disc is a great spherical mass of stars forming what is called the nucleus. (The appearance has been likened to that of two fried eggs placed back-to-back.)

How big is our Galaxy?

To cross the Galaxy in a straight line a spaceship would have to travel for 100,000 years at the speed of light. The Galaxy revolves on its own axis once every 225 million years. It carries with it the Sun and its planets, so that we are in fact all cosmic travellers careering through space at a speed of almost 1 million km/h around the Galaxy. Overall, our Galaxy is composed of 100,000 million stars, but we can see only a few thousand of these with the naked eye.

How old are the galaxies?

Galaxies are of two main types, elliptical and spiral. Elliptical galaxies mainly consist of very old stars formed about 10,000 million years ago when "protogalaxies" (large clouds of gas resulting from the "big bang" which it is believed was the beginning of the Universe), started to contract under the effect of their own gravitational fields. In spiral galaxies, like the Milky Way, the stars in the centre are up to about 10,000 million years old, while the stars in the spiral arms are much younger, presumably because the arms were created after the galactic centre.

What are nebulae?

It is not possible to see as far as the centre of the Galaxy because between it and us there are obscuring clouds of gas and "dust", so-called interstellar material. These clouds are found in other parts of the sky too. They are called "nebulae", the Latin word for clouds. There are bright nebulae and dark nebulae.

The so-called Sword of Orion in the constellation Orion is quite a conspicuous bright nebula. It is a shining cloud which glows because of the radiation from stars embedded within it. Other bright nebulae glow simply by reflecting starlight.

Above: The famous Lagoon nebula which is more than 4,850 light years away

How is distance measured in space?

The nearest star (except the Sun) is called Proxima Centauri and lies about 40 million million km away. Expressing such distances in terms of kilometres is very inconvenient. It is like expressing the width of the Atlantic Ocean in millimetres! To simplify matters, therefore, astronomers express distances in terms of the distance light travels in a year – about $9\frac{1}{2}$ million million km. They call this unit a light year. Using this measurement, things are much simpler. Proxima Centauri, for example, lies just over 4 light years away.

Below: A modern observatory with its radio, solar and optical telescopes. In the sky above it are aircraft and balloon probes and satellites, which are all used for astronomical research.

When were the planets discovered?

Five of the planets, the "wandering" stars, were known to the ancient world because they can be seen with the naked eye. They are, going outwards from the Sun, Mercury, Venus, Mars, Jupiter and Saturn. Beyond Saturn, in the depths of the solar system, lie three more planets which have been discovered comparatively recently: Uranus (1781), Neptune (1846) and Pluto (1930). Earth itself lies between Venus and Mars.

How many planets are visible from Earth?

Venus, Mars, Jupiter and Saturn are among the brightest objects in the sky. Mercury, too, can occasionally be seen shining bright very low on the horizon. You can sometimes see Uranus if you have keen eyes and the night is exceptionally clear. In order to see Neptune, you need a telescope, but Pluto is beyond all but the most powerful telescopes.

The planets vary greatly in size, mass and distance from the Sun. Mercury and Pluto are much smaller than the Earth, yet Jupiter is more than 1,300 times bigger than the Earth.

What are asteroids?

There appears to be a "gap" between Mars and the inner planets and Jupiter and the outer planets. Within this gap, circling around the Sun in orbit, is a belt of small bodies called "asteroids", also known as minor planets and "planetoids". More than 3,000 asteroids have been found, but it has been estimated that there may be hundreds of thousands. Many which have been identified are only a few kilometres in diameter, and the rest may be smaller, which is why they have not been found.

Most asteroids are thought to be rocky fragments, some of which may be covered in ice or frozen gas. Originally, it was thought that asteroids were the remains of a large planet, but this now seems unlikely. It is likely that they were formed at the same time as the planets.

Below left: In the early days of astronomy, scientists had only very basic equipment.

Below right: An ancient observatory of the Mayan civilization in Central America

Which is the biggest asteroid?

The biggest asteroid and the first to be discovered (1801) was Ceres, which has a diameter of about 1,000 km. Within six years, three more were discovered: Pallas (540 km), Vesta (515 km), and Juno (225 km). One of the best-known asteroids is Eros, which is a cigar-shaped body about 30 km long. It is interesting historically because earlier this century observations of it were used in estimating the distance of the Earth from the Sun. Eros approaches within 25 million km of the Earth, while some asteroids approach even closer.

Which planet has the longest orbit?

Like the Earth, the planets have a dual motion, travelling in orbit around the Sun to make their "year" and turning on their own axes to make their "day". The farther the planets are from the Sun, the longer is their orbit, and therefore their orbital period, or year. At an average distance of 5,900 million km, Pluto has the longest orbit and its year is equivalent to almost 248 Earth-years.

Pluto is usually the most distant planet, but at some points in its orbit it is nearer to the Sun than Neptune. Its distance and the fact that it is the smallest planet, smaller even than our Moon, make it very difficult to observe from Earth.

Facing page: This diagram illustrates the distances of the planets from the Sun. As the orbits are elliptical, the distances are not constant. The values shown are minimum and maximum distances expressed in millions of kilometres.

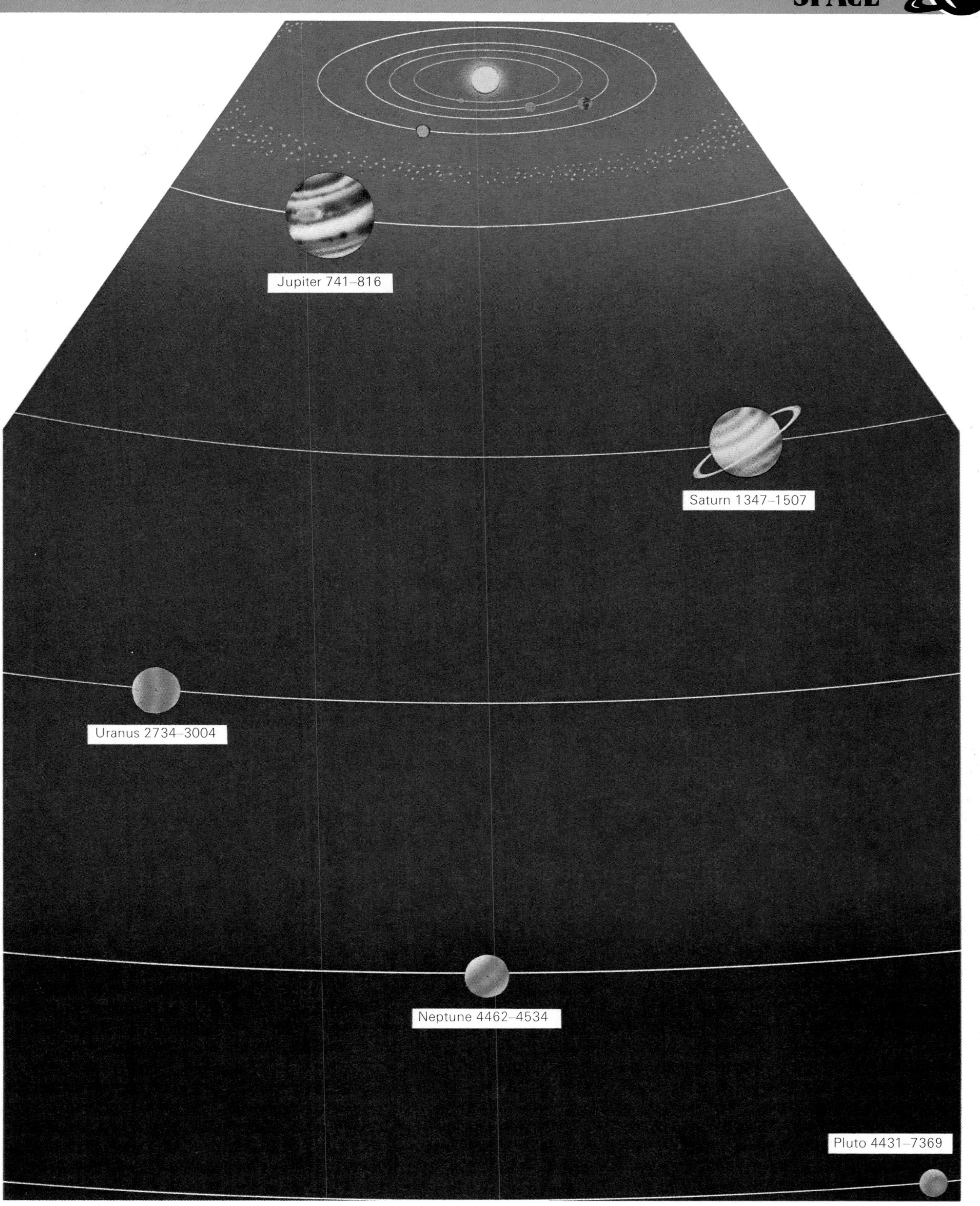
Jupiter 741–816
Saturn 1347–1507
Uranus 2734–3004
Neptune 4462–4534
Pluto 4431–7369

What are Saturn's rings made of?

Saturn is the planet in the solar system sixth furthest from the Sun. The most striking characteristic of this planet is its rings, which appear through a telescope as three separate, concentric and luminous bands closely encircling the planet and extending to a distance of 77,000 km from its equator.

The pictures taken by the Voyager space probes show that in fact these bands extend for 200,000 km and are made up of a multitude of thinner rings of dust, ice crystals and sometimes rock fragments.

Top right: Saturn photographed by the probe Voyager 1 using a technique that intensifies colours and highlights detail

Above: The atmosphere around Venus is thick with clouds.

Why did space probes visit Venus?

Venus approaches closer to Earth than any other planet. Despite this, little was known about it until recently because it is shrouded in dense cloud. This reflects much of the sunlight falling on it, making it appear bright, but also hiding its surface. However, the surface has now been mapped using radar and a number of probes have visited Venus. Its size and density are similar to Earth's, and it seems to have a similar composition. The radar maps show many large craters, huge basins, mountain ranges, volcanoes and canyons including one 1,500 km long. The rocky surface is very hot, about 480°C.

How hot is Mercury?

Being so close to the Sun, Mercury is difficult to observe from Earth and most information about it has come from the Mariner 10 probe. Like the Moon, its surface is heavily cratered from meteorite bombardment, and it contains basins similar to the Moon's "maria" (see page 38), including the 1,400 km wide Caloris basin. The surface temperature can rise to over 400°C on the sunlit face and falls to −170°C on the opposite side. Since it also has no permanent atmosphere, Mercury is a most inhospitable planet.

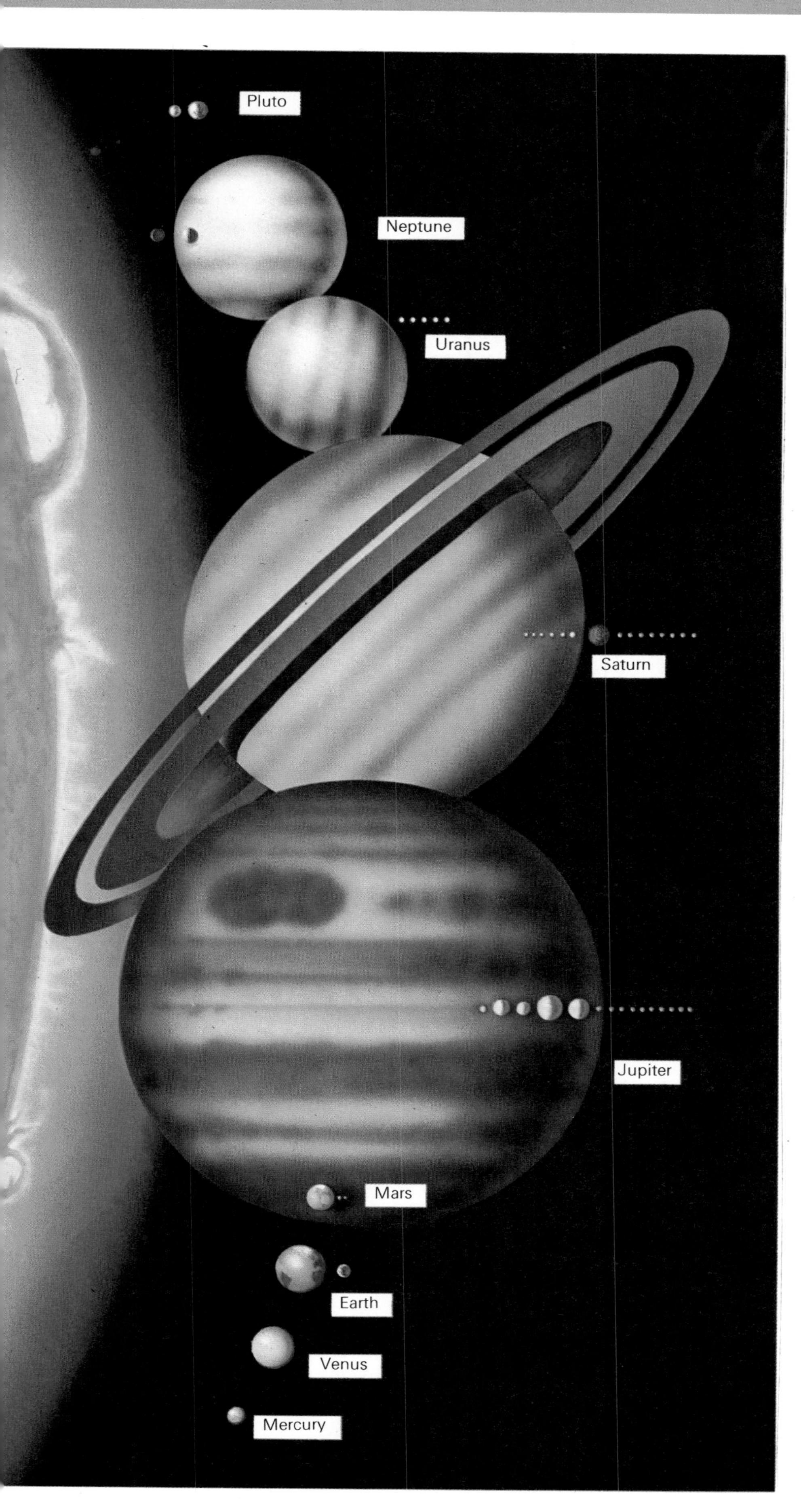

Which is the biggest planet?

Beyond the orbit of Mars (and separated from it by a wide asteroid belt containing innumerable fragments of rock and frozen gases) lies Jupiter, the largest of all the celestial bodies orbiting the Sun. This enormous spherical mass of gas is more than a planet, it is a "failed" star. Its chemical composition of 80 per cent hydrogen and 20 per cent helium is, in fact, similar to that of the Sun, and it is very likely that Jupiter would have become a star had it been bigger. However, its mass was not sufficient to set off the thermonuclear reactions that occur within stars and fuel them for thousands of millions of years.

Jupiter is bigger than all the other planets put together. Its most prominent feature – the Great Red Spot – has a surface area as big as the Earth's, and is a vast whirling eddy of cloud.

Has there ever been life on Mars?

Beyond Earth lies Mars, the planet closest to us. Often called the Red Planet, it is much smaller than Earth. It has only a thin atmosphere, and so its surface can be seen through a telescope. Its clouds, polar icecaps, the seasonal changes in the size of the icecaps and in some surface markings, led people years ago to compare it to Earth and to imagine the existence of Martian civilizations. Unfortunately, later evidence, particularly from the 1976 Viking landings, has dispelled this myth. Indeed, nó trace of any kind of life has yet been found on Mars – though scientists are keen to examine the polar icecaps more closely.

Left: A diagram showing the nine planets of the solar system to scale with their respective satellites, as though they travelled in the same orbit. This clearly shows the contrast in size, not only between the planets themselves, but also in relation to the Sun, part of which can be seen on the far left. In reality, the orbits of the planets are millions of kilometres apart and hence a great distance from the Sun.

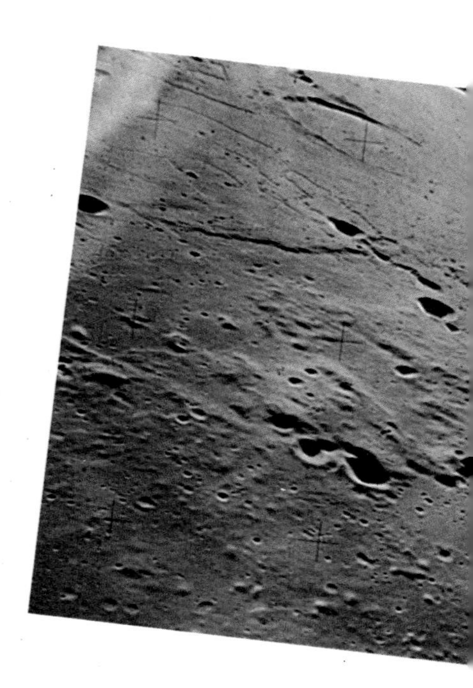

Above: A photograph of the Schröter valley on the moon's surface, taken in 1971 by Apollo 15

Left: The Moon photographed by Apollo 8 in 1968

What keeps the Moon in place?

Just as the Sun's gravity holds the Earth in its orbit around the Sun, so the Earth's gravity holds the Moon in its orbit around the Earth. As far as the Earth is concerned, the Moon is very special. It is our nearest neighbour in space, it is our only natural satellite, and it was the first heavenly body which humans reached and set foot upon.

The Moon lies on average about 384,000 km from the Earth. Its diameter is only 3,475 km, about a quarter that of the Earth and it has less than one-eightieth of the Earth's mass. The Moon's gravity, therefore, is much less strong than the Earth's, only one-sixth of the strength, in fact. Astronauts on the Moon feel light on their feet because they weigh only one-sixth of their weight on Earth.

Why does the Moon have craters?

The most common lunar features are the craters. The largest, Clavius, is about 240 km in diameter. These large craters are often called "ring mountains". Some of them have one or more mountain peaks rising from the crater floor, which is much lower than the general surrounding level. Several of the largest craters, such as Tycho and Copernicus, have conspicuous bright rays issuing from them.

At least 300,000 craters on the Moon's face are large enough to be seen from Earth, while some are little more than shallow pits. It is thought that many of the craters have been caused by the impact of meteorites (rocks from outer space). There is no atmosphere to protect the Moon from such bombardment, as there is on Earth. Some authorities consider that the larger lunar craters may be volcanic in origin.

What are lunar seas?

Covering half of the surface of the Moon are enormous plains called "maria" (singular "mare"), or seas. Early astronomers (believing these dry plains to be oceans) gave them such delightful

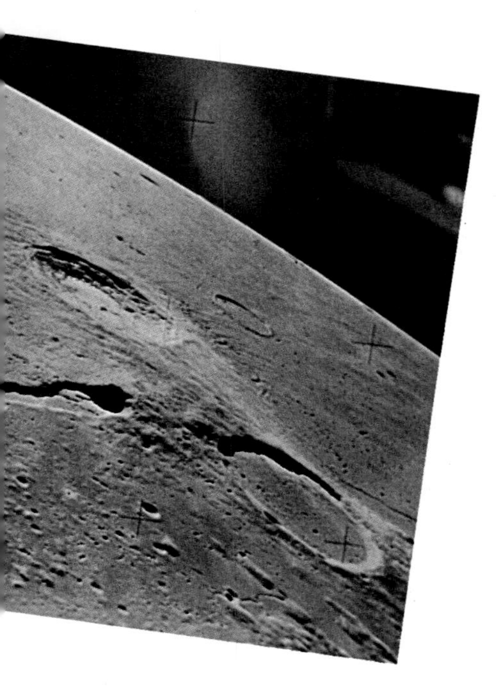

Right: The American astronaut Buzz Aldrin at work on the surface of the Moon

names as Sea of Showers, Sea of Serenity, Sea of Tranquillity, and Sea of Fertility. You can see these with the naked eye from Earth as dark patches against the brighter body. In places across the maria run long, low ridges and narrow, crooked clefts, or valleys, called "rilles". A few marias are bordered by jagged mountain ridges, some of which tower well over 6,000 m high.

Why is there no life on the Moon?

Gravity on the Moon is so weak that it has not been able to hold back any gases to form an atmosphere. This means that there can be no wind, no weather, no sound and no life. The Moon is silent and barren. As there is no insulating atmosphere, there is a wide variation in temperature between day and night. In the merciless heat of the "lunar day", the temperature of the surface reaches more than 100°C, which is the temperature of boiling water. During the "lunar night" the temperature falls drastically to 150°C below zero.

Whose footprints are on the Moon?

The Moon's surface material is a fine black dust. The Apollo astronauts who first set foot upon it in the Sea of Tranquillity in 1969 described it as finely powdered charcoal. Fortunately, they found that the dust covering was only thin and tended to stick together like damp soil. The astronauts' footprints will remain in the dust for a very long time, since there is no wind or rain to obliterate them, but will eventually be worn away by meteorite particles from space.

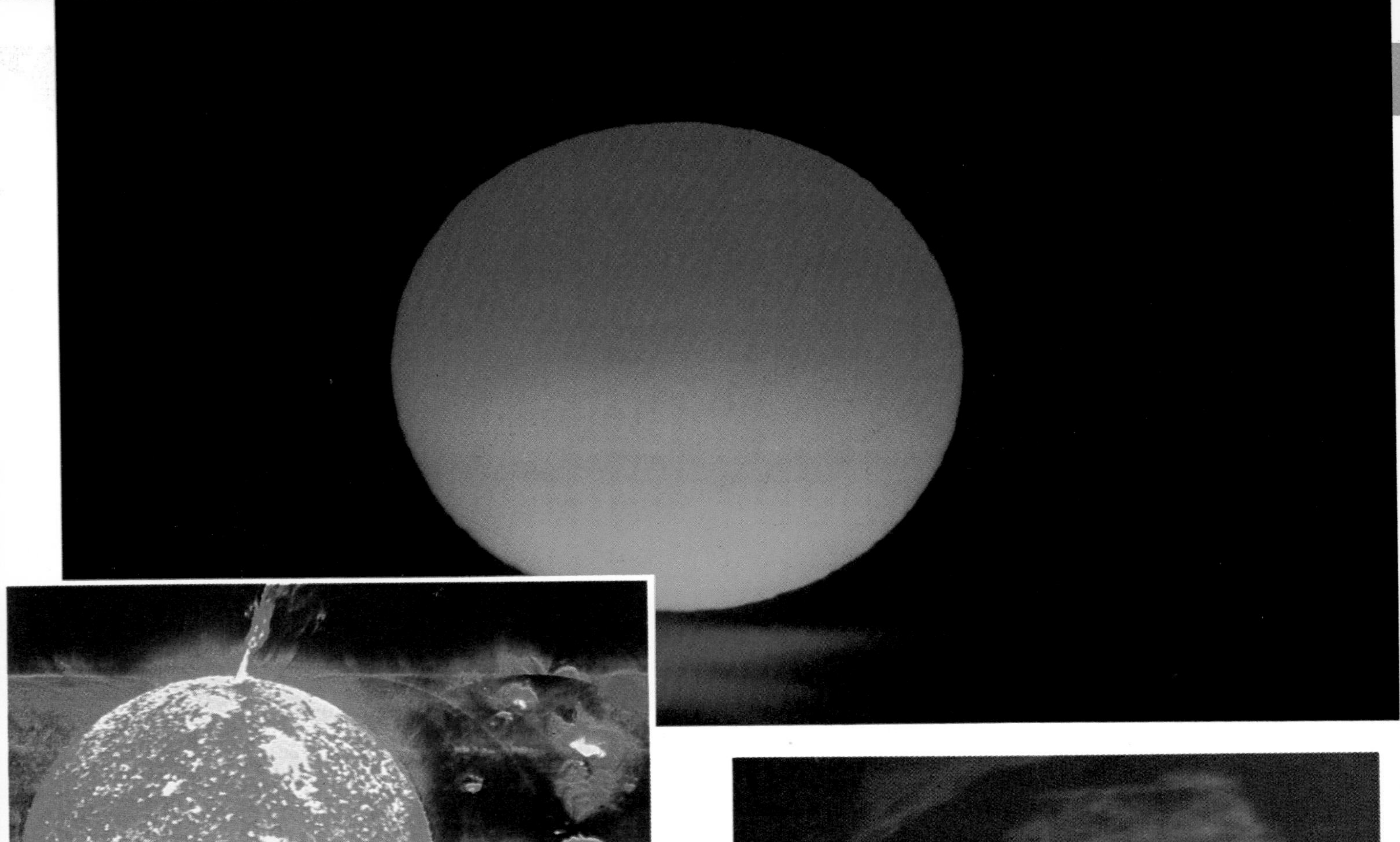

Main picture: The Sun as it is visible from the Earth
Inset left: The Sun viewed from space, with a vast eruption of gas rising from its surface
Inset right: A gas eruption falling back to the Sun's surface

Is the Sun at the centre of our galaxy?

At first, astronomers assumed the Sun was near the centre of the Galaxy, but it is now known that it is a great distance from the centre, about 30,000 light years in fact.

For thousands of millions of years, the Sun has taken the Earth and its other planets along a vast orbit, 33,000 light years in radius, which it describes once every 225 million years around the centre of the Galaxy. Its orbital speed is fantastic – 250 km/s. From Earth, the Sun appears to be the biggest and the brightest star in the whole Universe but this is only because it is so close – a mere 150 million km away. From it, the light and heat which support life on Earth are received.

What is the Sun made of?

The Sun is an enormous sphere of incandescent gas composed mainly of hydrogen (73 per cent) and helium (23 per cent) with small quantities of heavier elements which are also in the gaseous state. It behaves like a giant atomic furnace "consuming" atoms, the tiny, basic particles of matter. At the intensely hot centre of the Sun, four atoms of hydrogen, the simplest of all atoms, combine together to form one atom of the next simplest element, helium. This process is known as "nuclear fusion", and releases so much energy that the Sun's core temperature is at least 14 million°C.

As far as stars go, the Sun is very ordinary, neither particularly big nor particularly bright. There are stars very much bigger and brighter but there are

also many that are much smaller and dimmer.

The diameter of the main "ball" of the Sun is 1,390,000 km or 109 times the diameter of the Earth. The Sun is over 333,000 times more massive than the Earth, but it has only one-quarter of the density.

What are sunspots?

The Sun appears to be a smooth and brilliant disc. However, here and there its surface is marred by small black spots which stand out against the dazzling background. These are sunspots, which were discovered by Galileo in 1610. They appear to be areas of wildly whirling gases. The smallest, called pores, are only a few hundred kilometres in diameter. They may last for just a few hours, or a day or so. But the large ones, which grow rapidly to tens of thousands of kilometres across, may last for weeks or even months. Typical large sunspots have a dark centre, or "umbra", surrounded by a lighter region, or "penumbra". The temperature of these spots is about 4,500°C.

What are eclipses?

An eclipse is a fairly frequent astronomical phenomenon which can be observed with the naked eye. In an eclipse, the Sun or Moon is temporarily obscured. An eclipse of the Sun occurs when the Moon passes between the Earth and the Sun as it moves round the Earth. Its shadow falls on the surface of the Earth and blocks out the Sun's rays. Eclipses of the Sun may be total or partial, depending on the position of the Moon and the point from which the eclipse is observed.

An eclipse of the Moon takes place when the Earth passes between the Sun and the Moon, so that the Moon travels through the cone of shadow cast by the Earth. Eclipses of the Moon are visible in the hemisphere of the Earth opposite the Sun. They too may be total or partial.

Does the Sun move?

The Sun rises in the east and sets in the west, but this is only an apparent movement caused by the rotation of the Earth itself. It has nothing to do with the Sun. The Sun, nevertheless, does move. It moves in two ways: it rotates about its own axis, and it moves in an orbit around the centre of one of the great star systems, or galaxies, of the Universe. Its dual motion resembles that of the planets, which rotate on their own axes as well as moving in orbit around the Sun.

Bottom left: A cross section of the Sun

Below: An eclipse of the Moon (top) and an eclipse of the Sun (bottom)

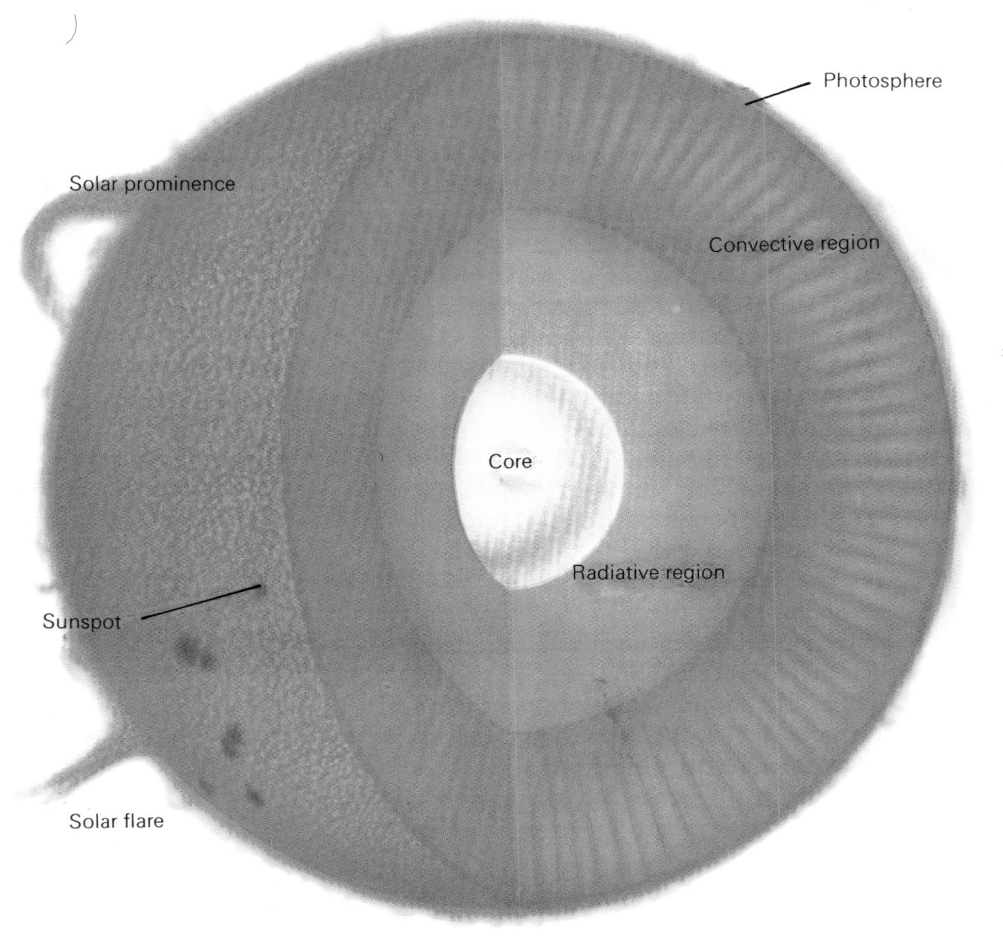

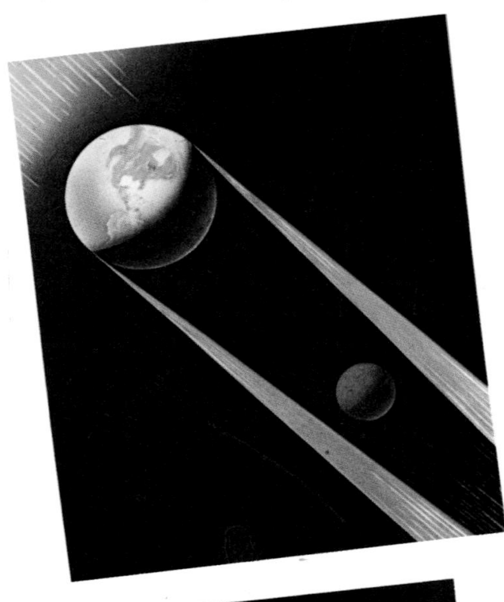

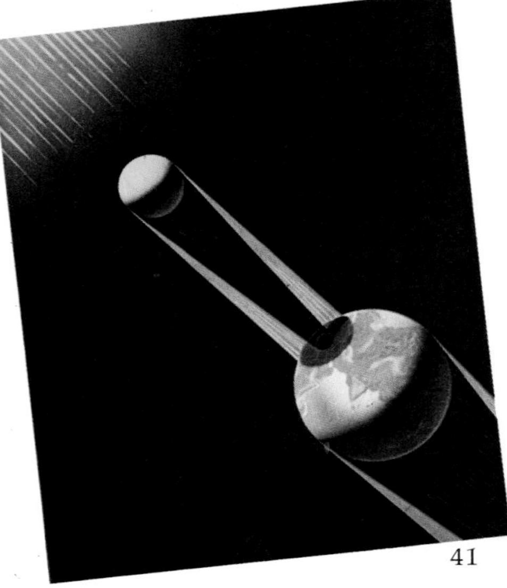

Above: An enormous crater in Arizona, USA, formed when a meteorite hit the earth about 50,000 years ago

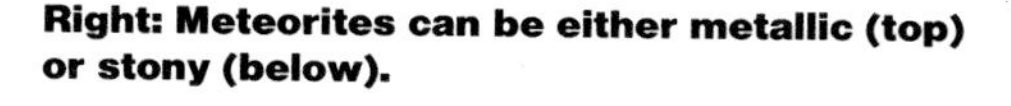

Right: Meteorites can be either metallic (top) or stony (below).

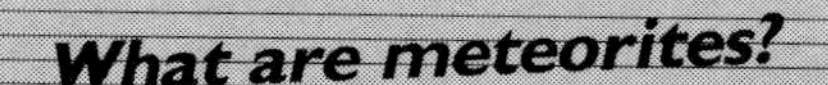

What are meteorites?

The majority of the particles entering the Earth's atmosphere are small and literally burn up when they are still 80 km or more up. But occasionally, larger lumps manage to survive the normally destructive passage through the atmosphere and reach the ground reduced in size, but whole. They are called meteorites. They are found to be of two main sorts – stony and metallic. The metallic ones contain mainly nickel and iron.

The most famous meteorite crater is in Arizona in the USA. It is 1,280 m in diameter, 174 m deep and probably about 50,000 years old.

Two suspected meteorite falls occurred this century in Siberia – in 1908 and 1947. The 1908 impact flattened over 50 sq km of forest. However some authorities now believe a comet, not a meteorite, was responsible.

What are shooting stars?

Wandering through the solar system are particles and chunks of material called "meteoroids". When you look up at the night sky you often see bright streaks as though a star were "falling" from the sky or "shooting" upwards. Those streaks are the result of meteoroids entering the Earth's atmosphere at very high speed from outer space. The friction, or rubbing effect of the atmosphere, heats up the meteoroid until it begins to glow white hot and destroys itself in a luminous streak. That is when we see the falling or shooting star, properly called a "meteor".

From time to time meteors become more frequent. Such "meteor showers" happen when the Earth encounters a whole stream, or swarm, of meteoroids. These swarms travel around the Sun in definite orbits and are associated with comets.

Why did people fear comets?

A comet appears to be a very large bright star with a massive, luminous "tail" streaming out behind it. Such a spectacle is an awe-inspiring sight. Small wonder that our ancestors regarded a comet with fear, believing it to be an evil omen and an indication of the wrath of God.

A comet appeared in 1066 just before the Battle of Hastings – the English may well have blamed their defeat by William the Conqueror on the evil influence of the comet. The idea that a comet is a bad omen has taken a long time to die out. A wave of terror convulsed the world at the passage of Halley's Comet in April 1910. Dozens of people committed suicide.

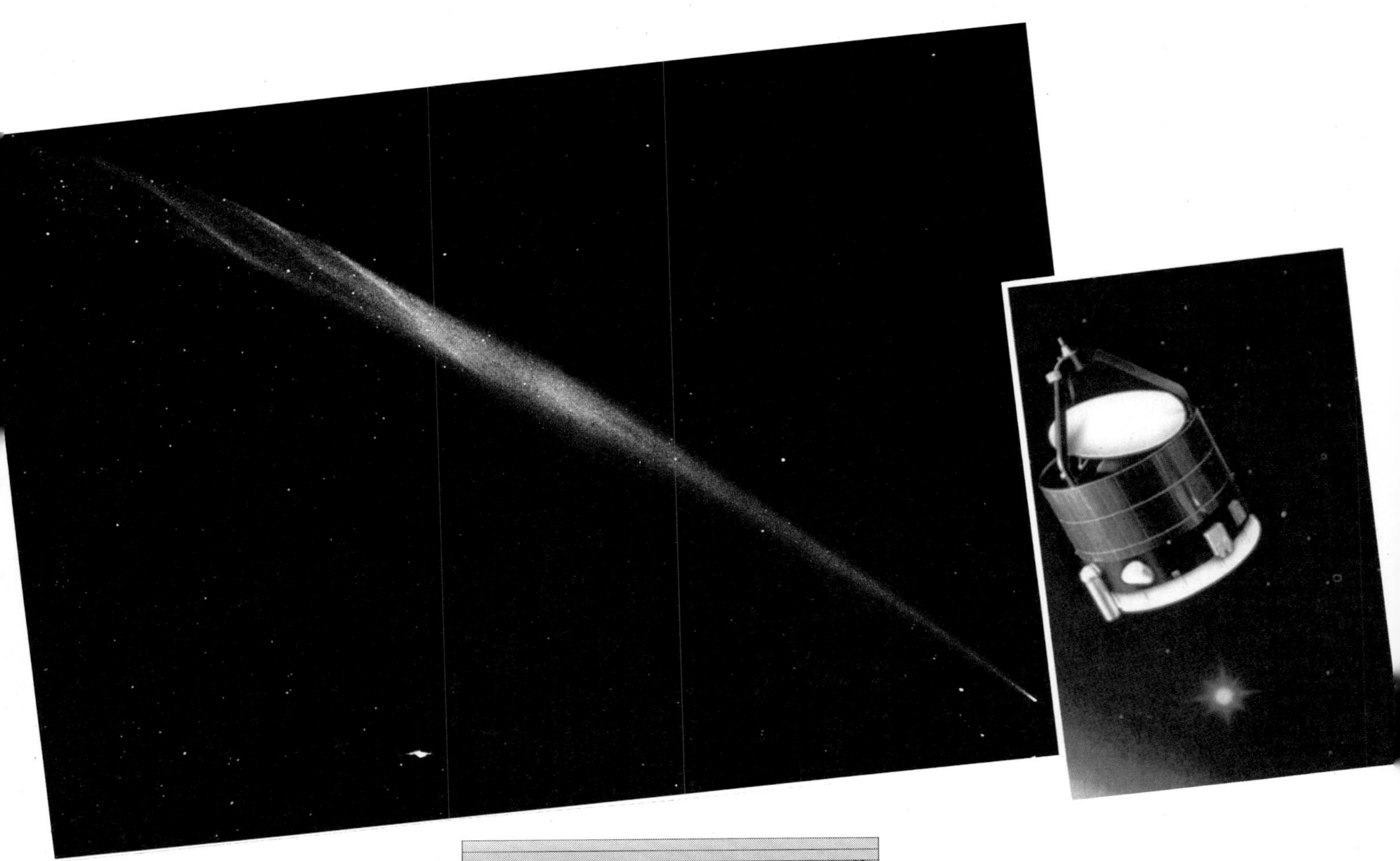

Main picture: The comet Ikeya-Seki photographed in 1965
Inset: The probe Giotto which went to meet Halley's Comet in 1986

How long is a comet's tail?

When a comet approaches the Sun, some of it is vaporized by the Sun's heat. The pressure of the stream of particles from the Sun called the solar wind, forces the vaporized particles away from the nucleus in a great tail. The tail, therefore, does not stream out behind the comet, but away from the direction of the Sun. As it approaches the Sun, the comet travels faster and faster, with its "halo" growing bigger all the time, until it stretches for hundreds and then thousands of kilometres.

Once it is past the orbit of Mars, the grand finale of this "cosmic firework" begins. At the stage of its maximum splendour, when the comet is closest to the Sun, the tail may stretch out for hundreds of millions of kilometres. This all takes place in a few days.

Why do comets enter our solar system?

There are billions of comets in the universe and they usually remain outside our solar system. However, every so often, through the gravitational effect exercised by the nearer planets or star systems, a cometary nucleus leaves its cold, remote position and ventures towards the centre of our solar system. The central core of a comet, the "nucleus", consists of a kind of dirty snowball made up of an agglomeration of rocks and dust, ice and frozen gases, usually only a few kilometres in size. The long, trailing light that we see is not the nucleus of the comet but illuminated gases which evaporate as a result of the Sun's radiation.

The comet's journey will take years to accomplish, and is full of unknown hazards. When we see them, comets have already completed nine-tenths of their journey.

How often does Halley's Comet return?

One of the most famous comets is Halley's Comet, named after the astronomer Edmond Halley (1656–1742), who accurately calculated its time of orbit (about seventy-six years) around the Sun. It was this same comet which appeared in 1066 to alarm the English before their battle with William the Conqueror. In 1705, Halley predicted it would reappear in 1758, and it did so. Its last appearance was in 1986, so it should return in 2062.

The most frequent comet is in fact Encke's comet, which has been recorded forty-eight times, against twenty-nine times for Halley's Comet.

What is a radio telescope?

In 1931 an American engineer, Karl Jansky, detected radio waves coming from space, somewhere in the Milky Way. From this has developed one of the most important and fastest-growing branches of astronomy – radio astronomy. Radio waves have now been found to come from certain stars and galaxies in many parts of the Universe.

The instrument astronomers use to study them is called a radio telescope. It consists basically of an aerial, or antenna, and some kind of reflector, which may be bowl-shaped. The reflector of a radio telescope collects and focuses radio waves in much the same way as the mirror of a reflecting telescope collects and focuses light waves.

Above left: The large parabolic aerial of a radio telescope. Instruments of this type are used to detect various radio sources scattered through space.

Left: The main dome of a large observatory.

How does a modern telescope work?

A modern astronomical observatory has a large dome that can rotate through 360 degrees in a horizontal plane with a vertical opening that can be closed hydraulically. It is through this that the observatory's telescope is able to explore the heavens. The electronically-controlled vertical movement of the telescope and rotation of the dome allow the telescope to follow heavenly bodies as they move.

Although the orientating mechanism weighs several hundred tonnes, it is so finely balanced that only a small electric motor is needed to point the instruments in different directions. Inside the telescope's optical system, light from a star (guided by a series of mirrors) reaches a spectrograph, where it is split into a spectrum and photographed. The spectrum helps identify the features of the star from which the light comes by displaying dark lines against a rainbow of colour. The position and thickness of the lines and the brightness of the various points of the spectrum indicate the star's chemical composition, temperature, density, speed, etc.

Below: Powerful telescopes from the observatories in Arcetri, near Florence, Italy (top left and right), Edinburgh (top centre) and Merate, Italy (bottom)

When did the Space Age begin?

The story of the conquest of space began during the Second World War with the fearfully destructive German V2 weapons, the forerunners of today's rocket missiles. After the War, German technology was adopted and improved by the Russians and Americans. On 4 October 1957, the USSR put the first artificial satellite into orbit: Sputnik 1, a sphere weighing a little over 83 kg orbiting the Earth at a maximum distance of 947 km, transmitted temperature and pressure data. It sent out a steady "bleep, bleep" of signals as it orbited the Earth every ninety six minutes. A month later the Russians launched Sputnik 2, weighing about 500 kg. It carried the very first space traveller – a dog named Laika.

The sheer size of the Sputniks amazed the Americans. The Russians' launching rockets were obviously much more powerful than theirs. When the Americans launched their first satellite, Explorer 1, on 31 January 1958, it weighed only 14 kg.

Right: The Russian rockets Sputnik and Vostok

Who foresaw the space rocket?

In 1903, a Russian schoolmaster, Konstantin Tsiolkovski, published an article entitled "The exploration of space with rocket craft". It was the same year as the first flight by the Wright brothers, a mere hop of 32 m, and very few people who had read the article took it seriously. Tsiolkovski nonetheless foresaw that the rocket had to be the scientific basis for space travel and he is now regarded as the founder of astronautics, the science of space flight. Other pioneers include the American Robert H. Goddard and the Germans Wernher von Braun, Hermann Oberth, Walter Riedel and Walter Dornberger. It is thanks to them and to technological progress that space flight became a reality.

Will there be nuclear spacecraft?

Small nuclear power plants are already used in satellites. It is a likely assumption that, for journeys beyond the Moon, spacecraft propelled by nuclear power will be used. Such craft would have engines capable of producing more power than existing rockets, like those of the Space Shuttle, which are propelled by chemical fuels. These nuclear spacecraft could possibly be used to carry passengers and freight on direct flights from the Earth to the planets.

Some experts think this is a perfectly realistic picture of the prospects that lie ahead for manned spaceflight, at least from the technological viewpoint. The question of cost is another matter.

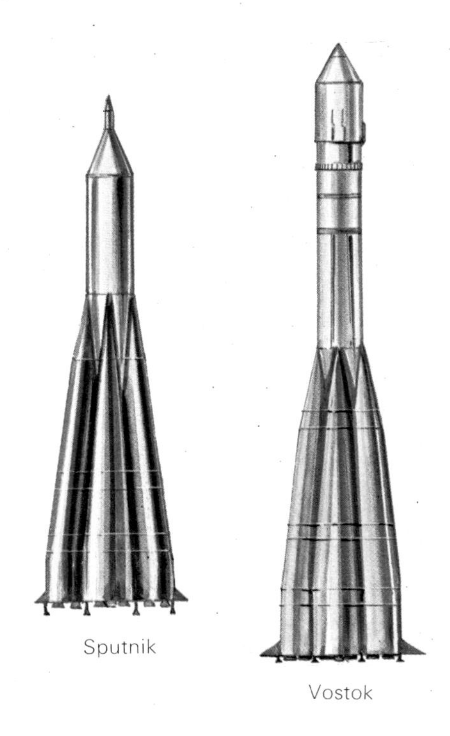

Who was the first astronaut?

On 12 April 1961, a human being ventured into space for the first time and returned alive. Major Yuri Gagarin, a Russian pilot, became the world's first astronaut (or "cosmonaut", as the Russians say) when he made one orbit of the Earth in his spacecraft Vostok I (Vostok means East). Four months later another Russian cosmonaut, Gherman Titov, circled the Earth seventeen times in Vostok 2 before returning safely. It was not until 20 February 1962 that the USA launched a man into orbit. He was Colonel John Glenn, who made three orbits in Friendship 7.

How do astronauts train for weightlessness?

In space, a spacecraft travels in orbit. It may be a more or less circular orbit close to the Earth or an elongated orbit which extends to the Moon. In orbit the forces on the spacecraft are balanced. The outward force, due to motion, balances the inward pull of gravity. This means that there is no effective gravity acting on the craft or anything inside it. When there is no gravity, there can be no weight. Thus, astronauts in space are weightless, and can float effortlessly in all directions.

The best way of simulating weightlessness on Earth is to fly a plane at high speed up and over in a steep arc. For a short time, trainee astronauts inside the plane experience the effects of being weightless. What is actually happening, however, is that they are falling at the same time as the plane is, but the effect is more or less similar to weightlessness. Training under water, in huge tanks, also helps astronauts to be prepared for zero gravity conditions.

Facing page: The astronaut Bruce McCandless "walking" in space. His carefully designed spacesuit protects him from the hostile environment.
Inset: Buzz Aldrin, pilot of the Apollo 11 expedition which was the first to land men on the moon on 21 July 1969

Why do astronauts wear spacesuits?

When astronauts leave their craft to "walk" in space, or explore the Moon, or if the pressure system fails, they must wear carefully-designed spacesuits to give them protection against the hostile environment of space.

The spacesuit is made up of a number of separate layers. Cooling water circulates through the thin undergarment next to the astronaut's skin to keep the body temperature steady. Another layer is made airtight and supplied with air. Above this is a pressure "skin" which keeps the air at more or less the same pressure as that on Earth. Thick padding and a tough outer garment protect the inner layers. The outer garment is coated with a shiny material such as gold to help reflect the strong heat and radiation coming from the Sun. On the head, an astronaut wears a helmet with a transparent visor in front, which has a fine gold coating, too. Inside the helmet are the earphones and microphones by which the wearer can keep in contact with his fellow astronauts and base.

Right: The Saturn V rocket, the biggest ever to fly, which launched various craft including the Apollo spacecraft

Who was the first man on the Moon?

The most moving moment in space history was undoubtedly Monday, 21 July 1969, when the American astronaut Neil Armstrong became the first human being to step on to the Moon. Descending the ladder from the Apollo 11 lunar module, lightened by the reduced gravity of the Moon, Armstrong put his left foot on the arid soil and uttered the words which millions of people watching on television heard directly on the Earth: "That's one small step for a man, one giant leap for mankind."

After a further five landings on the Moon, which brought the total cost of the American manned space programme to 25,500 million dollars, the Americans began to develop a reusable space plane, the Space Shuttle. The Russians, however, concentrated on space laboratories in Earth orbit.

How does a rocket work?

A rocket works on the same principle as the jet engine used in aircraft. Burning a fuel inside the engine produces hot gases which shoot out backwards at high speed. Reaction to the escaping gases thrusts the engine forwards. This is the principle of jet propulsion.

A jet engine needs oxygen from the air to burn its fuel, whereas a rocket carries its own oxygen. That is why a rocket can work in space where there is no air. The substance a rocket carries to provide oxygen is called an oxidant. Both the rocket fuel and the oxidant are known as "propellants".

Powerful space rockets have liquid propellants and the oxidant normally used is oxygen in its very cold, liquid form. Solid-fuel boosters may also be used, for extra power at take-off.

Which was the first space laboratory?

The world's first orbital space laboratory to be launched was the Russian Salyut 1 in April 1971. Space laboratories are helping astronauts learn to live and work for long periods in space. In later Salyut stations, and their successor, Mir, Russians have remained in space for up to a year.

The American Skylab was launched in May 1973. Three teams of astronauts visited Skylab, the last returning to Earth in February 1974. In 1975, the first joint space venture between the Russians and Americans took place – an Apollo–Soyuz link-up in space.

In 1983, the first Spacelab was taken into orbit by the Space Shuttle. Built by the European Space Agency, Spacelab is not left in space but remains on board the Shuttle in orbit for a week and is then returned to Earth.

Facing page.
Right: Some of the world's most important satellites.
Inset: A satellite in circular equatorial orbit which lasts for 23 hours, 56 minutes and 4 seconds, a time identical to that of the Earth's rotation

How are satellites powered?

Communications satellites, like all kinds of satellites, are powered by special batteries which get their power from sunlight. The Sun is always shining in space, and therefore the batteries never run down.

These solar batteries consist of a very large number of cells of a chemical element called silicon. When sunlight falls on silicon, a tiny electric current is produced. Joining hundreds of these

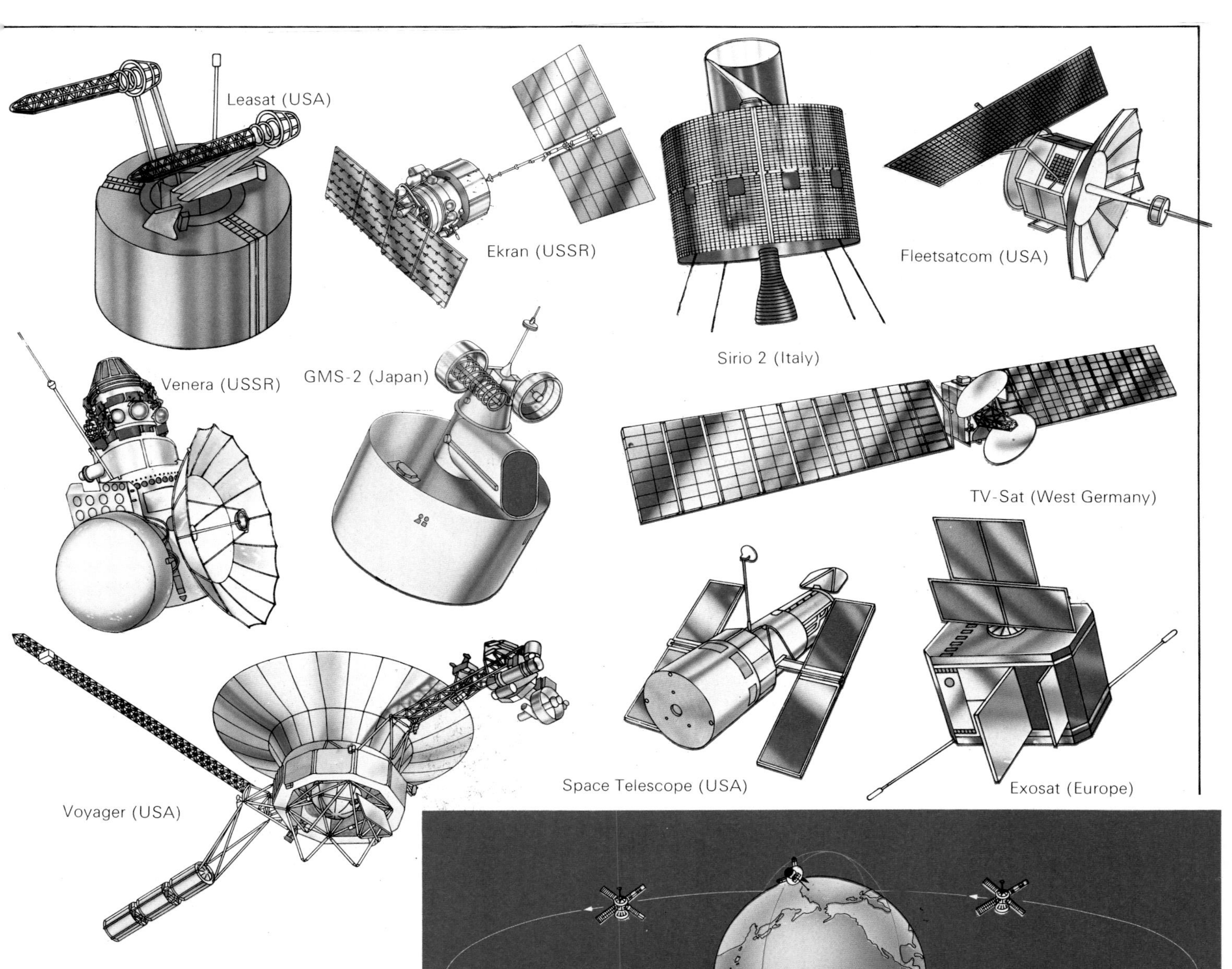

solar cells together produces enough electricity to power a satellite's equipment. In some satellites, the cells form part of the outer surface of the satellite itself. In others, the cells are arranged in flat panels which stick out of the sides of the satellite like wings.

How does a satellite stay in orbit?

If you throw a ball through the air, it travels a certain distance and then falls. The Earth's gravity pulls it back. The harder you throw the ball, the faster and further it goes before falling back.

To keep a satellite in orbit, it must reach such a high speed that it "falls" only the same amount as the Earth curves. In effect the satellite remains travelling parallel to the Earth, that is in orbit. The outward force on the satellite (due to its motion) is equal and opposite to the inward pull on it (due to gravity). This is the same as natural satellites travelling around parent planets, such as the Moon around the Earth.

Gravitational pull on an object gets weaker the farther the object travels from the Earth. Therefore, the force, and hence the speed, required to keep a satellite in orbit is less the higher up it is. The speed a satellite must achieve to stay in orbit is called the orbital velocity. At 160 km above the Earth, the orbital velocity is about 28,000 km/h.

Will astronauts ever travel to the stars?

In the euphoria that followed the first landing of astronauts on the Moon in 1969, people looked ahead to a new era in which humans would be able to travel out among the planets of the solar system and then beyond to the stars. But could human beings ever achieve such an epic journey? Light, which travels at 300,000 km/s, takes over four years to reach the nearest star. So, an interstellar astronaut would need to approach the speed of light itself. Not even nuclear energy is capable of producing such a speed. A spaceship travelling at 40,000 km/h, the speed at which the US Apollo astronauts began their voyage to the Moon, would take more than 110,000 years to reach even the nearest star. Nevertheless, it may one day be possible for interplanetary spaceships to be built at orbiting space stations, perhaps driven by ion engines or by sails to catch the solar wind.

Is there life on other planets?

Life as it is known on Earth definitely could not exist on Mercury because it is too hot, and Jupiter and the outer planets are much too cold. The only planets where life has been considered possible are Venus and Mars, but the available evidence from Russian and American space probes makes the possibility remote.

What about life outside the solar system? The Sun is but one of millions of stars in the heavens. It would be incredible if there were not other stars with planetary systems like the solar system. Some dark, planet-like bodies have in fact been identified, associated with some of the nearer stars. Therefore, it is likely that there are, within the Universe, planets on which conditions are much like those we experience on Earth. Future space exploration may give us some more definite information.

Facing page: An artist's view of the interplanetary spaceships we might see in the future. Power for these craft could come from advanced engines or they may be equipped with sails to catch the solar wind.

Above: Professor Gerard O'Neill's plan for a space colony designed to accommodate 200,000 people

When did interplanetary exploration begin?

The Russians launched the first interplanetary probe, to Venus, in February 1961. Although the flight path was accurate, the communication system failed. The USA scored the first success with their Mariner 2 probe, launched in August 1962, which passed within about 34,000 km of Venus. In 1976, the American Viking 1 and Viking 2 craft landed on Mars. They conducted life-seeking experiments on the soil and sent back pictures of the surface.

For a probe to travel to the planets, it must leave the vicinity of the Earth and escape from the Earth's gravitational pull. To be able to do this, the probe must be given an initial speed of at least 40,000 km/h or 11 km/s. This speed is known as the escape velocity.

Which planets did Voyager explore?

In 1977, American space scientists at NASA launched the Voyager 1 and 2 space probes on journeys of exploration to the outer planets and moons of the solar system. Many extremely interesting photographs were sent back from Jupiter and Saturn by the spacecraft, and much important new information was gained. Voyager 2 flew on to look at Uranus in 1986. There it discovered that the planet had rings and unknown satellites. It journeyed on towards Neptune, twelve years after leaving Earth.

What is camouflage?

Many animals protect themselves from the threats and attacks of predators by taking on the colours and shapes of the surroundings in which they live. This phenomenon is called "camouflage". The chameleon is generally reckoned to be the superstar of animal camouflage: it can change its colour to suit the different surroundings in which it finds itself.

The commonest form of camouflage is when the individual animal takes on the colours of its surroundings. Animals that live in the snow, like the stoat and the mountain hare, grow a white coat during the winter so that predators will not be able to see them; similarly, the ptarmigan moults to an all-white plumage at the first hint of winter cold. The dark patches on the giraffe mingle with the dappled pattern of sun and shade among the trees where it feeds. Most animals which live in the desert have a colour somewhere between grey and yellow, so that they do not stand out against the background. In the tropical rainforests there is an abundance of green insects, birds and reptiles which hide in the leaves of the trees.

What is the difference between jungle and rainforest?

The terms "jungle" and "rainforest" are sometimes used to describe the same thing, but there is a difference. A jungle is a tangled forest often separated by areas of desert, such as in India. A rainforest is a moist tropical forest like those found in the Amazon and South East Asia.

Tropical rainforests are perhaps the most amazing habitat on Earth. They are packed with countless thousands of animals and plants and the number of different species is so great that they have not yet all been named. Most rainforests occur between the two tropics of Capricorn and Cancer, with small intrusions into North-East India. There are fifty countries which possess rainforests and these encircle the world around the Equator. Rainforests are being cut down (for timber and grazing land) at such a rate that it is causing worldwide concern.

Why is balance within an ecosystem important?

Green plants, which make food by photosynthesis, are considered to be "producers" of energy, while animals are considered to be "consumers". Producers and consumers live in a delicate biological balance within an "ecosystem" (plant and animal community and its habitat). This avoids the over-development of any one population and promotes natural selection. If, for example, plant-eating animals were to disappear from an ecosystem, in a few years it would be overwhelmed by vegetation, because there would be no way of limiting its development. If, on the other hand, carnivorous animals were to disappear from the same ecosystem, the number of plant-eating animals would increase because of the lack of predators. Sooner or later, all the vegetation would be eaten and destroyed, with extremely serious consequences.

What is a habitat?

Each place that living things occupy is called a habitat. Some habitats are very small – the damp, dark region under a stone, an abandoned bird's nest or even the fork of a tree. All these places have their own community of plants and animals, but because they are so small they are called "microhabitats". Bigger habitats, such as a forest floor or a meadow, are made up of several microhabitats. A community of different living things, together with their habitat, is called an "ecosystem".

Another word used to describe a particular area within the living world is "environment". This is used when talking about the general nature of a place such as a desert, forest or ocean, where a habitat is located.

Facing page: A chameleon, a fish and a leaf insect show some of the varied forms camouflage can take.

Above right: Chamois walking agilely among the rocks which are their home
Inset: The Gibson desert in Australia provides a less hospitable habitat

Below right: Factory chimneys emitting gas waste into the atmosphere

What is a food web?

Plants and insects play a vital role in the natural sequence of "eater" and "eaten". A small creature such as an aphid may eat plant sap, and a ladybird may eat the aphid, and in turn be eaten by a bird, and then the bird be eaten by a fox. This sequence is called a "food chain", for food has passed, in a chain-like fashion, from the plant sap to the fox. In nature, many such chains exist, but normally the chains are linked, invisibly of course, to other food chains. For instance, the aphid in our example may be eaten directly by a bird which is already part of another food chain. This complicated series of connecting food chains is called a "food web".

Could the balance of nature be overthrown?

For millions of years, the balance of nature has been maintained: changes, when they occur, have taken place very slowly. Now humans are threatening this carefully controlled balance. Chemical and radioactive pollution, unreasonable hunting and fishing, the destruction of whole ecosystems, and the uncontrolled introduction of harmful species into new environments are the most serious problems created by human beings.

The future of the Earth could be one of disaster, unless the damage already caused is remedied and the pollution of the environment is controlled. Otherwise, there will be seas like immense oil slicks, rivers without life and rationed and unpleasant-tasting drinking water. There will be a sky streaked black and yellow by smog, disastrous accumulations of silt, the countryside devoid of greenery, wild animals extinct and sparrows a rarity. Only rats and cockroaches may survive.

We must change our whole attitude towards our environment and find once again our place in the balance of nature – or else we too could go the way of the dinosaurs.

How tall can trees grow?

The tallest trees in the world are the coast redwoods (*Sequoia*). They are native to California, and reach up to 110 m tall. In Europe, where they are planted ornamentally, they often lose their tops as they are usually the tallest vegetation and attract lightning. Named after their red spongy bark, redwoods are fairly unusual among trees in having fireproof bark – a survival aid against natural fires. Their limbs only branch some 50 m from the ground, where they can escape fires.

There are two species of sequoia: *Sequoiadendrum giganteum*, and *Sequoia sempervirens*. The former is commonly known as the giant sequoia. It grows at altitudes between 1,500 and 2,400 m in the Sierra Nevada.

How can you tell a tree's age?

The age of a tree can be worked out by looking at a cross section of its trunk. There is a seasonal difference in the average diameter of the cells of a certain type of plant tissue (xylem). The cells are at their largest when the water supply is greatest once a year and this difference in size can easily be seen as alternate light and dark rings. In order to tell the age of a tree, simply count the dark rings. The number will correspond to how old the tree is – for example, the diagram on the right shows a cross section of a three-year-old tree.

The favourableness of different years can be compared by looking at the relative thickness of the growth rings: a wet year will produce a thick ring, while a drought year produces a thin one.

Top right: The giant sequoia (*Sequoiadendrum giganteum*), the larger of the two sequoia species

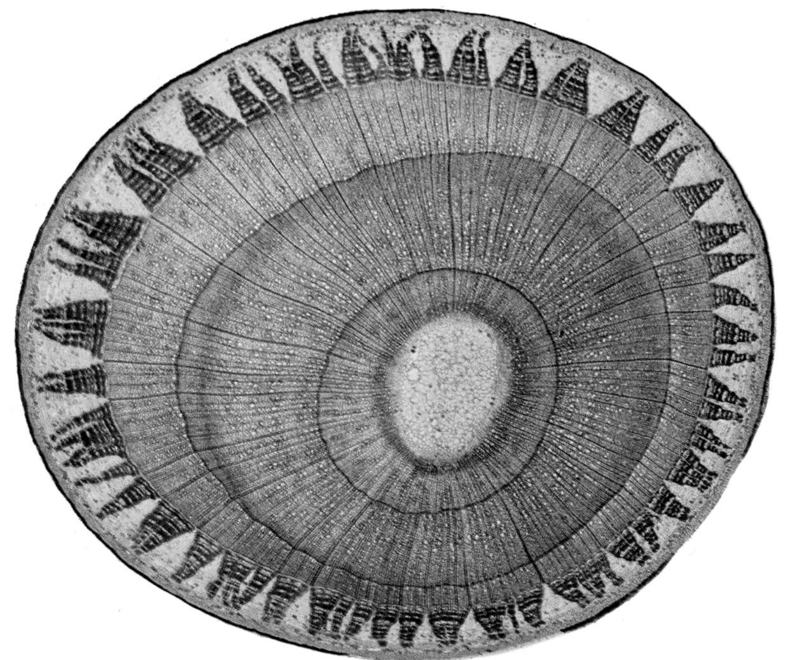

Right: A diagram of a tree cross section showing the alternate dark and light rings. The number of dark rings indicates that the tree is three years old.

What is Dutch Elm disease?

There are various species of elm, found all over the world. They include: the American elm (*Ulmus americana*) which can reach a height of 30 m, and has pendulous branches whose strong fibres were used by American Indians to make rope; the mountain elm, found in the Alps, which has red or golden leaves; the English elm (*U. procera*), whose shape was, until recently, so characteristic of the British countryside; and the Siberian elm (*U. pumila*), which grows quickly but never exceeds a height of 10 m.

The fungus *Ceratocystis ulmi*, which reached America from Holland around 1930, exterminated 40 per cent of the 25 million elm trees growing there. This fungus entered Britain from Canada and killed millions of elm trees. The disease it causes is known as Dutch Elm disease, and though work is being done to develop resistant strains, the damage done to the traditional English countryside may never be repaired.

How big can pine cones grow?

Most cone-bearing (coniferous) trees are evergreen trees which have unenclosed seeds. The reproductive organs are cones, which are either male or female. Male and female cones are carried on the same plant, though are often some distance apart. The male pollen is blown by the wind to the ripe female cones. There fertilization takes place, but it is some time before seeds form.

Some cones can be enormous, as in the "kilo cones" of the Californian coulter pine (*Pinus coulteri*). These cones may be several kilograms in weight, sufficient to kill if one fell on a person's head. In another Californian pine species, the bishop pine (*P. muricata*), the cones have evolved to stay on the tree for up to twenty-five years until a natural fire releases the seeds. The fire will clear the forest floor, giving room for the seeds to germinate and grow.

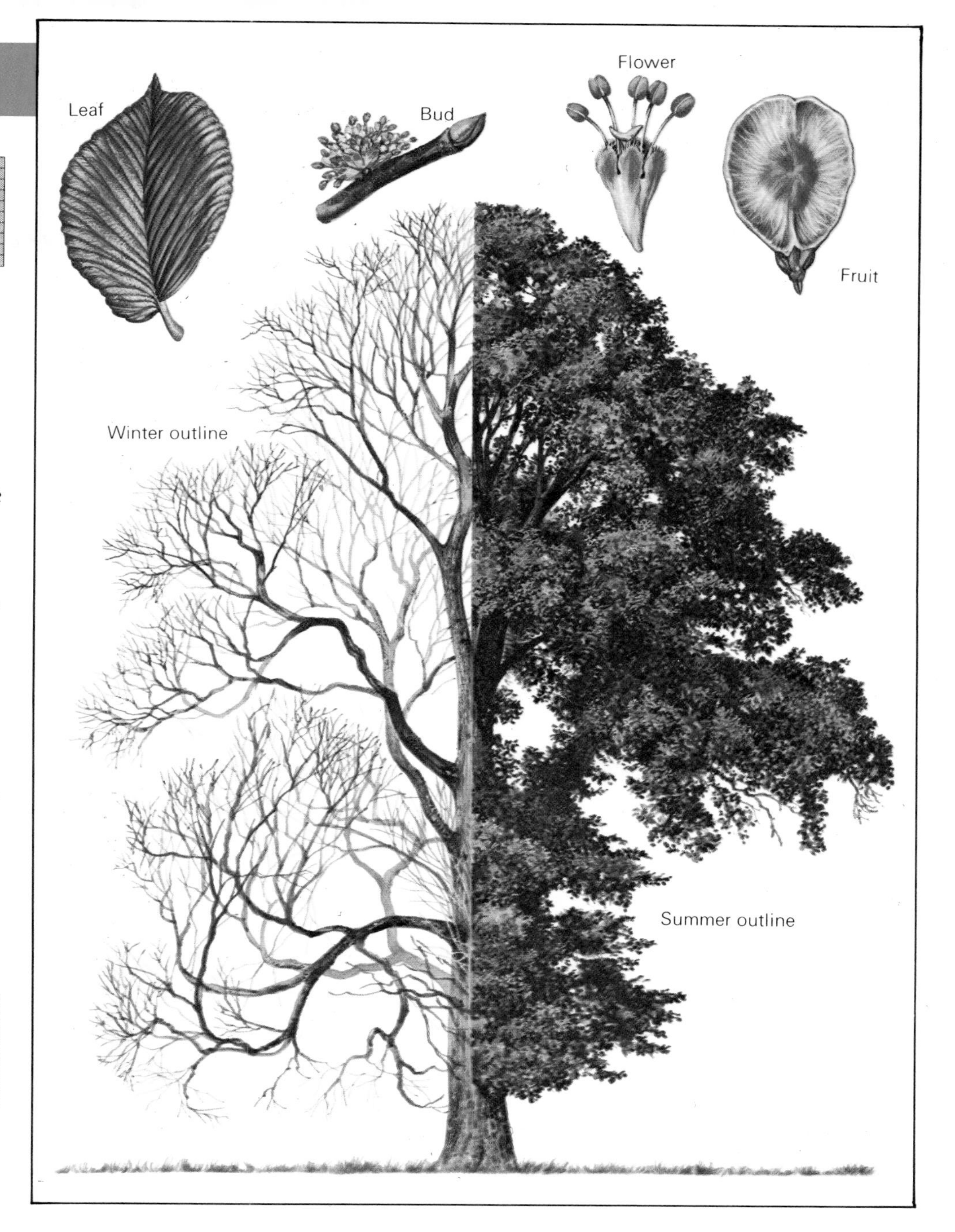

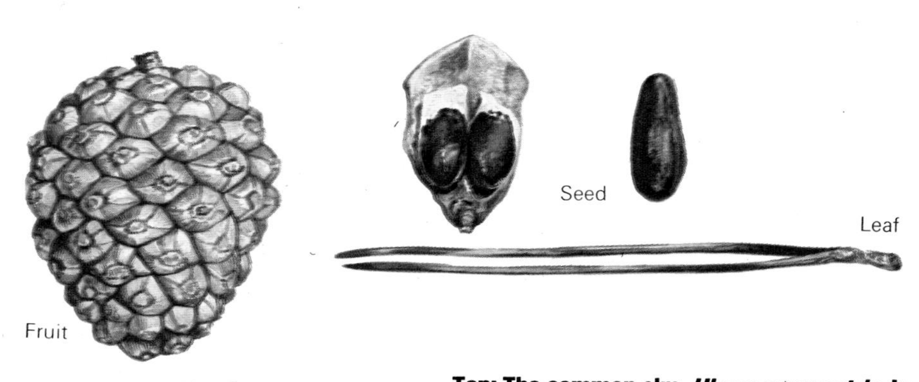

Top: The common elm, *Ulmus campestris*. In spring, it is covered with small yellow and pink blossoms.

Above: The fruit, seed and leaf of the domestic pine, *Pinus pinea*

How can you tell a plant from an animal?

Even today the dividing line between very primitive animals and plants is indistinct. A basic difference between the two is that plants manufacture their own proteins, while animals must eat proteins which have already been produced by other organisms. Yet there are some single-celled plants which cannot make protein, whereas there are a few microscopic animals which can. Even more confusingly, there are some viruses which are still little more than scraps of basic protein.

Which are the oldest plants?

Plants are divided into lower or higher plants according to their evolutionary history. Algae, diatoms, bacteria, mosses and liverworts are the oldest forms of plant still alive today. They are known from fossils 500 million years old. Conifers appeared about 200 million years ago, and soon afterwards the modern ferns evolved. Flowering plants, known as "angiosperms", first grew about 120 million years ago.

Why do plants have roots?

Roots anchor plants in the ground and absorb water and nutrients (needed for photosynthesis and growth) from the soil. Roots divide into rootlets which push between the soil particles, so increasing the surface area which is available for absorption. Water and dissolved nutrients are absorbed into the roots through millions of fine root hairs which are extensions of the root cells.

Some plants have roots that penetrate many metres into the soil. Roots of the horsetail ferns (*Equisetum*) reach down about 6 m. Tamarisk roots have been found at 30 m.

Why are most plants green?

Chlorophyll is a green substance used in photosynthesis and is the pigment that makes plants green. It is found in chloroplasts which occur in cells. Those cells nearer to the surfaces of leaves have more chloroplasts than those deeper inside. Chlorophyll also occurs in stems. Chloroplasts move around in the cytoplasm of the cells to be in the best place for absorbing light energy during photosynthesis.

Photosynthesis is a chemical process during which carbon dioxide, water and sunlight are, in the presence of chlorophyll, combined to make starch and oxygen. Sometimes oxygen can be seen bubbling from underwater plants in an aquarium. The starch produced may be changed into sugars.

Below left: A plant fossil

Below: The vast roots of a fig tree

Above: A reaper ant carrying a seed pod

Right: Green algae covered in white lime, which gives it a shiny appearance
Inset: Green and red algae

How are seeds dispersed?

Every fruit and seed is highly adapted for dispersal. The swollen succulent exteriors of fruits or the rich food reserves in a hard shell, are strategies evolved to encourage birds, mammals and insects to eat the seeds and disperse them away from the parent plant. The seeds of some tropical plants must pass through the gut of a mammal, where their outer layers are broken down by digestive juices, before they will germinate. Other seeds are eaten and passed out unchanged in the animal's dung. In this way they have a perfect fertilizer. Ants are great seed collectors and are responsible for dispersing hundreds of leguminous plant species. Many other seeds are also dispersed by insects.

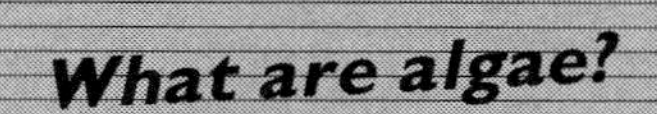

What are algae?

Algae are the most primitive plants. They range from microscopic species such as the filamentous algae through free-living algae to the giant seaweeds, which may be several hundred metres long. The floating mass of the Sargasso Sea, north of the West Indies, is mostly made up of brown seaweeds.

The 18,000 species of algae in the world are classified according to several features, such as: what pigments they have; how they reproduce; the type of cell wall; and the type of cell contents. Photosynthesis allows algae to grow using light energy from the sun and dissolved nutrients in the water. Reproduction may be by joining and exchanging cell contents, by cell division or by dispersal of spores.

What are crustaceans?

Sometimes called shellfish, crustaceans are invertebrates and have hard skins and many legs, some of which act as breathing organs. They live mostly in the sea and number about 25,000 species. The more familiar crustaceans are the ones caught for food, such as crabs, lobsters and shrimps. There are vast numbers of smaller crustaceans hiding in rock pools, or living as part of the floating world of plankton (a word meaning "wandering") – small drifting organisms in seas and rivers. The plankton in the Antarctic include the shrimp-like krill eaten by the giant whales that live there.

One of the largest crustaceans is the giant spider crab of tropical seas, which has legs up to a metre long.

What is coral?

Coral is really a whole mass of tiny sea creatures called coelenterates. The coral "polyps" join up as a branching colony. To protect and cover up this living coral, lime is taken from the sea water and built into a hard skeleton. This can form a reef which may be 100 m deep. Since coral builds very slowly, some reefs must be millions of years old.

As the sea-bed slowly sinks, the living coral grows to keep level with the surface of the sea. A reef which forms along a tropical coastline cuts off some of the sea to form a lagoon. In the clear and still water live a great variety of fish and other sea life, including worms, molluscs, anemones and sea-urchins. The sandy beaches which form on the reef may be visited by sea birds and turtles which go there to lay their eggs.

Bottom: An enormous crab found on Africa's Ivory Coast.
Inset: Close-up of a coral

What are echinoderms?

Echinoderms are a group of about 4,000 sea creatures consisting of starfish, sea-urchins and sea-cucumbers. The term "echinoderm" comes from two Greek words meaning spiny and skin.

Starfish usually have five arms, and creep about slowly on rocks; their underside is covered with hundreds of little suckers, called "tube feet". With these, a starfish can grip the shell of a mussel and slowly force it open to get at the contents. Sea-urchins get their name from the old English word urchin, meaning a hedgehog. Their globe-like shells are covered with spines. They cling to rocks and move about slowly. Some can burrow into the sand. Sea-cucumbers also have spiny skins and live on the sea-bed. Their bodies are shaped like cucumbers, and are collected by divers for food, called *bêche-de-mer*.

Which animal can turn itself inside-out?

Sea-cucumbers use various methods to protect themselves. One of these is the release of poison. Some species cannot be put into an aquarium with fish because the poison they give out kills the fish. It is not known whether this method is as effective in the open sea.

Some large sea-cucumbers have a second set of tentacles, at the rear, which can throw a net of sticky threads over any attacker. The sea-cucumber then wanders away, leaving its enemy helplessly trussed up. If more violently provoked, these sea-cucumbers can turn their back end almost inside-out, hurling out a lot of their body organs over the attacker.

Left: A beautiful *Linckia laevigata* starfish. Famous for its regenerative powers, it can produce a complete individual from a single one of its arms.

Two types of tropical fish, a Harlequin Sweetlip (below) and a Butterfly Fish (bottom)

Why are tropical fish so colourful?

Many tropical fish which live on coral reefs have brightly coloured scales which serve as camouflage in the colourful landscape of the reef. Because they are so pretty, a great number of them are kept in aquariums.

In their natural habitat, such fish show a great variety of lifestyles. For example, angelfish drift among the coral, feeding on sponges and sea-squirts during the day, while at night they sleep in coral caves. Butterfly fish mate for life and are always found swimming in pairs.

How many insects are there?

Insects are the biggest class of animals, numbering nearly 1 million species. The number of individuals is beyond calculation. They are found everywhere, even in the sea. Insects (from the Latin *secare*, to cut) have six legs, bodies divided into three parts (head, thorax and abdomen) and go through several stages in their life history – egg, larva, pupa and adult. Insects provide one of the major food sources for other animals. There are about thirty groups or orders of insects. Beetles form the largest order with over 250,000 species.

Above, from top: A wasp, a beetle and a mosquito laying eggs on water

Left: A praying mantis

Which insect carried the Black Death?

Fleas are parasitic, living on other warm-blooded animals and feeding on blood. Not only are humans attacked by fleas but almost all other mammals and most birds have their individual fleas. A flea has hooked legs for hanging on to its host, and a body flattened sideways for creeping between hair or feathers. Usually, a flea species sticks to one kind of host, but dogs and cats may pick up fleas from rabbits, hedgehogs and rats. The flea from the rat can be very dangerous, as it may carry the germ of bubonic plague – the Black Death which killed millions of people during the Middle Ages.

Which is the most destructive insect?

Of all insect pests, the locust is perhaps the most destructive. Resembling a large grasshopper, a locust and its offspring will do no harm for years. Then, mysteriously, a swarm begins to build up as the locusts increase and remain together. At first they move on the ground, as their wings have not yet developed. At this stage they are called "hoppers". Then, with the last moult, the flying locusts emerge to make a swarm, which can be so thick that the Sun is blotted out. An average swarm can weigh more than 1 million kg, and the locusts eat this amount of food each day. To fight the locusts, poisoned bait is put in the path of the hoppers. Aeroplanes attack the flying swarm with contact poison, but by then it is usually too late to stop them destroying huge areas of crops.

Left: A spider spinning a web

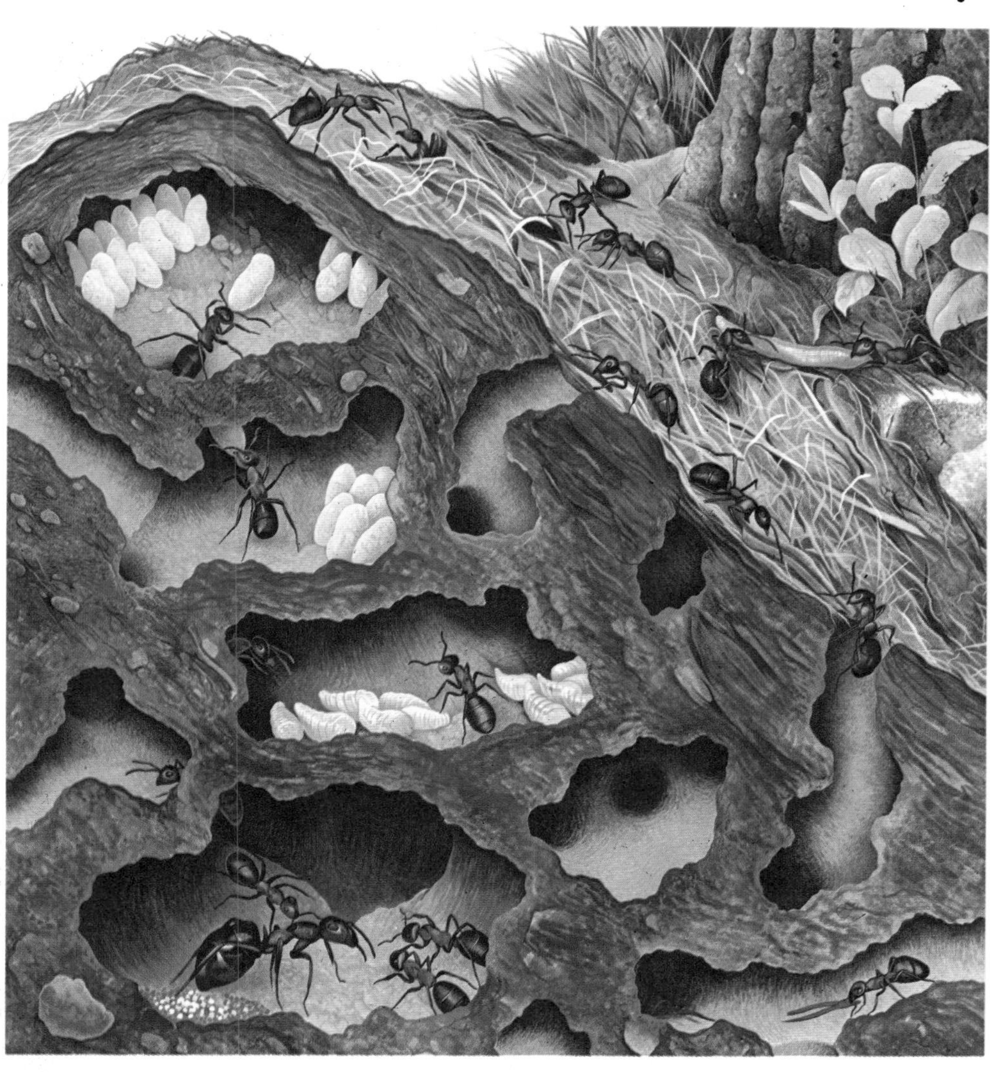

Above: The inside of an ant's nest. The workers are filling the larders. Others are looking after the larvae and the queen.

Are spiders insects?

Spiders, with their relatives the mites and scorpions, are not insects. They belong to a class of arthropods called "arachnids". Spiders have eight legs and a body in two parts: the head and thorax joined and the abdomen. The orb-spinning spiders, so called because the web they spin is circular and wheel-like, are well known.

But not all spiders spin webs. The most primitive are the hunting spiders which merely pounce on their prey. Others build simple traps of a funnel shape, and can be found in grass along the hedgerows, or in cellars. Trap-door spiders build tunnels which are lined with silk and covered with a door on a hinge which fits so well that it cannot be seen. When something comes close, the trap-door spider darts out and catches its victim.

What are social insects?

Bees, wasps, termites and ants are called social insects because each group lives and works together in colonies. Each individual insect has a job to do and this is done by instinct. In the beehive the "queen" bee lays eggs, surrounded by "workers". Some workers look after the queen and feed her, some act as nurses to the grubs, and others go out and gather nectar and pollen. There are workers which cool the hive by standing in the doorway and beating their wings, and others on guard outside it. The job of the "drones" (or males) is to mate with the young queens each year.

Ants also live in colonies, making tunnels underground or in heaped-up nests. In Europe, the large wood ant uses pine needles, piling them into a heap. In the garden, there may be a nest of the small black ant beneath a concrete path. Sometimes on a warm summer day, as if by a signal, thousands of winged females appear. They fly off, land and bite off their wings. They then start a new colony.

When was the Age of Dinosaurs?

About 150 million years ago in the Jurassic period, great reptiles flourished, especially the dinosaurs (the name means terrible lizards). From simple beginnings in the Triassic period, they evolved into monsters like *Brontosaurus* and *Diplodocus*.

Dinosaurs came in all shapes and sizes: the largest may have weighed as much as 40 t and measured more than 25 m long, but some were very small.

iguànadon

Some dinosaurs were carnivores, eating the flesh of other dinosaurs which fed only on plants. In the sea the ichthyosaurs flourished, joined by long-necked plesiosaurs. Plesiosaurs used their fins like oars.

Of all the giants, one of the most terrifying must surely have been *Tyrannosaurus rex*. This carnivorous dinosaur stood about 6 m tall and measured some 12 m from nose to tail. Its teeth were 15 cm long and it had great claws on its toes. Peaceful vegetarians like *Iguanodon* and *Trachodon* could escape enemies by running away or leaping into the water. Other dinosaurs were equipped for defence. The armoured kinds had thick coats of bony plates and scales, and were like living tanks. Others like *Triceratops* had horns on their heads, and a curved bony hood over the neck.

The age of dinosaurs ended in mass extinctions some 65 million years ago, but no-one is sure why.

styracosaurus

brontosaurus

tracodon
tyrannosaurus
coritosaurus
triceratops
diplodocus

Above: A crocodile on the banks of the River Nile in Egypt

How can you tell a crocodile from an alligator?

The main difference between a crocodile and an alligator is in the way their teeth are arranged. The upper teeth of a crocodile are in line with its lower teeth. When its mouth is closed, the big fourth tooth in its lower jaw fits into a notch in the outside of its snout and can be clearly seen. An alligator's bottom teeth fit inside its upper teeth. When an alligator's mouth is closed, the big tooth cannot be seen.

Crocodiles cannot chew and are not very good at biting off pieces of meat. To tackle prey as large as a cow, or a human being, the crocodile gets a firm grip with its sharp teeth and then spins its whole body in the water. This twists off an arm or leg that the crocodile can then swallow whole.

Why are tortoises unique?

Tortoises are land reptiles with domed shells and stumpy legs. They move about clumsily and feed mostly on plants and fruit. The largest are the giant tortoises of the Galapagos Islands in the Pacific, and the Aldabra Islands in the Indian Ocean. They can weigh up to 550 kg and measure almost 2 m in length.

Tortoises and turtles are unique among animals, having their whole bodies enclosed in a bony box. This is built from the rib cage which grows and joins up outside the limbs. The earliest tortoises show separate ribs but even these are already flattened as if about to join together. This peculiarity goes back even before the dinosaurs. Chelonians (the order to which tortoises belong) are the oldest group of reptiles and are of three kinds, tortoises, turtles and terrapins. They even include the oldest individuals on Earth today – the giant tortoises which can live to 150 years or more.

Below: A land tortoise

How do snakes catch their prey?

Sight is not as important to snakes as are their senses of taste and smell. They are also very sensitive to vibrations transmitted to their body through the ground or tree branches. The forked tongue of a snake is its "nose".

Having no legs could make catching prey difficult. A struggling animal in a snake's mouth would be very hard to control without some way for the snake to keep its body steady. Some snakes have solved this problem in either of two different ways. One method is to have a venomous bite, so that the prey is poisoned and paralyzed when the snake eats it. The second is for the snake to wrap its whole body round the prey to hold it steady while it gets a grip with its mouth.

How do lizards run?

Lizards are the sprinters of the reptile world. They occupy many different habitats on every continent except Antarctica. There are marine lizards, climbing lizards, desert lizards, big ones and small ones, fast ones and slow ones, and even one or two that can nearly fly.

The shape of a typical lizard is long and flexible, with a long, tapering tail and a short neck. Its short legs stick out at right angles to the body, which is not as strong an arrangement as that of some mammals' legs that can support the body like stilts. When a lizard runs, it curves its back from side to side to increase the length of its stride.

Below: A clamidosaur from Australia

What are amphibians?

All truly aquatic vertebrates have "gills" at some time during their lives for extracting oxygen from water. Gills are feathery, thin-skinned structures that float in the water. In air, gills droop, stick together and dry up. Take a fish out of water and it simply suffocates because it does not have equipment for breathing in air.

Amphibians (such as frogs, toads newts and salamanders) spend the first part of their life in water, with gills, but when they are mature they can survive out of water and breathe air. Their name means, literally, "either life".

Among the 2,500 species of amphibians, there is a wide variety of ways of life. Some species hardly go near water while others hardly ever leave it. Nearly all amphibians, however, need to breed in water.

Below: A tree frog

What is migration?

Migration is one of the most impressive and mysterious wonders of nature. Movement across land and sea, to find fresh food supplies or to reach traditional breeding grounds, occurs in a number of species – some of which make truly amazing journeys.

The most remarkable and the most important migrants are birds. Their travelling capacity is quite incredible. For example, the Arctic tern is known to be capable of flying from the USSR to Australia via the Atlantic, a journey of some 22,000 km. The golden plover is thought to exceed even this distance in its flight from the Arctic to South America. Just how they find their way, in many cases returning year after year to the same nest sites, is one of the miracles of the natural world. It is probable that birds use whatever signs are available – stars, Moon, Sun, as well as landmarks – to get their bearings. Some people believe that birds can also use the Earth's magnetic field to guide them to their destination.

What can you tell from a bird's beak?

The shape of the beak in the various species of birds varies according to their eating habits. Ducks have a beak shaped like a shovel, for digging around in the mud; the sparrow's and the hen's beak is shaped for pecking up grain; the insect eater's beak may often gape open so that it can catch as many insects as possible in flight; the wader's beak is long and thin for probing the mud; the parrot's beak is hooked, so that it can crack seeds and grasp branches. Birds of prey, with their hooked beaks, feed on animals such as snakes, frogs, fish and rodents; the woodpecker knocks on the bark of trees with its beak to find larvae, and its tongue, 10 cm long, can get into tiny cracks in the trunk.

Top: The toucan's large beak is designed for squeezing fruit

Above right: The parrot's hard beak is used to crack seeds

Below: A flight of common cranes migrating to Africa
Inset: White storks fly from Africa to northern Europe every year to breed.

Above: Although they cannot fly, ostriches are very powerful runners.

Why are parrots so noisy?

The long tail, bright colours, and loud voice of a typical parrot are all adaptations for living in dense forest. The long tail makes a good rudder, for manoeuvring between closely-packed branches. Bright colours enable the birds to find one another in the dim light of a tropical forest. The loud voice of the parrot also helps it to keep in touch with other birds, and to give them warning of possible danger.

How is a bird's wing constructed?

A bird's wings are really only the forelimbs covered in feathers. The skeleton of a wing is anatomically similar to that of the forelimb of all the vertebrates – there is a forearm, an arm and a hand with very reduced fingers. On to this framework of light but strong bones are fixed the large flight feathers that go by the name of "remiges". Under the heavy outer, or "contour" feathers, which are often oiled so as to be waterproof, are the smaller "down" feathers which are light and fluffy, and designed to keep the bird's body warm.

Both kinds of feathers are changed once or twice a year as the seasons change. Among the 9,000 species of birds in existence, there are many beautiful plumages of every colour of the rainbow.

Left: Flamingos use their beaks to sift animals and plants from water.

How does a flamingo feed?

Flamingos are birds that feed in a specialized way. Their curiously shaped beak is constructed to sieve out very small animals and plant material from mud and water. The beaks of the two most common types of flamingo are shaped slightly differently, so that they can feed side by side without actually competing. The pink colour of flamingo feathers is caused by the crustaceans that make up a large proportion of the diet of these birds.

Can all birds fly?

Although all birds have feathers, not all of them fly. Some live in ways that do not require the ability to fly, and others have a lifestyle that may make it positively dangerous to fly. These species have given up flight in favour of other ways of travelling.

The group of birds called "ratites", including ostriches, emus, rheas and cassowaries, are all large birds that have very small useless wings. Instead, these birds are powerful runners. Ratites are put together in one group because of their resemblance to one another, but we do not know whether or not they are really closely related.

Ostriches have long, powerful legs with two-toed, hoof-like feet. An ostrich can travel at a speed of 65 km/h.

Which are the most primitive mammals?

Monotremes are the most primitive mammals. They have features in common with both reptiles and mammals. One monotreme, the platypus, inhabits the fresh waters of Australia and Tasmania. Its soft, duck-billed snout is used for finding worms, and it swims with the aid of its webbed feet and flattened tail. The spiny anteaters from Australia and Papua New Guinea, also monotremes, have long snouts and sticky tongues for feeding on worms and ants which they extract from burrows. All these curious mammals lay eggs, instead of giving birth to live young like all other mammals.

What is a marsupial?

The main difference between marsupials and other mammals is that they keep their babies in a pouch. This is much more than just a pocket of skin, for it has one or more teats inside for feeding the young animals. Herbivorous marsupials such as the kangaroo have a forward-opening pouch. Carnivorous ones such as the Tasmanian devil have a backward-opening pouch.

Nearly all the marsupials in the world today live in Australia, New Guinea and Tasmania. There are only about 175 species of marsupial in the whole world, but they were once much more common. In America, there remains the opossum.

Top: A giant panda

Below: A mother kangaroo with her young

Why are giant pandas so rare?

There are only two species of panda: the small red panda and the famous giant panda. They may be related to the raccoons, and the red panda does look like a raccoon, but they live in Asia, where there are no true raccoons.

The red panda is also called the "cat-bear". It lives in mountain forests, sleeping in a tree during the day and feeding at night on acorns, roots, lichens and bamboo shoots on the forest floor.

Giant pandas eat only bamboo shoots. One major problem they have is that the bamboo dies after flowering. If most of the bamboo plants flower at once, then the pandas starve afterwards. Unfortunately, this has happened recently, and fewer than 500 pandas now exist in China. Successful breedings of captive pandas have been rare.

Which are the most successful mammals?

Of all the groups of mammals, rodents are the most successful. There are over 1,700 species of rodent, from the tiny harvest mouse to the capybara, the giant of the order at $1\frac{1}{4}$ m long and 50 cm high.

Their name means "gnawing", and this is what all rodents have in common. The front teeth, or incisors, are chisel-shaped, and grow continuously throughout a rodent's life, so that they are never worn away. Rodents have no teeth between these incisors and their grinding molar teeth at the back of the mouth. When they are gnawing on the hard food they eat, the gap between their incisors and back teeth is filled in by their cheeks. This means that the back teeth, which do not keep on growing, are not worn out.

Why did primates develop a large brain?

The primate body is basically built for climbing. It is believed that the earliest ancestor of living primates (monkeys, apes and humans) was a tree-climbing insectivore rather like the eighteen species of tree shrews that still live in the forests of Java, Borneo, Sumatra and south-east Asia. These small, squirrel-like creatures move quickly among the branches, feeding on insects, together with some fruit and seeds.

Living in trees requires good eyesight. This in turn necessitates a larger brain to handle the information fed in by the eyes, as well as to deal with the problems of moving accurately in a three-dimensional world.

Climbing also calls for special adaptations for clinging on. One way of solving this problem was the development of fingers that could grip instead of claws, and fingers also had the potential ability to hold on to and make tools.

Which is the most deadly animal?

The most poisonous animal is a north Australian jellyfish known as the sea wasp (*Chironex fleckeri*). It has been estimated that its poison is more than 350 times more potent than that of the Portuguese man o'war. The poison acts so quickly – death usually occurs only a few minutes after being stung – that there is usually no chance to attempt treatment.

The most venomous land animal is the funnelweb spider (*Atrax robustus*), a large south Australian species. No really effective treatment has been found for its venom, which is far more potent than that of the most deadly snake.

How do dolphins navigate?

Dolphins are among the most intelligent of mammals. In captivity, dolphins play with their keepers and quickly learn all sorts of tricks. Like bats, dolphins rely on a sound-echo, or "sonar", navigation system. Tests have shown that a blind-folded dolphin can move about quite easily without hitting any obstacles.

Dolphins and porpoises are not generally found together. Porpoises belong in the north, whereas dolphins tend to keep to warmer seas. They often accompany ships by swimming just in front of the bows.

Right: Dolphins playing in an aquarium in San Diego, USA

Why do giraffes have long necks?

Giraffes feed largely on prickly acacia trees, stripping the leaves off with their lobed teeth and working round the thorns with their long tongue and mobile lips. The long legs and neck of a giraffe enable it to feed on leaves other browsers cannot reach, but also cause something of a problem. When a giraffe drinks, it must stand with its front legs widely spread so that it can reach down to the water. Giraffes do bend their legs at night, to chew the cud with their head erect. They sleep with their head folded down along their back for a few moments at a time.

In spite of having such a long neck, giraffes have no more neck bones than any other mammals.

How many toes has a rhinoceros?

The rhinoceros is an "ungulate". The name ungulate means "hoofed", and the so-called odd-toed ungulates are hoofed mammals whose feet are centred on one particular toe. In some species, like horses and zebras, this toe is very big and the animal actually stands on it; in other species, like rhinoceroses, there are three large toes.

There are only sixteen species of odd-toed ungulates alive in the world today. We know 152 species from fossils, which means that this group of mammals has probably had the highest rate of extinction of all the mammal orders.

These mammals fall into three groups: the horse, ass and zebras; the tapirs; and the rhinoceroses. Of these, the rhinoceros is by far the most endangered. It is hunted illegally by poachers, chiefly for its horn.

Which is the largest land animal?

Elephants are the biggest living land animals and have enormous appetites. Elephants in zoos require about 45 kg of hay each day; in the wild, they feed on green shoots and leaves and eat a far greater amount. Elephants also require a lot of water, nearly 200 l daily.

African elephants are larger than the Asian ones; they have bigger ears and a straighter back, and are far less easy to tame. In the wild, elephants tend to live in well-organized groups. These may be family units of about four animals or herds of two or three dozen individuals. These herds are usually led by an old female and will include several other females and their young, together with a number of young bulls. Old bulls lead solitary lives away from the herd.

Why did bison nearly vanish from the Earth?

The American bison or "buffalo" once roamed across the plains of North America in herds so large that it was said they took hours or even days to pass by. In the 1800s, they were slaughtered for their meat and hides at the rate of thousands daily. From the 60 million animals that were alive at the beginning of the nineteenth century, only a few hundred were left before the twentieth century began. Today the bison survives, but only in semi-captive herds within national parks.

The European bison, or "wisent" fared even worse than the American bison, and was very nearly destroyed

Above: The European bison, a magnificent animal now only found in parks and reservations

Right: An Arab rides his camel through the desert

Facing page: A female giraffe feeding her young

altogether during the First World War. A careful breeding programme has now produced about 200 animals in the Bialowieza Forest reserve in Poland.

Why do camels have humps?

The camel's hump serves as a fat store to be drawn on when there is no food. The camel can get some water from the fat as this is processed in its body, but it drinks enormous quantities of water whenever it gets the chance.

Bactrian camels have two humps, and live in the cold, rocky deserts of Asia. They have a thick, warm coat. Arabian camels, or dromedaries, have one hump. They have short hair and like the desert heat. Their feet are adapted to spreading over the surface of the sand.

Why do hunting animals grow up slowly?

Hunting animals need to be intelligent. First they have to find their prey. When they have located it, they then have to catch it in spite of all its efforts to escape. On the other hand, large hunters do not have to worry too much about being hunted themselves. Apart from humans, their natural enemies are very few.

Such carnivorous animals tend to grow up slowly. They spend their infancy practising hunting and learning to use their bodies. They develop skills that will help them to survive when they must fend for themselves.

Do male lions hunt prey?

Unlike most cats, lions live and hunt in groups called "prides". A pride may contain up to thirty lions, consisting of at least one male, together with several lionesses and their young.

The maned male lion does not do much hunting. He saves his energy for chasing away rivals who may steal his mates. The lionesses do the hunting for the pride, working as a team to stalk and kill a zebra or antelope. Generally, the leading male has first choice of the carcass, while the younger animals are left with the scraps.

Top: Lion cubs grow up slowly so that they have time to learn the hunting skills they need.

Below: A grizzly bear in Canada

What do bears eat?

Bears are "omnivorous" animals. They feed on roots, plants, berries, nuts, fruit, eggs, insects, young livestock, and can even catch trout and leaping salmon. However, they have one particular passion – honey. Only polar bears are exclusively meat-eaters.

Bears are intelligent animals, and of a fairly peaceable nature. However, if disturbed in their den, or otherwise upset, they can be extremely dangerous.

In the winter a bear dozes in its den, but it is not a true hibernator and gets up for a sleepy foray on warm days. The female has a gestation period of seven to eight months, and gives birth in the depth of winter to two or three cubs. At birth the cubs are tiny, but at four or five months they are able to forage with their mother.

How do cheetahs hunt?

The cheetah is the most dog-like of the cats. It hunts in open country in Asia and Africa, where there is not enough cover for it to stalk close to its prey. Cheetahs may hunt alone or in pairs. They stalk as near as they can get to a chosen victim and then cover the remaining distance at a sprint, sometimes reaching a speed of over 100 km/h. They cannot keep this speed up for long, however, and if their first rush does not succeed they will generally give up after travelling about 400 m.

Which are the biggest cats?

Tigers are the biggest cats. They live on the continent of Eurasia, hunting in forests from Siberia to India. There are several different races, of which the Siberian tiger is the largest. The tiger's coat is striped to match the pattern of light and shade in woodland, and it spends much of its time in the shade. Tigers do not like great heat; in India, they may even lie in water to keep cool and they are excellent swimmers. Tigers nearly always hunt alone, though a male tiger may help his mate to hunt when she has cubs.

Why do wolves hunt in packs?

The ancestors of our domestic dogs were probably wolves. These dogs hunt in well-organized packs. They cooperate to trail and kill large prey, such as moose and caribou. Their social life is equally well ordered. Within the pack, male and female wolves often pair for life. The female digs a hole to shelter her young, generally helped by the father and some other adult wolves. At breeding time the packs are broken up by this activity, and wolves may hunt the plentiful small prey of spring and summer in small groups or even alone.

Each wolf pack has its own territory, an area that consists of about $2\frac{1}{2}$ sq km. They patrol this area regularly over a number of weeks, leaving scent marks on rocks and trees as they go along.

Below: A pack of wolves in a forest in Northern Europe

Bottom: A tiger, one of the big cats

Do cats have good eyesight?

A cat's eyes are designed to spot the smallest movement. They are also positioned on the front of the face to give good stereoscopic vision, enabling the cat to judge distances very accurately. The large ears can pick up the tiniest noise and detect the direction of the sound. Although cats' noses are not as sensitive as dogs', they are probably more acute than those of humans. Their whiskers help them to sense their own position when the other senses are concentrated on the hunt.

Below: Early men and women gradually learnt how to make fire and to use simple tools for hunting. They ate the meat of the animals they caught and used the skins for clothing.

Right: Six stages in the progression from hominoids (the primitive family from which present-day apes and people developed) to modern human beings. The change from a partially to a fully upright posture and the gradual growth in skull size can be seen.

Below right: Prehistoric people usually lived in caves, but they sometimes also built primitive shelters. The one shown here consists of a framework of mammoth tusks covered in animal skins and is based on an actual shelter whose remains were found in the USSR.

Australopithecus, height: 1.20 m

Paranthropus, height: 1.25–1.5

How have humans developed?

Humans emerged from a huge group of mammals known as primates. Among this group are the apes, all of which are tailless and resemble humans quite closely. The African great apes (gorillas and chimpanzees) belong to the same group of animals as humans.

The African great apes and humans have a common ancestor, a type of ape called *Australopithecus*, who lived in prehistoric Africa. This creature walked upright and knew how to use its hands. It had a larger skull than the chimpanzee and teeth similar to a modern human's. *Australopithecus* was only 120 cm tall and communicated by means of gestures and grunts. A type of primitive man, *Homo neanderthalensis*, thrived during the third great ice age, and Cro-Magnon man, an early type of modern human, finally emerged about 35,000 years ago.

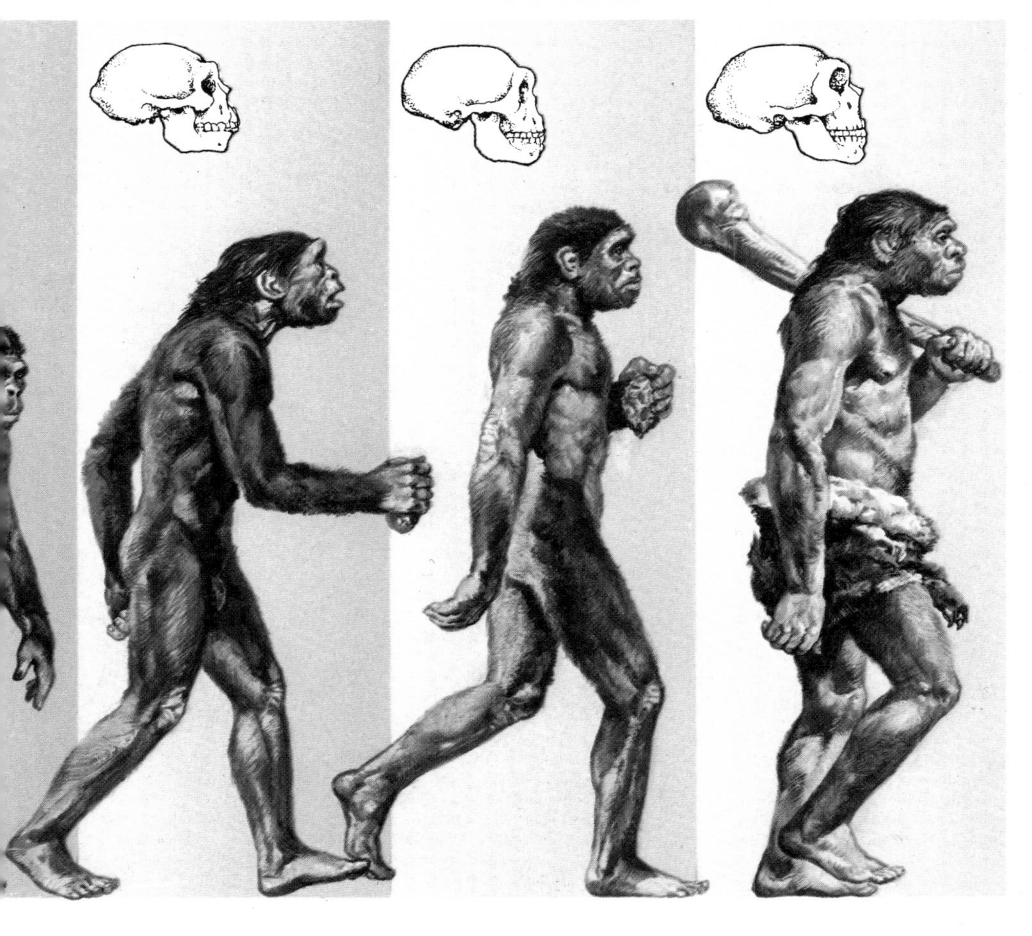

Pithecanthropus,
height: 1.60 m

Homo sapiens,
height: 1.60 m

Neanderthal man,
height: 1.60 m

Cro-Magnon man,
height: 1.82 m

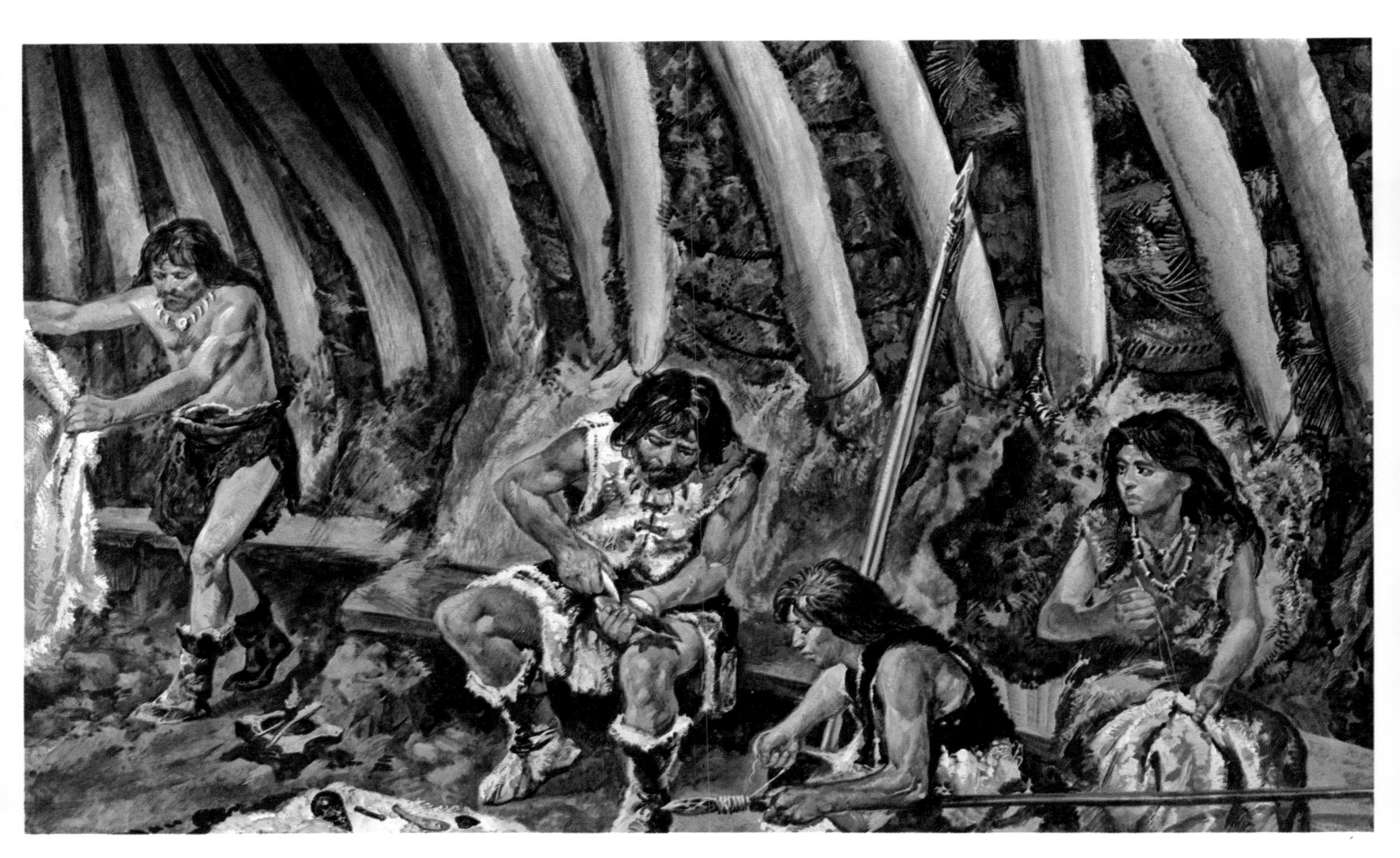

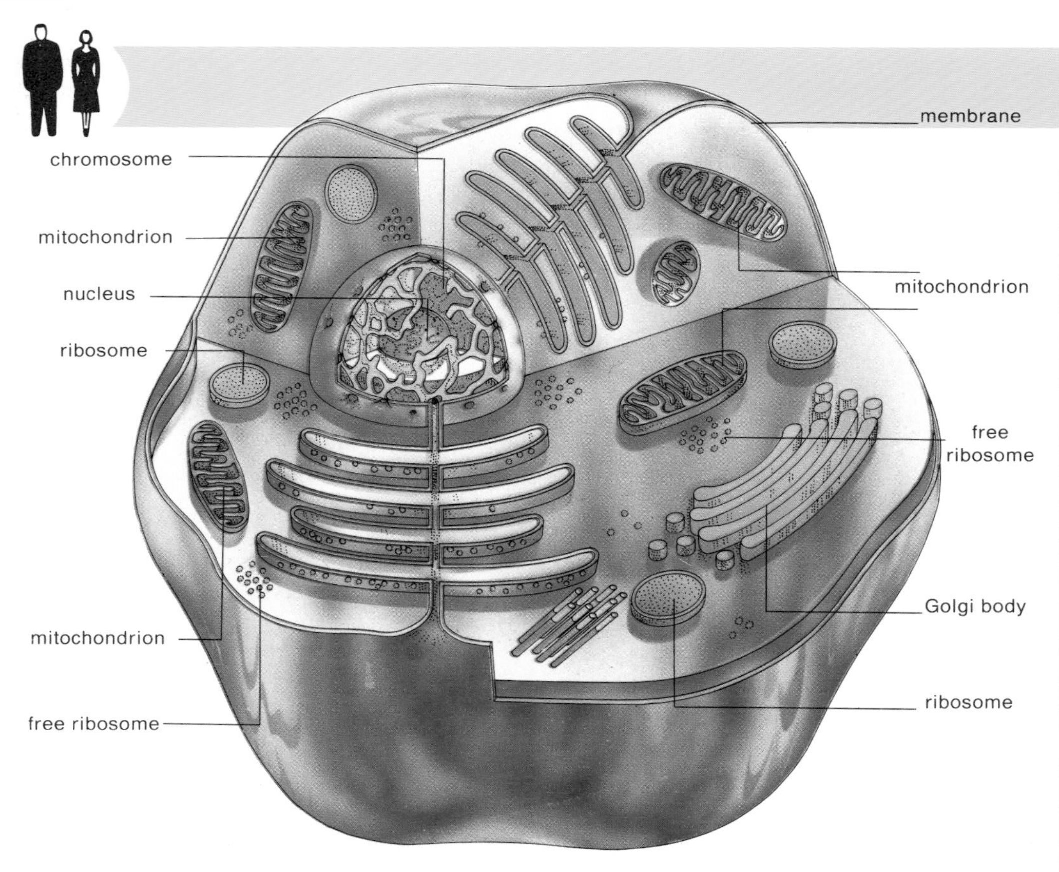

Above: A cross section of a body cell. Each of the labelled structures has a particular task to carry out.

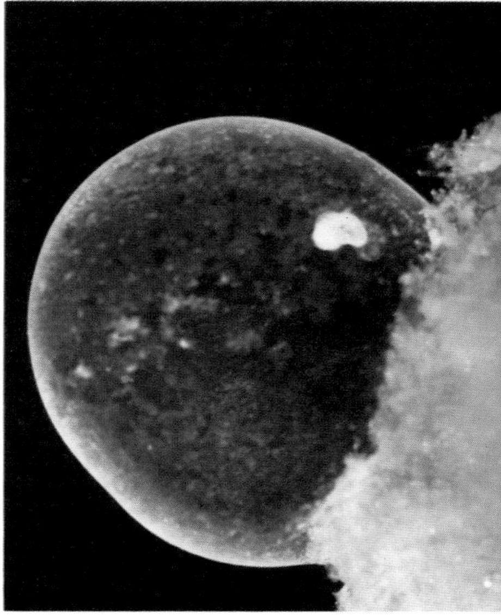

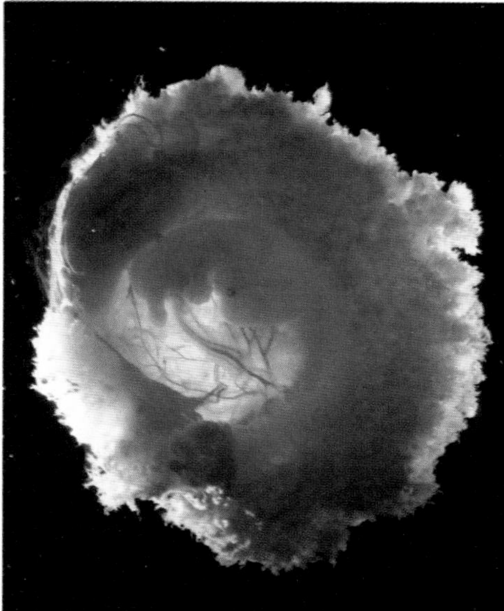

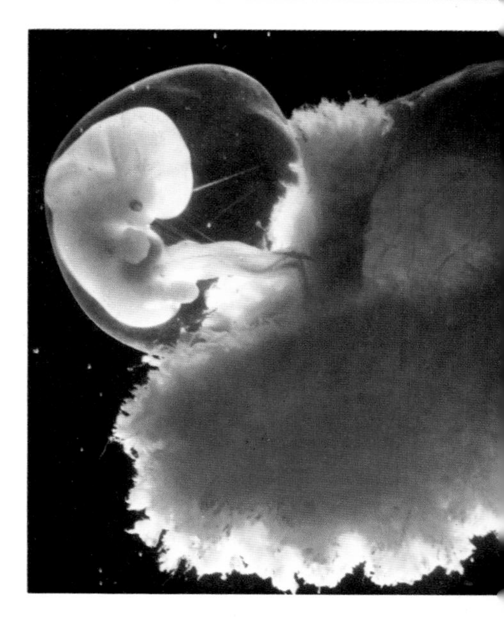

Right: Three stages in the development of a human embryo

What does a body cell do?

A cell consists of a membrane surrounding a jelly-like fluid. It is a hive of activity that can be likened to a chemical factory. In it, chemicals are built up, exported to one set of cells, imported from other cells, used to provide energy and broken down into waste products. All these activities are controlled by the cell nucleus which contains the chemical blueprints for all the instructions that the other cell structures need. The illustration above shows some of these structures.

How long do body cells live?

Cells are not all the same. In the human body there are many different kinds: large cells, small cells, round cells, flattened cells, star-shaped cells, long, many-branched cells and even cells that swim like tadpoles. Most of these cells have only a very short life. Every day, old cells wear out and are replaced by new ones. Some live for several months, but others last less than one day. Only nerve cells live for many years and are never replaced.

How does a baby grow from a cell?

The process of sexual reproduction involves creating special sex cells. A male and a female sex cell are then brought together so that their nuclei fuse, a process known as fertilization.

The cell resulting from this process develops into a new individual. In about nine days, it has grown into a ball of cells, which becomes implanted in the wall of the mother's womb. By eight weeks, the developing embryo has a skeleton, muscles and nervous system. It continues to develop in the womb for another seven months and then, nine months after fertilization, the baby is born.

What does blood do?

The purpose of circulating blood around the body is to carry chemicals to where they are needed. Oxygen is carried from the lungs to the rest of the body's tissues and carbon dioxide is taken to the lungs. Food chemicals are carried to the liver and other tissues, and waste materials are carried from the liver to the kidneys. Blood also carries the chemical messengers known as "hormones" for distribution throughout the body. White blood cells in particular are responsible for fighting disease and infection and are able to flatten themselves in order to pass through "capillaries" (small blood vessels) to where their assistance is needed.

What does blood consist of?

Blood consists of several kinds of cell suspended in a clear liquid known as "plasma". The most common cells are the red blood cells, which are disc-shaped and have no nuclei. They contain the pigment haemoglobin, which is the chemical responsible for carrying oxygen around the body. There are also white cells in the blood which help protect the body from infection and "platelets" which are not really true cells but minute cellular fragments without a nucleus. They play an important part in the process of clotting.

How many blood groups are there?

Not everybody has the same type of blood. There are four blood groups, known by letters of the alphabet: groups O, A, B and AB. Most people can receive and give blood only of their own group. Exceptions are people of group AB, who can receive blood of all other groups, and those of group O who can give their blood to people of all other groups.

Why is blood red?

There are about 4.5–6 l of blood in a human body. The most numerous cells in the blood are the red corpuscles

cu mm. The pigment responsible for their colour is called haemoglobin, and it is this which makes blood red. The white corpuscles ("leucocytes") are much less numerous (about 8,000 per cu mm).

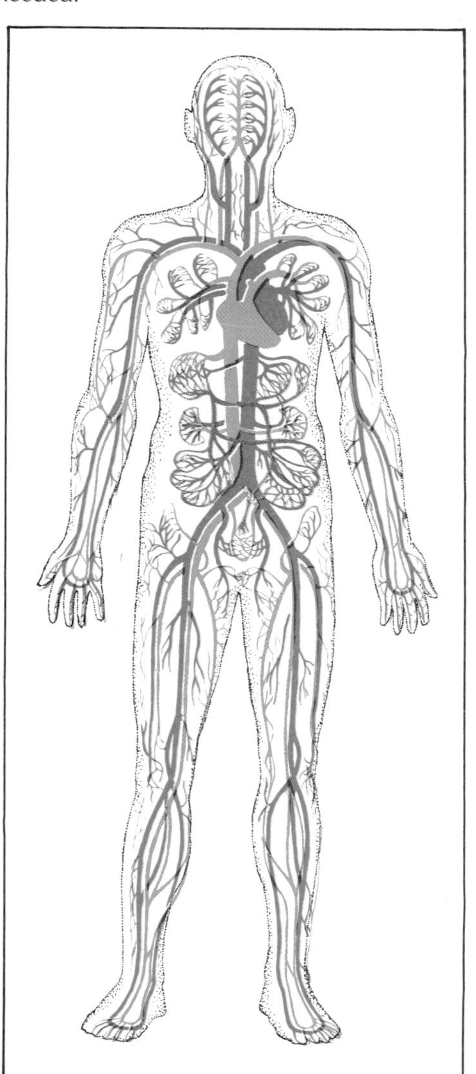

Left: The blood vessels of the human body. Those shown in red are arteries and carry oxygenated blood from the heart to various parts of the body. Those shown in blue are veins which carry deoxygenated blood back to the heart.

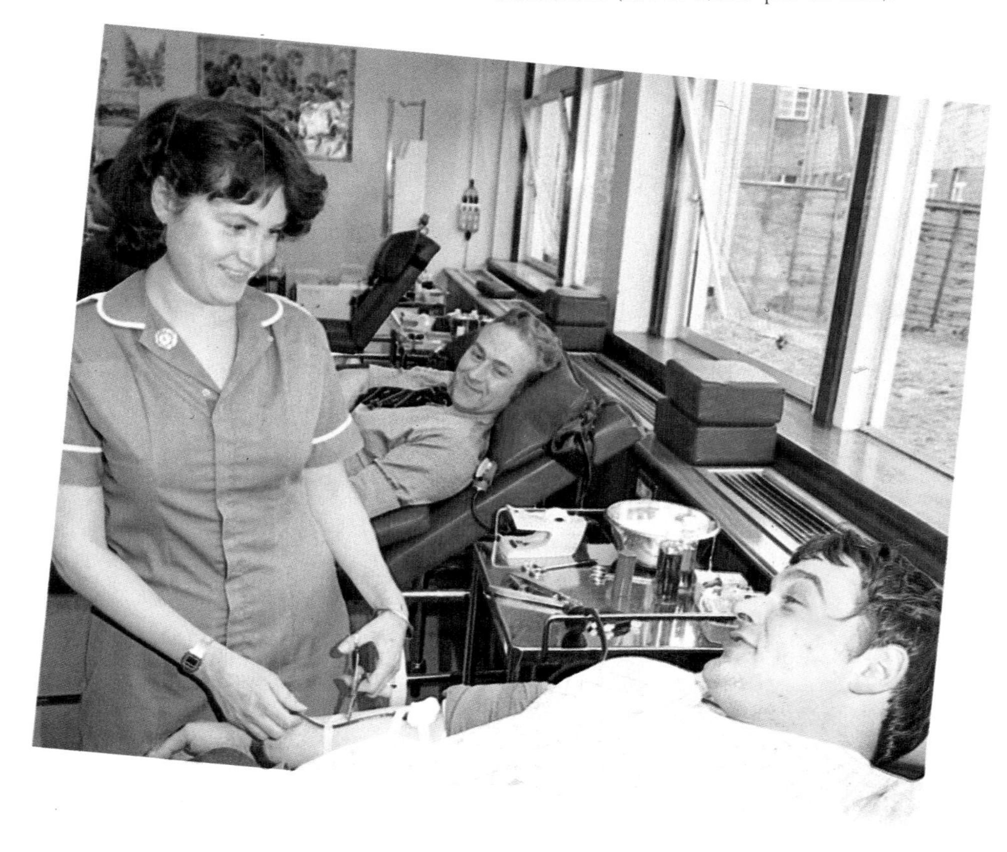

Below: Many people regularly donate up to a pint of their blood for later use in hospitals.

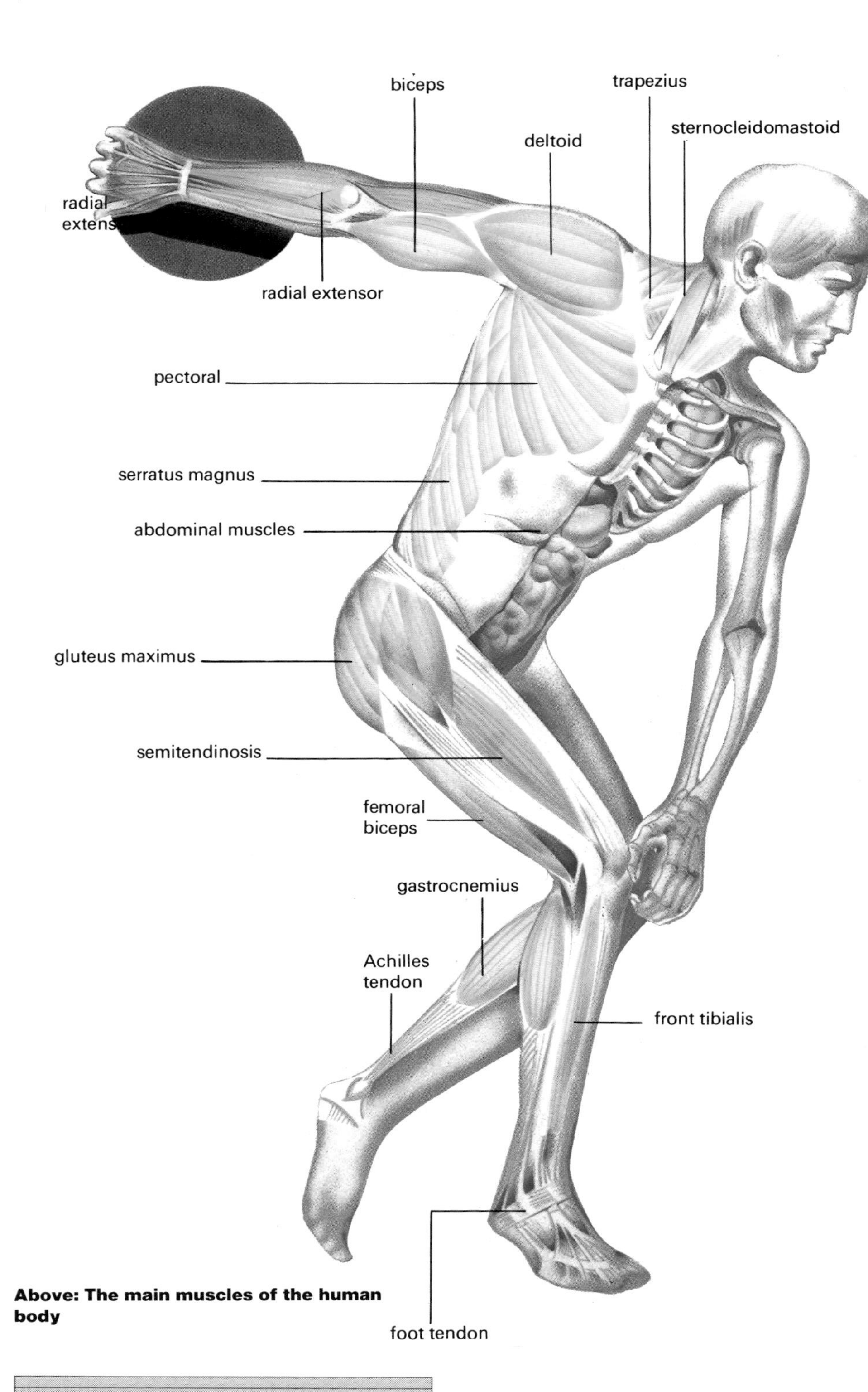

Above: The main muscles of the human body

How do muscles move?

Every body muscle is made up of several muscle bundles. Each bundle contains a number of muscle fibres, and each of these has a large number of short filaments. Nerve impulses cause the overlapping filaments to slide over one another. As a result, the muscle fibres become shorter and the whole muscle contracts.

A muscle can only contract. It is expanded again when it is relaxed and then stretched.

What does muscle look like?

There are three kinds of muscle tissue, of which the most common is called "striped" muscle. This makes up all the skeletal (bone-moving) muscles of the body. It is so-called because, when seen under the microscope, it has a striped appearance.

The gut lining, the walls of the arteries and the iris of the eye are made of "smooth" muscle, which consists of long, tapering cells. Striped muscle can be consciously controlled, but the action of smooth muscle is automatic and is controlled by the autonomic nervous system.

The third type of muscle is the cardiac muscle which makes up the heart. Its structure is between that of striped and smooth muscle.

How many muscles are needed to move an arm?

To operate a part of the body, at least two opposing muscles are needed. The simplest example of this can be seen in the arm. Here, the contraction of the biceps muscle at the front pulls the forearm up towards the upper arm. The arm is straightened again when the triceps muscle at the back contracts. Where more complicated movements are needed, there are two opposing sets of muscles instead of just two muscles.

What makes bones move?

Muscles do not move bones directly because they are not attached to them. Instead, each end of a muscle is joined to a tendon, which is attached to and moves the bone. Some tendons are very long – for example, some of the tendons that link the bones of the fingers to muscles in the forearm. A ligament is a flexible band of tissue that links two bones at a joint to keep them in place.

How many muscles are there in the human body?

There are over 600 muscles in the human body and together they make up about 40 per cent of a person's total weight. Muscles may be divided into two types – "voluntary" and "involuntary". Voluntary muscles, such as those in the arms, legs and face, can be made to move when required – they are sent an order consciously by the brain. Involuntary muscle, such as that which pushes food through the intestines, works automatically and needs no conscious order.

Which muscle controls breathing?

The movement of air into the lungs is controlled by the diaphragm. This is a sheet of muscle stretched across the bottom of the ribcage. When it contracts, the lungs expand so that the pressure in the chest cavity is reduced, and air is drawn in. The expansion of the chest cavity is also helped by the contraction of the muscles between the ribs, which lifts the ribs upwards and outwards. Breathing out is achieved by relaxing all the muscles. The lungs then shrink and force out the air.

How does the human heart work?

The heart is a powerful muscle, normally capable of beating rhythmically between fifty and eighty times per minute. It pumps the 5 or 6 l of blood in the human body through an incredible network of blood vessels. Over a period of seventy years, the heart contracts about 2,500 million times and pumps about 180 million l of blood.

The heart has four chambers, two "atria" (or "auricles") and two "ventricles". Blood enters the heart from the body via the right atrium. A small squeeze from the muscles of the atrium wall then pushes the blood into the right ventricle. The one-way valve between the atrium and ventricle then closes, and the wall of the ventricle contracts powerfully, forcing the blood out via the pulmonary artery. This carries the blood to the lungs where it picks up oxygen. The pulmonary vein then carries the oxygenated blood back to the heart, where it enters the left atrium and left ventricle.

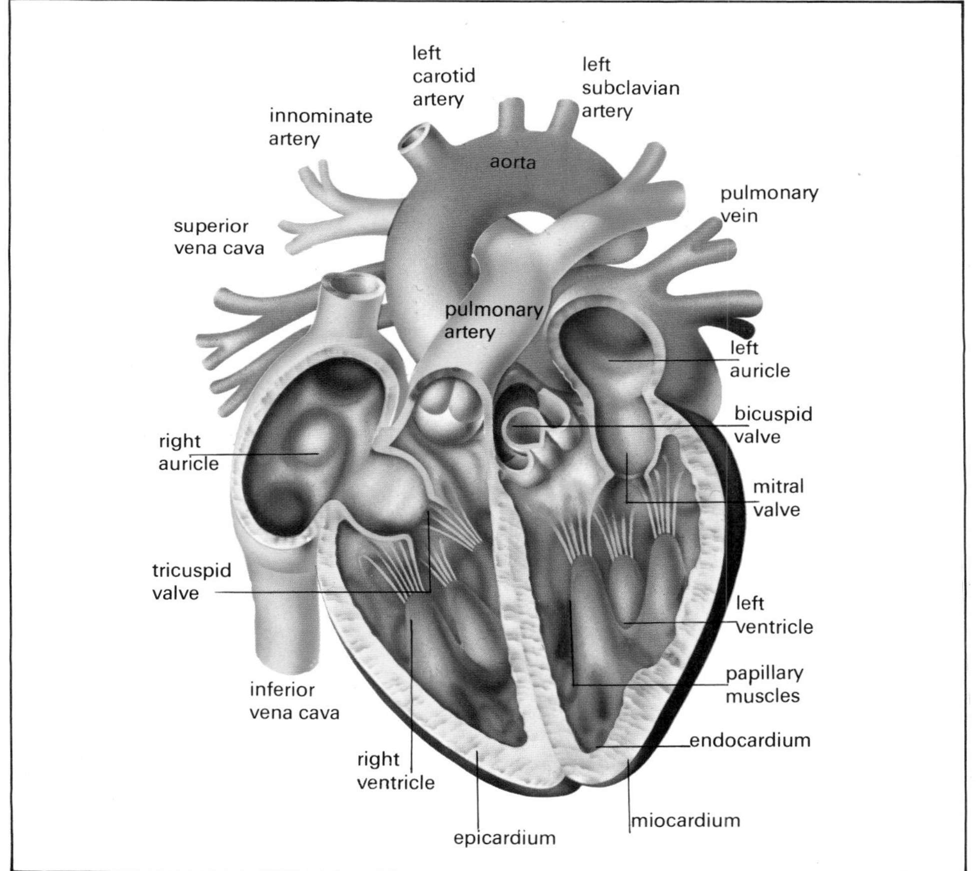
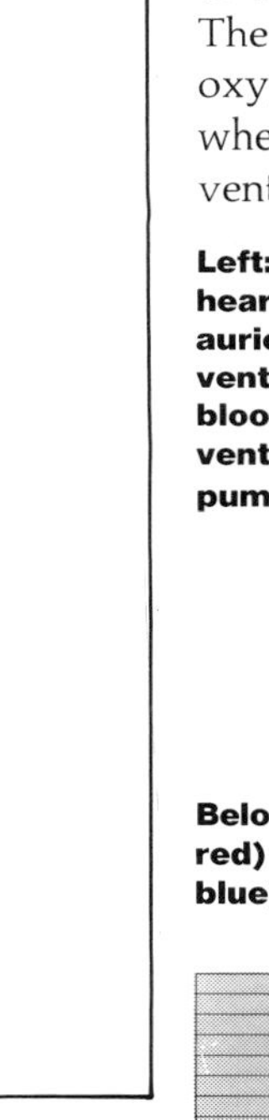

Left: A diagram of the human heart. The heart is divided into four cavities, two auricles, or atria, at the top and two ventricles below. The auricles collect the blood reaching the heart, while the ventricles, with their thick, muscular walls, pump it out.

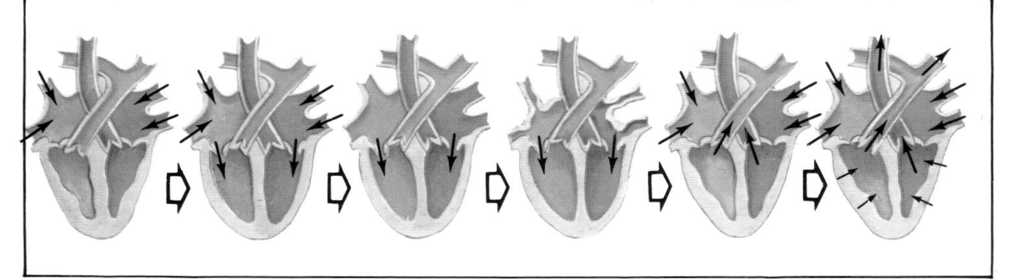

Below left: How oxygenated blood (shown in red) and deoxygenated blood (shown in blue) is pumped through the heart

What makes the heart beat?

Cardiac muscle is found only in the walls of the heart. It is very powerful and its most important characteristic is that it can contract regularly without being stimulated by nerve impulses. In a human being, it contracts regularly about sixty to one hundred times each minute, thus making the heart beat.

Left: Skin forms a protective layer all over the body.

How much skin covers the human body?

From the outside, the most obvious feature of the human body is the skin. This waterproof, elastic covering forms a vital protective layer all over the body – some 18,000 sq cm. It keeps out germs, dirt and moisture and, at the same time, helps protect the more delicate tissues inside from being damaged and from losing precious moisture – about 60 per cent of the human body is water. In addition, the skin helps to control the temperature of the body and acts as a sense organ.

What is human skin made of?

The skin consists of two layers. The outer layer, the "epidermis", varies considerably in thickness. The tough skin on the soles of the feet may have an epidermis of over 3 mm thick, whereas on the eyelids it is often less than $\frac{1}{2}$ mm. The outer layers of the epidermis consist of dead cells that are continually being shed. Only the innermost epidermal cells are living. Here, new cells are formed to replace those lost from the outside. The whole epidermis is replaced once every few weeks.

The inner layer of skin is called the "dermis". It is mainly composed of blood vessels, nerve endings and fat.

How does skin keep people cool?

There are tiny glands in the dermis (inner layer of the skin) which are able to produce a watery fluid, known as sweat. Sweat consists of water and waste substances; it helps to keep the body both clean on the inside and at a constant temperature. On hot days, the evaporation of sweat helps to cool the body down. Cooling is helped by the fact that the blood vessels in the dermis swell and fill with blood. Heat then passes more easily from the blood to the outside.

How does skin keep people warm?

On cold days the blood vessels in the skin contract and sweating stops. If the skin gets too cold, some of the body muscles start to contract and relax rapidly, causing people to shiver. This muscle action helps to generate more heat. At the same time, the hair muscles contract, pulling the hairs upright and the skin into "goose pimples". The inner layer of the skin consists mostly of cells containing large amounts of fat. This is the layer that does most to insulate the body from cold.

Below: A cross section of human skin. The skin consists of two layers, the outer epidermis and the inner dermis.

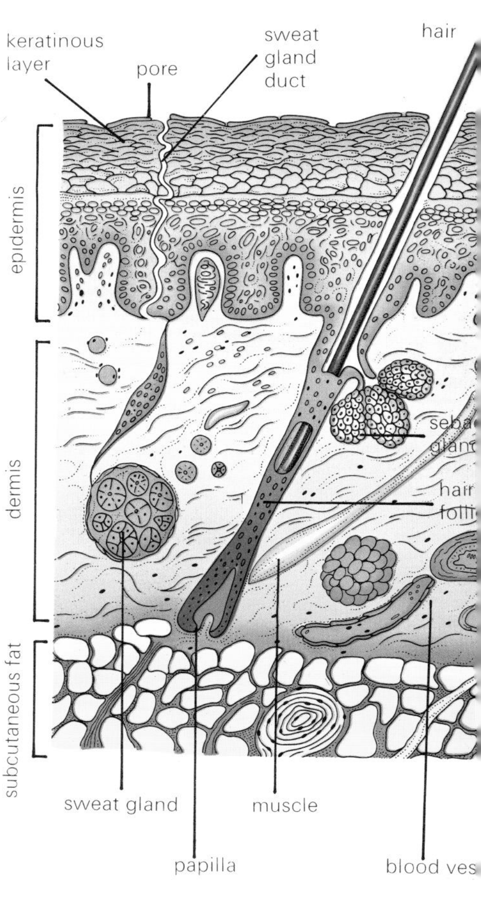

Why does skin colour vary?

In the epidermis (the thin, outer layer of the skin) are star-shaped cells called "melanocytes". These control the amount of melanin, a dark pigment which is present in the skin. Dark-skinned people have very active melanocytes whereas those of fair-skinned people are less active.

Over human history, the pigment in skin has reacted to the rays of the Sun, adapting the human body to its

environment. In countries where there was little hot sun, people with light-coloured skins could live comfortably, and a dark skin was no advantage. But where the Sun was very hot, people with darker skins were at an advantage, as they did not burn. This meant that they were able to hunt more, and by getting more food, generally thrive and reproduce. Any skin colour is simply a sign of human adaptation to the environment.

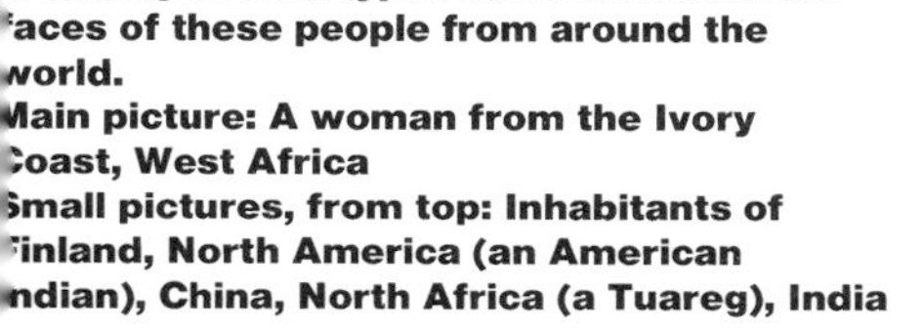

A variety of skin types can be seen on the faces of these people from around the world.
Main picture: A woman from the Ivory Coast, West Africa
Small pictures, from top: Inhabitants of Finland, North America (an American Indian), China, North Africa (a Tuareg), India

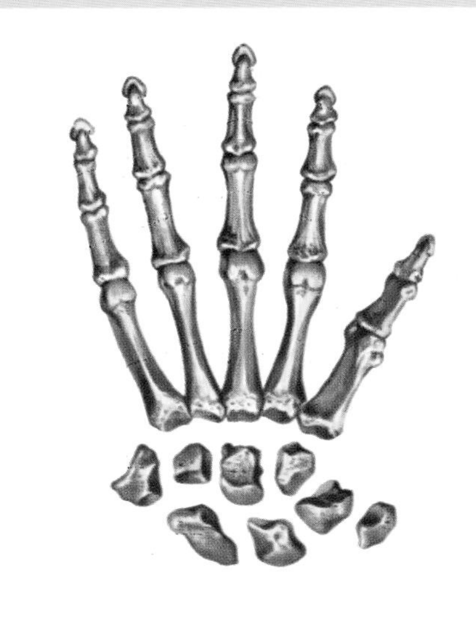

Above and right: The twenty-seven bones of the human hand make it flexible enough to perform intricate tasks such as sculpting and writing.

What makes human hands unique?

The hand is a masterpiece of engineering, particularly the position of the thumb in relation to the fingers. Anthropologists believe that the "opposable" thumb, which enabled our ancestors to grasp tools, was one of the reasons for the development of human intelligence, which is unique in the animal world.

The hand can be used in many different ways. It can mend a tiny watch or carry out a delicate surgical operation; it can grip a heavy suitcase; it can wrench the top off a bottle or grip a crowbar; it can help to pull its owner up a rope or a pole.

Below: A human skeleton seen from the front, the side and the rear

How many bones are there in the human body?

The human skeleton consists of 206 bones. The largest is the "femur" (thigh bone) and the smallest are the bones in the inner ear.

The central supporting part of the skeleton is the spinal column, which has thirty-three separate bones called

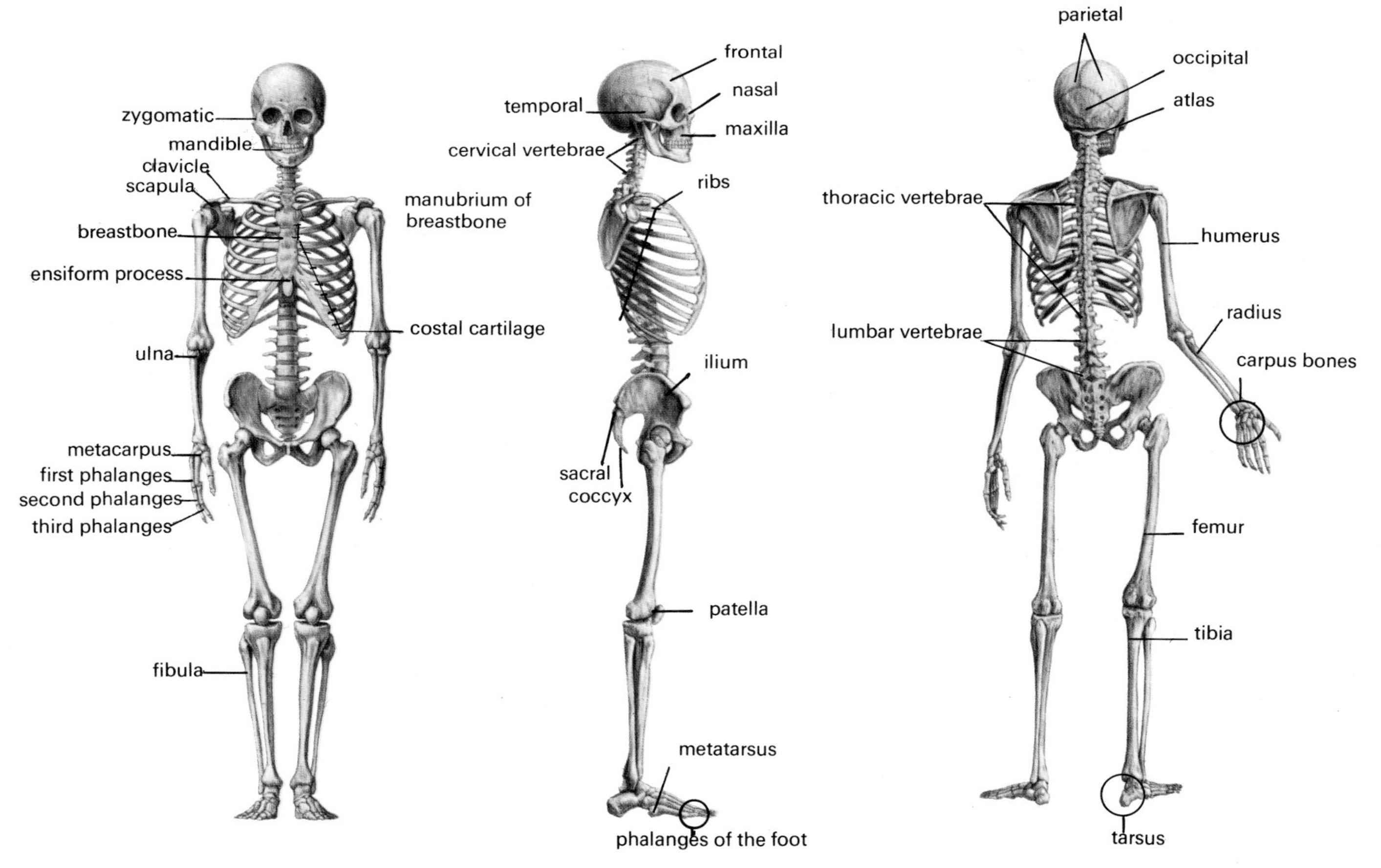

"vertebrae". At the top of this column, seven neck vertebrae support the skull, which is made up of several bones fused together. Below the neck are twelve thoracic vertebrae, which have curved projections – the ribs.

How can hands "speak"?

Hands are not just used for gripping – they assist a person's balance when necessary, and are even used for communication. Everyone resorts to "sign language" when the language they are speaking is not understood. People also use hand gestures to underline the meaning of the spoken word and hand contact with other humans can signal peaceful intent, affection or agreement. The deaf can learn to communicate with each other by a series of hand signals.

What are wisdom teeth?

A human's permanent teeth consist of four "incisors" (front teeth which bite off food), two "canines" (pointed biting teeth), four "premolars" and six "molars" (back teeth which chew food) in each jaw – thirty-two teeth altogether. The last four molars (the eighth tooth on the right and left of each jaw) do not appear before the age of eighteen to twenty, and for this reason they are known as "wisdom teeth".

How do people feel heat and cold?

When a part of the body comes into contact with an object, we feel sensations including touch, pressure, heat and cold. These are detected by nerves that end in organized receptors. There are some 500,000 touch receptors compared with over 3 million pain receptors. Cold receptors number about 150,000, but there are only 16,000 receptors for warmth. Touch receptors are most numerous in the fingers, where there are about 200 per sq cm.

How is the tongue able to taste?

The surface of the tongue is covered with "papillae" (tiny lumps). On the sides of many of these are "taste buds", each of which consists of a group (four to twenty) of taste cells. These send nerve impulses to the brain when stimulated by chemicals in the saliva.

There are about 10,000 taste buds on the human tongue and different areas of the tongue respond to different sorts of taste. Sweetness is tasted at the front of the tongue, bitterness at the back. Sour things are tasted along the sides of the tongue. Salty things are tasted all over the tongue, but especially at the tip.

Above: To be able to judge the age and quality of wine, experts must cultivate their senses of taste and smell.

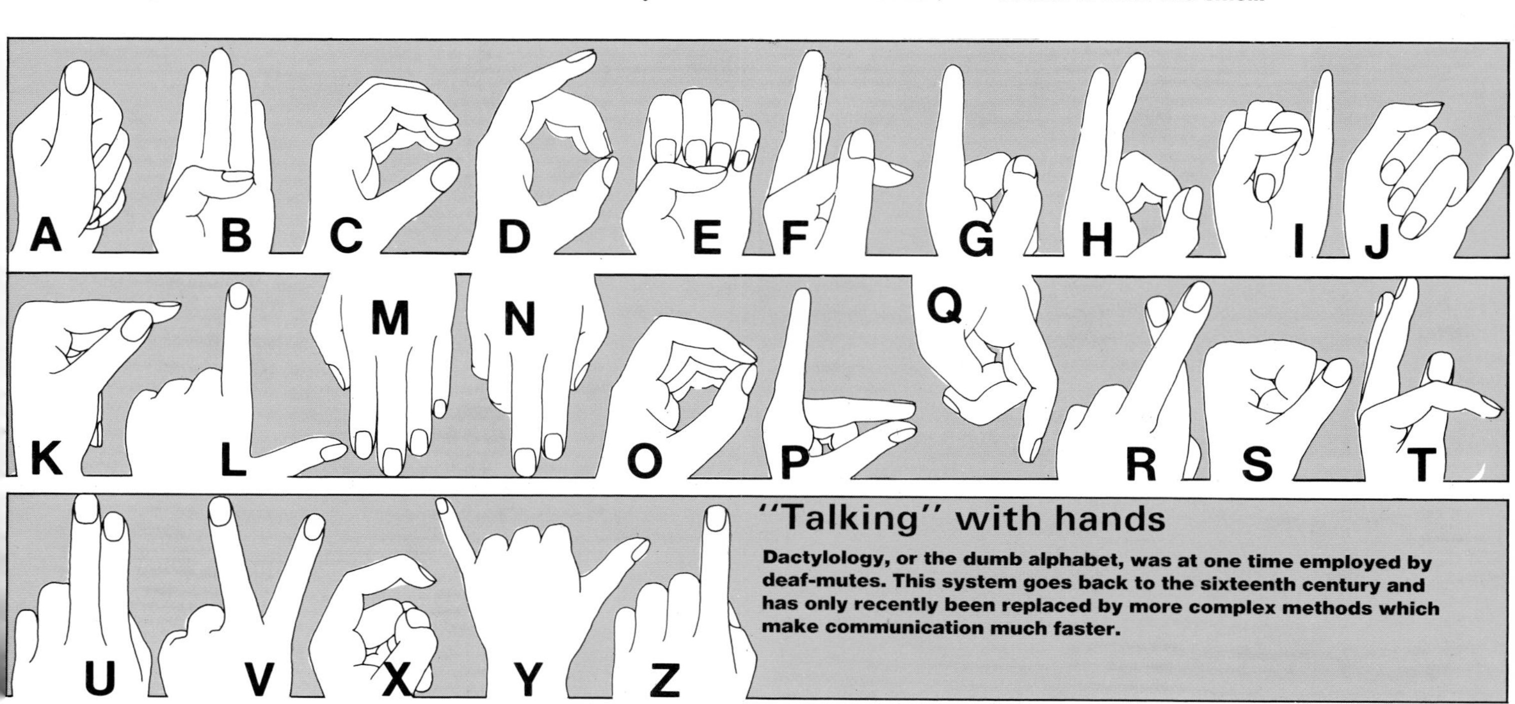

"Talking" with hands

Dactylology, or the dumb alphabet, was at one time employed by deaf-mutes. This system goes back to the sixteenth century and has only recently been replaced by more complex methods which make communication much faster.

How do the eyes see?

At the front of the eye is a transparent window called the "cornea". Light enters the eye through the cornea and passes through a hole (the "pupil"), in a coloured disc known as the "iris". Next, the light passes through the "lens". When the eye is focused on distant objects, the lens is flattened. When it focuses on nearby objects, the lens becomes rounder.

The focused light forms an image at the back of the eye. Here, there is a light-sensitive layer of cells called the "retina". Light falling on these cells causes them to send impulses to the brain, which "sees" the image formed on the retina.

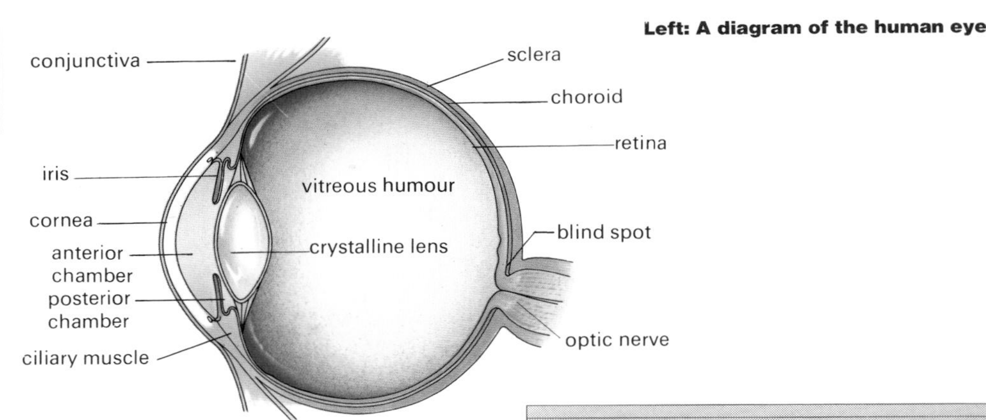

Left: A diagram of the human eye

Why do eye surgeons use lasers?

A laser is an instrument which produces a beam of light. However, laser light is much more powerful than ordinary light. It has such high energy that it can cut through very hard substances such as metal and diamond.

Lasers are also useful in medicine. For example an eye surgeon can use narrow beams of laser light to operate on the eye without cutting it open.

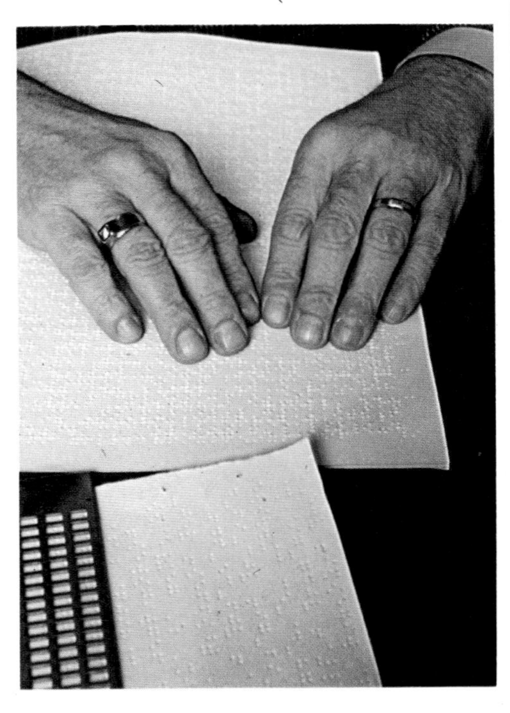

Above: A blind person reading the raised letters of the Braille alphabet with their fingertips

Below: Preparations being made with the aid of a laser for an eye operation to reattach a retina

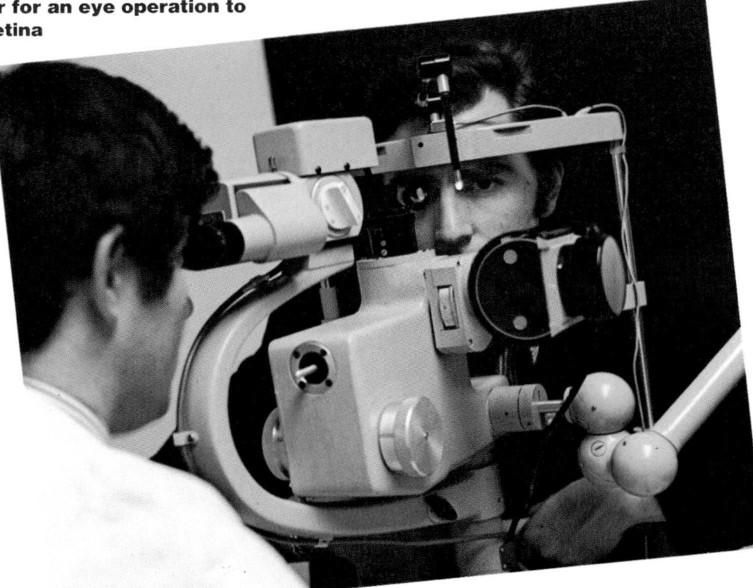

How can blind people read?

The blind can read thanks to an alphabet invented in 1829 by the Frenchman Louis Braille, who was himself blind. Each letter is made up of a group of between one and six small dots which are arranged in different ways. The dots are raised up from the paper, and are "read" by being touched gently with the fingertips.

Today Braille typewriters enable the blind to write, and many books, newspapers and magazines are published in Braille in nearly every country in the world. There are also Braille codes for music and mathematics.

How can the eye see movement?

Under normal conditions, our eyes provide us with precise and detailed images, but if something moving quickly is observed, then only a blur is seen, as shown in the photograph on the right. This is because the image remains on the retina for about a tenth of a second, and in this small fraction of time the retina cannot clearly fix any other new image. Instead, it partially superimposes a second image on the first, giving a confused picture which is out of focus. This is, in fact, a good thing, because it gives a person a sense of movement. It is thanks to this that the eye is able to convert a rapid series of "frames" into an animated sequence; in fact, the cinema makes use of this very effect.

How many senses are there?

Humans are often said to have five senses: sight, hearing, smell, taste and touch. In fact, there are many more. In addition to the sense of touch, the skin has four other kinds of receptors, while sense organs in the head give a person a sense of balance. Sense receptors in the muscles give information about the position of the limbs and the activity of the muscles.

Nerve endings in the stomach tell whether it is empty or full, giving a sensation of hunger when it is empty. Other receptors are concerned with thirst.

Below: Trapeze artists must have an excellent sense of balance.

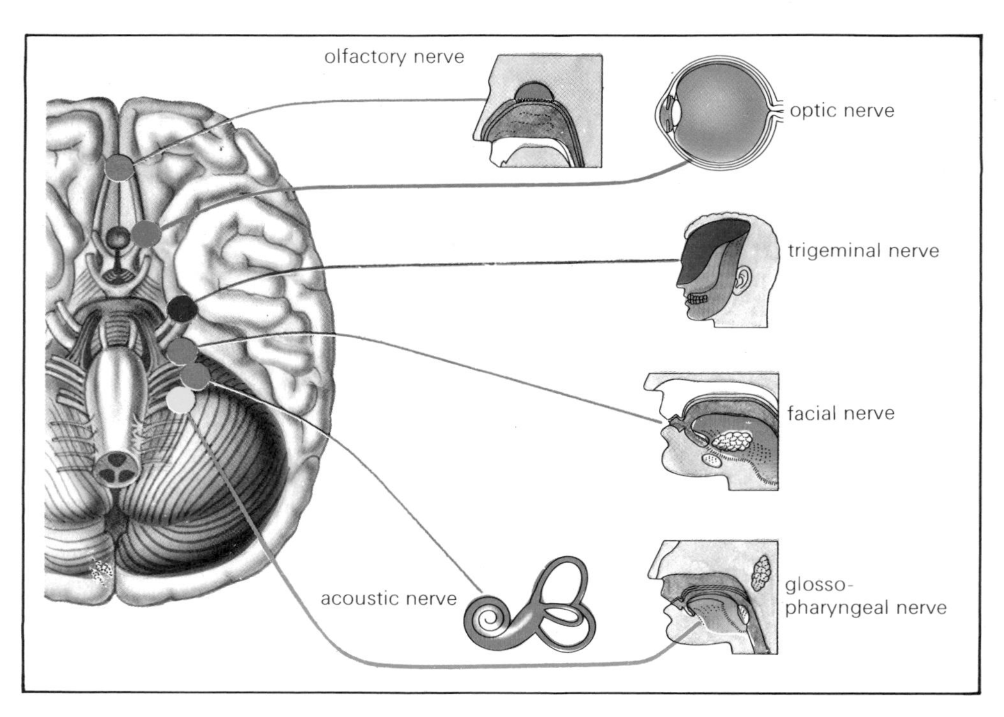

Above: The six cranial nerves which carry signals from the sense organs to the brain. The trigeminal nerve is responsible for the sensitivity of the eye, the glosso-pharyngeal nerve for taste.

How does the body send messages?

Messages are sent around the body in two separate ways. Some are transmitted as electrical and chemical impulses along nerves, while others are transmitted by hormones in the blood.

Whereas nerve impulses have an instant effect, hormones take longer to act. However, their effects also last longer. Nerves are necessary when instant action is needed, but hormones are used to control the day-to-day running of the body.

Why do people get giddy?

The ear contains the sense organs concerned with balance and with detecting the position of the head. Minute hairs in the internal cavities of the ear are surrounded by fluid. These move with the slightest change in position of the head. Their movements stimulate a number of nerve endings which send messages to the brain. If a person spins around on one spot, the result is a giddy feeling. This happens because the liquid in the ears has been shaken up, and the little hairs are pushed first in one direction and then in another. The brain suddenly receives contradictory signals that disturb the usual patterns. The giddy feeling is the warning that the body can no longer maintain its usual balance.

How does hearing work?

Ears convert sound into nerve impulses. Sound entering the "outer ear" causes the eardrum to vibrate and this vibration is then passed on via the three small bones of the "middle ear". The last of these delivers the vibrations to a long, coiled organ called the "cochlea".

The cochlea contains sensory cells that send impulses to the brain when the membrane on which they rest vibrates. Different parts of this membrane respond to different pitches of sound. At the tip of the cochlea it responds to low notes, while the part nearest the middle ear responds to high notes. The brain "hears" the sound by detecting which sensory cells are being stimulated.

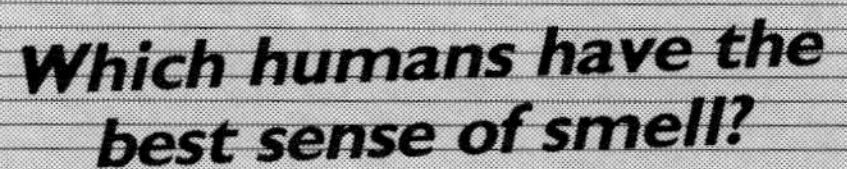

Which humans have the best sense of smell?

Over the centuries the sense of smell, like hearing, has deteriorated. People no longer depend on a sense of smell for survival, as hunters did to locate game during a hunt. Various peoples that have followed the traditional life of the hunter into modern times have retained an acute sense of smell. North American Indians, such as the Sioux, astounded pioneers in the last century by being able to locate and avoid a rattlesnake at night by detecting its musky smell.

Why can strong smells sometimes be ignored?

Various sense organs can receive a wide variety of messages, but if the stimulus remains constant over a period of time, it can no longer be singled out. For example, a strong perfume or even a continuous noise are, after a time, hardly noticed by the sense organs.

Why does having a cold affect taste?

The organ of smell is in the roof of the nasal cavity (the nose). It consists of a group of cells with branching, sensory hairs that project into the mucus that lines the cavity. Airborne chemicals dissolve in this mucus and are detected by the sensory cells.

The senses of taste and smell are closely related, and it is sometimes impossible to determine the nature of a piece of food by taste alone. This is why food often seems tasteless when you have a bad cold. Other sensations, such as texture, heat and cold, also play a part in the enjoyment of food and drink. In some people, such as professional wine tasters, this range of senses is particularly well-developed.

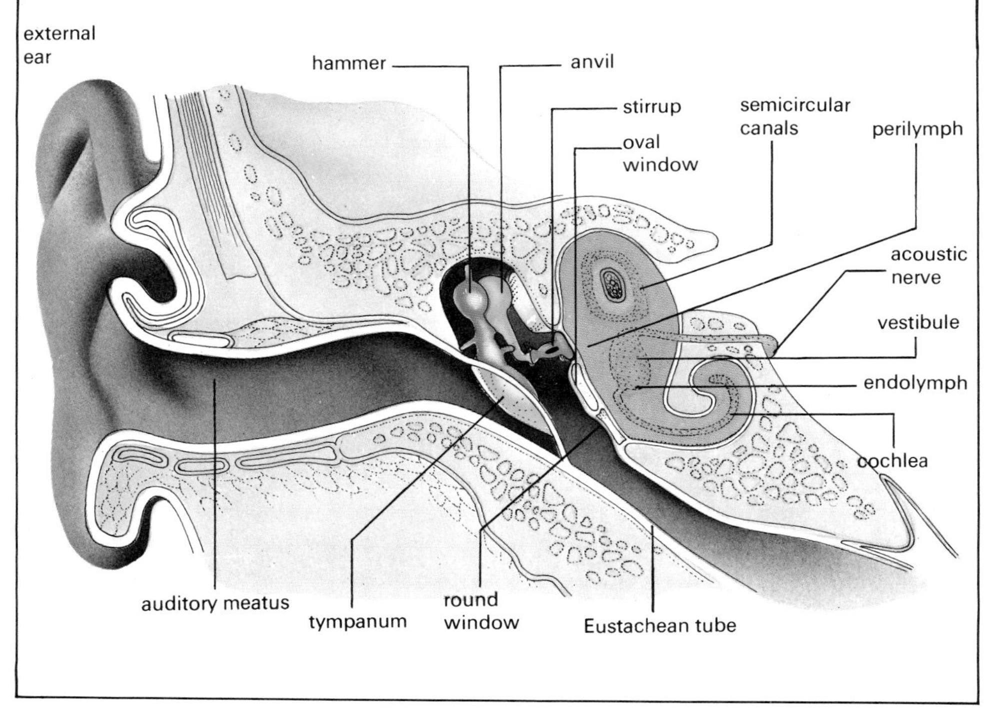

Top left: American Indians hunting bison
Left: A diagram of the human ear

Which chemicals are found in food?

There are five main types of food chemical: carbohydrates, fats, proteins, vitamins and minerals. Carbohydrates include such things as sugars and starches and consist of carbon and hydrogen only. Fats contain oxygen, as well as carbon and hydrogen, and are found in dairy products and fatty meats. Together, carbohydrates and fats form the main energy-giving part of the human diet.

A protein contains nitrogen as well as carbon, hydrogen and oxygen. Every day more than 1 million cells die in the human body, but the proteins carefully rebuild them. Proteins are found in such foods as meat, eggs and cheese.

Vitamins and minerals are present in the body in only tiny amounts, but they are essential for good health. Lack of particular vitamins can lead to deficiency diseases – for example, beri-beri is a disease of the nerves caused by the lack of vitamin B_1. Minerals, such as calcium and phosphorus, are essential for the growth of healthy bones and teeth. Vitamins and minerals are obtained by including fresh fruit and vegetables in the diet.

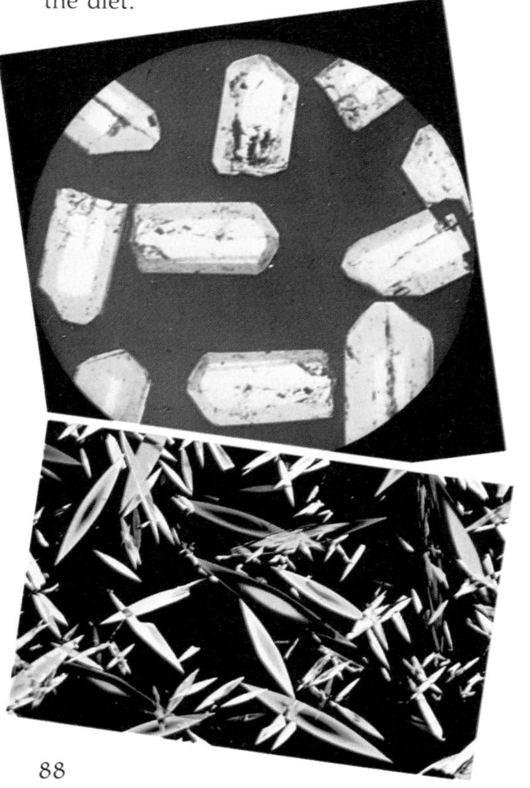

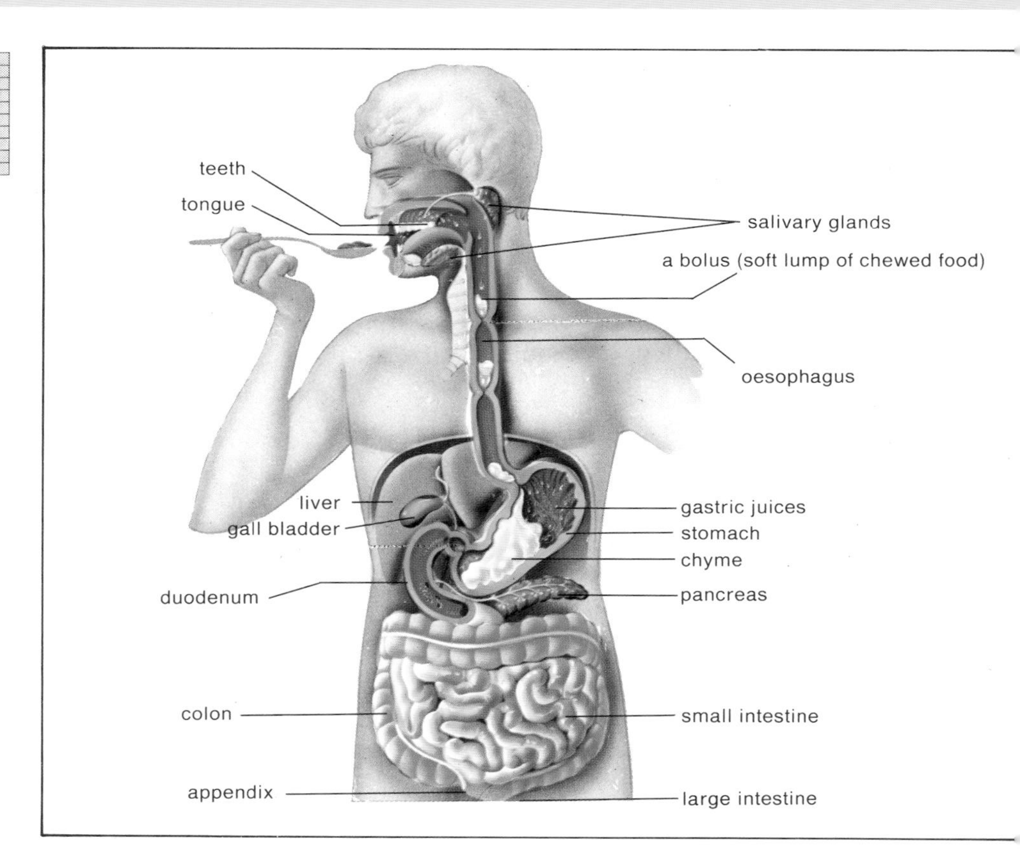

Above: The human digestive system

Below left: Crystals of two types of Vitamin B seen through a microscope

How is food digested?

Digestion begins as soon as food is chewed. The food then passes down the gullet to the stomach, where it is churned into a mixture known as "chyme". Small amounts of chyme are passed regularly from the stomach to the small intestine.

Once in the intestine, the food is bombarded with enzymes, each of which triggers a particular breakdown reaction. Eventually, all the carbohydrates that can be digested (humans cannot digest plant cellulose) are broken down into simple sugars. Fats are broken down into fatty acids and glycerol, proteins into amino acids.

How much food does a person need each day?

A human being needs to drink at least 2 l of water a day. It is taken in by drinking, but also occurs in solid foods such as meat, bread, fruit, greens and so on. Where does all this water go? It replaces water which is lost all the time – through urinating, sweating and breathing out.

Living beings need water for the simple reason that they are very largely made of it. Each person consists of about 60 per cent water. In a person weighing 50 kg, about 30 kg are water. Water is not just in the blood, but throughout the body, even in the hair and bones.

How does the body dispose of waste?

The chemical processes that go on in the body produce a variety of waste chemicals in the blood. These are removed by the body's two kidneys, each of which contains some 2 million microscopic filtering units.

Useful chemicals are reabsorbed into the blood, together with a quantity of water. The remaining fluid, known as "urine", passes out of the kidneys to the bladder and is expelled at intervals. About 1,800 l of blood pass through the kidneys in the course of twenty-four hours, and an average of $1\frac{1}{2}$ l of urine a day is formed by the human body.

Solid food waste which cannot be digested in the stomach or small intestine moves into the large intestine and finally leaves the body through the rectum.

How much water does a person need each day?

On average, a person drinks more than 1,000 l of water and eats 500 kg of food each year. But the weight of the food alone does not indicate the amount of energy it provides. This is measured in units called "calories". A calorie is the amount of heat required to raise 1 g of water 1°C.

The human body requires varying numbers of calories according to the work and conditions with which it has to cope. An adult needs about 2,500 calories per day, but the requirement increases if the person has a very tiring job, or lives in a cold climate. An Eskimo, for example, consumes more energy (that is, more calories) than someone who lives in a temperate climate. This does not mean that he or she will have to eat more, but that foods with a higher number of calories will have to be consumed.

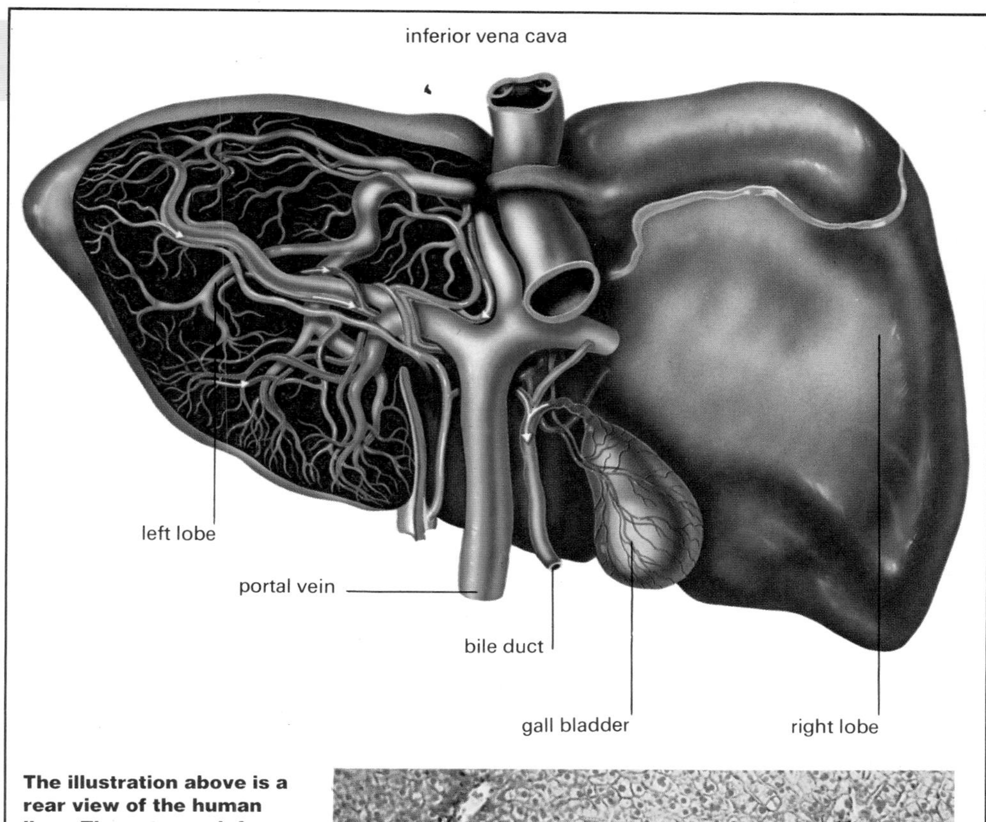

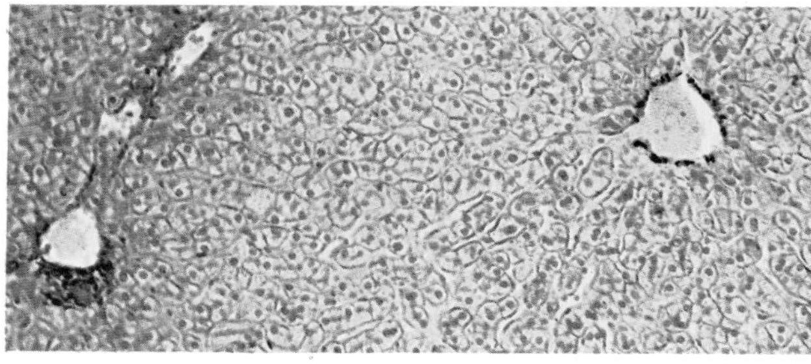

The illustration above is a rear view of the human liver. The cutaway left lobe gives an idea of the intricate web of blood vessels and bile ducts that spreads throughout the liver. On the right is a cross-section of liver tissues enlarged three hundred times.

Which is the body's largest internal organ?

The liver is the largest internal organ in the human body and one of the most important. In an adult, it weighs about $1\frac{1}{2}$ kg, and is made of soft reddish-brown tissue. All the carbohydrates absorbed from food are converted into glucose in the liver. Among its other tasks, the liver collects worn-out red blood cells and breaks them down, producing the greenish fluid known as "bile". This fluid helps in the digestion of fats.

The liver also helps to control the amount of sugar in the blood, deals with poisons such as alcohol, and joins in the fight against infectious diseases. Indeed, it is thought that the human liver can carry out over 100 totally separate functions.

Below: A child uses up about 1,500 calories per day simply to remain alive. The diagram shows the number of additional calories used per hour for various activities.

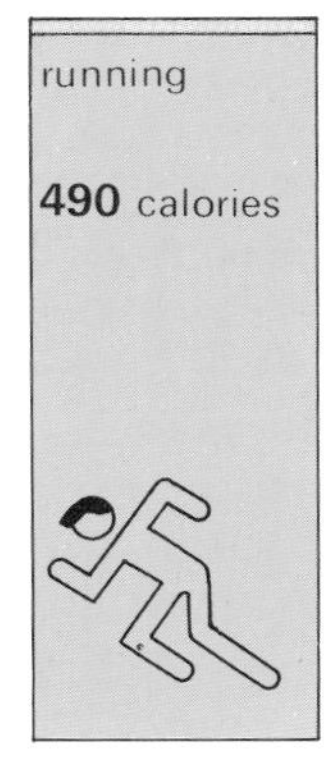

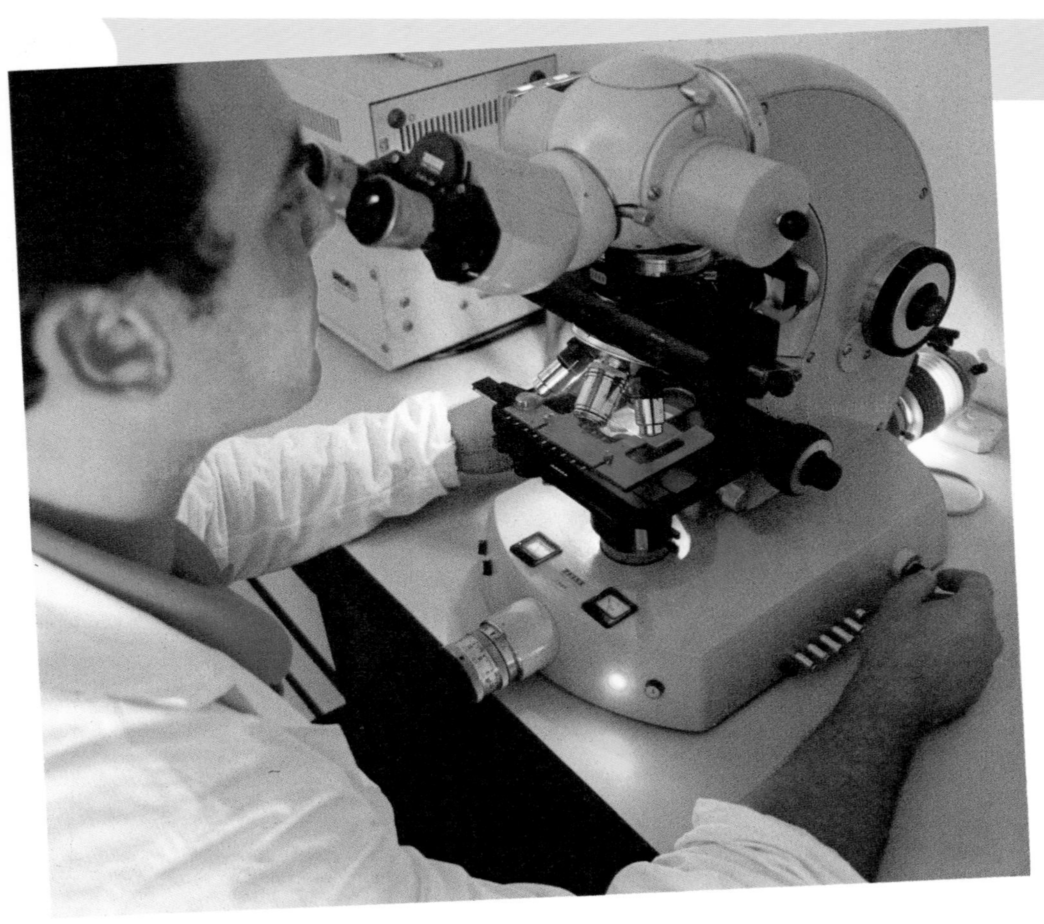

Above: A scientist studies bacteria under a powerful microscope

Bottom: Edward Jenner injecting an early vaccine

Which invention led to the discovery of bacteria?

The invention of the microscope by Zacharias Janssen, a Dutch lens maker, in 1590 and the substantial improvements made to it later, allowed the identification of living organisms invisible to the naked eye, some of them responsible for disease. This opened up certain lines of enquiry and led to the discovery in the nineteenth century, by the Frenchman Louis Pasteur, that many diseases were caused by even smaller living organisms – bacteria.

What is a vaccine?

A vaccine is a substance that causes the body's defence system to produce antibodies. These can then defend the body against any later invasion by a disease-causing germ. Some vaccines contain disease-causing germs that have been killed by heat or chemicals, while others contain modified forms of the poisons produced by germs. Yet others contain harmless live organisms that are closely related to the disease-causing types.

The Englishman Edward Jenner (1749–1823) discovered the principle of vaccination and began its use against smallpox.

Which substances kill bacteria?

Parasitic bacteria often cause disease, such as anthrax in animals, tetanus in humans and soft rots in plants. Some tiny plant organisms produce substances which are capable of killing bacteria – penicillin and streptomycin are two examples of these. The organisms producing these useful antibiotics are, in fact, fungi, and are cultivated in order to obtain large quantities for treating disease.

How does the body fight disease?

The first line of defence in the body is the skin. But, if germs do get into the body – through the mouth or wounds in the skin – they are rapidly attacked by the white cells in the blood.

A type of white cells called "neutrophils" first attack germs by engulfing them. Larger white cells called "monocytes" appear next and continue to engulf germs and debris. A single monocyte can engulf over 100 bacteria at a time. Pus consists of the remains of dead bacteria and white cells.

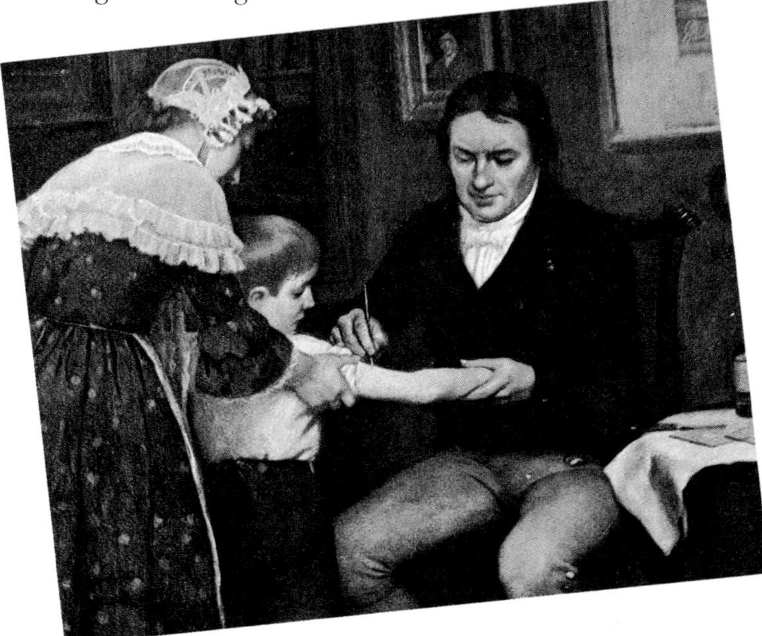

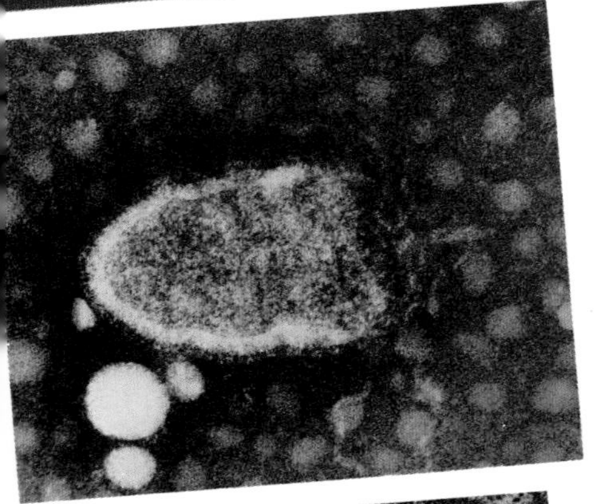

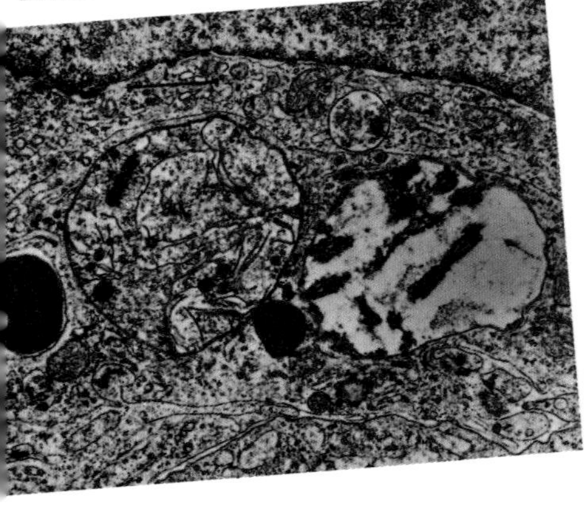

Above, from top: The *Streptomyces peucetius* bacteria; a parasite of the genus *Trypanosoma* which causes sleeping sickness; the rabies virus

What are viruses?

Viruses are organisms which are very much smaller than even bacteria and very little is known about them. They seem to be on the borderline between the living and non-living, although they do have the ability to increase and spread. They cause many diseases to plants and animals and are thought to be responsible for such things as colds, influenza and measles. Unlike a lot of bacterial and fungal diseases in plants, they cannot be killed by chemical sprays.

Who discovered antibiotics?

In 1928, the Scottish bacteriologist Alexander Fleming (1881–1955) discovered penicillin. In 1945, with Lord Florey and Ernst Chain, he was awarded the Nobel Prize for medicine.

From then on, antibiotics capable of countering almost any infection were developed. During the Second World War, top priority was given to the commercial production of penicillin which became widely available in a surprisingly short time. Penicillin is still one of the most commonly used antibiotics.

What are lymphocytes?

The body has a type of white blood cells called "lymphocytes" which help to defend it from disease. There are two kinds: B cells and T cells. When a B lymphocyte comes into contact with an invading germ, it reacts by forming antibodies. The B lymphocyte then divides repeatedly. If the germ reappears in the blood, these cells rapidly produce more antibodies and the person becomes immune to the disease. Sometimes, the immune system goes wrong. The disease AIDS (Acquired Immune Deficiency Syndrome) is caused by a virus that attacks certain T cells. As a result, the body becomes vulnerable to a large number of diseases.

What was Pasteur's great discovery?

Louis Pasteur (1822–1895) discovered that to inject a living creature with a very weakened preparation of disease-producing microbes would prevent that creature from ever developing the disease itself. Thus he made possible the new science of immunology. Vaccination, pioneered by Edward Jenner, is a part of immunology, but until Pasteur's discovery it had never been understood or regarded as useful, except in the case of smallpox. Pasteur's work was added to by Robert Koch (1843–1910), who identified the microbes responsible for tuberculosis, cholera and sleeping-sickness.

Left: Alexander Fleming (1881–1955)

Below: Louis Pasteur and his wife

When did surgery begin?

Trepanning (or trephining) is the oldest operation of which there is any trace. A hole was made in the patient's skull so that the demon believed to be causing the disease could escape. Trepanned skulls dating from prehistoric times have been found in Britain, France, other parts of Europe and Peru.

Other forms of surgery also have a long history. The discovery of metals led to the first modern type of surgical instruments, such as knives, scissors, forceps, scalpels and so on. These instruments were used by Assyrian, Babylonian, Phoenician, Egyptian, Indian and Jewish doctors many hundreds of years ago.

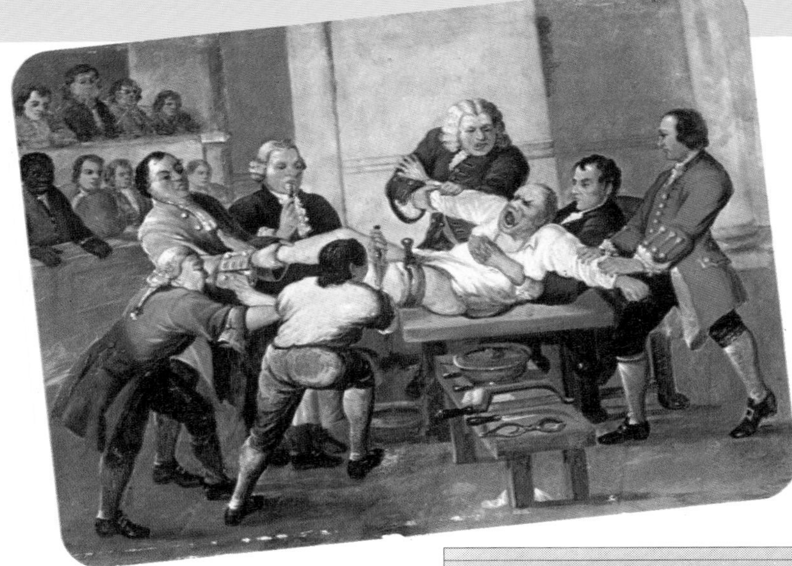

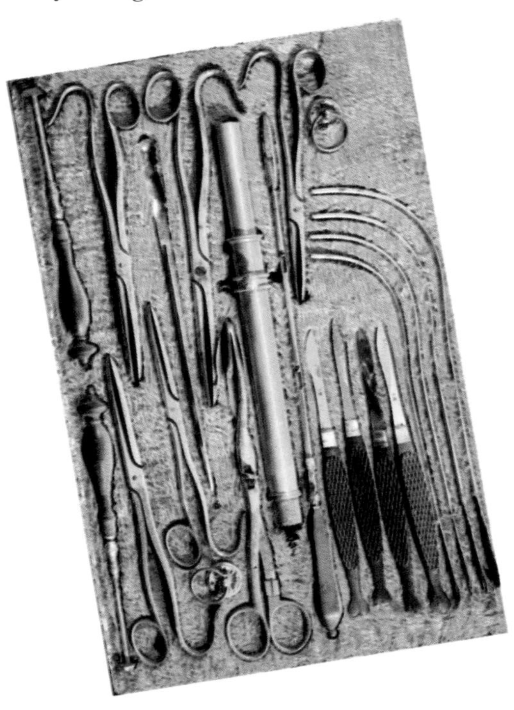

Top: Before anaesthetics were discovered, surgery was extremely painful. Patients were given a little alcohol to dull their senses and held down by a team of nurses.

Above: An operation during the First World War. By this time, gowns were sterilized and nurses wore rubber gloves.

Left: A surgical instrument box of the nineteenth century

When were anaesthetics first used?

An American dentist, William Thomas Morton (1819–1868), perfected systems of anaesthesia using ether, a substance which sent the patient to sleep and so spared him the pain of the operation. His first operation using this method was carried out in 1846. A second improvement in surgical techniques soon followed when an English surgeon, Joseph Lister (1827–1912), introduced chemical substances capable of killing bacteria to disinfect operating theatres. This prevented the infections which had previously often broken out after operations.

Who created the first modern nursing school?

From the Dark Ages until the Reformation, nursing was undertaken by monks and nuns, and all hospitals were religious institutions. In England there were no monasteries after the Reformation in the sixteenth century and nursing reached a very low ebb. When the Crimean War began in 1854, Florence Nightingale organized a nursing service to deal with sick and wounded soldiers, whose plight had been horrible. She then started a school for nurses at St Thomas's Hospital in London, and other hospitals rapidly followed suit. Nursing soon became one of the noblest professions.

Which is the oldest form of transplant?

Transplants can be made of skin (in the form of grafts), sections of blood vessels and organs like hearts and lungs. The use of artificial materials in "repair surgery" is also becoming widespread. Metal alloys and acrylic resins are used to replace heart valves and rebuild hip joints. Synthetic fibre tubes are used to replace sections of worn-out arteries.

Although not strictly speaking a transplant, the oldest medical replacement procedure is undoubtedly blood transfusion – every hospital is now equipped to transfer blood into the body of a patient who needs it.

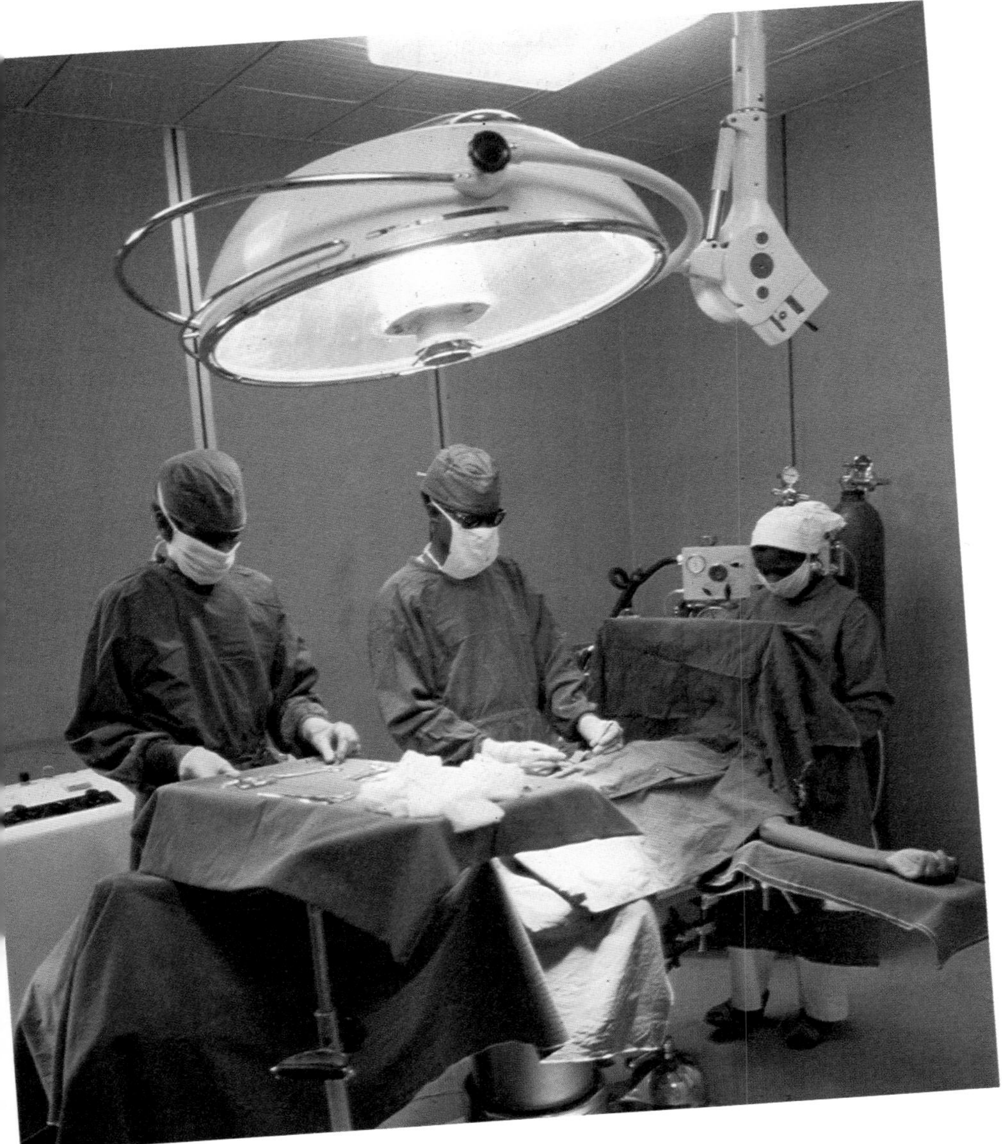

Which machines are used to diagnose disease?

There is a wide range of complex equipment available to diagnose disease. Examples include X-ray machines, which can take photographs of the inside of the human body – for example endoscopes examine the insides of body cavities, such as the stomach.

There are also several types of scanning machine, including computerized axial tomography (CAT) scanners, which use X-rays to make a picture of a "slice" of the body. The ultrasound scanner uses harmless, high-pitched sound waves to create pictures of internal organs, and is often used to examine unborn babies.

How can brainwaves be "seen"?

It is possible to register the very tiny electro-magnetic discharges produced by heart and brain activity and make a graph of them. The tracings which result from these investigations by special machines are called "electrocardiograms" and "electroencephalograms" respectively.

Above left: An operation underway in a modern operating theatre

Below left: X-ray photographs

Below: An image of a skull on a computer scan

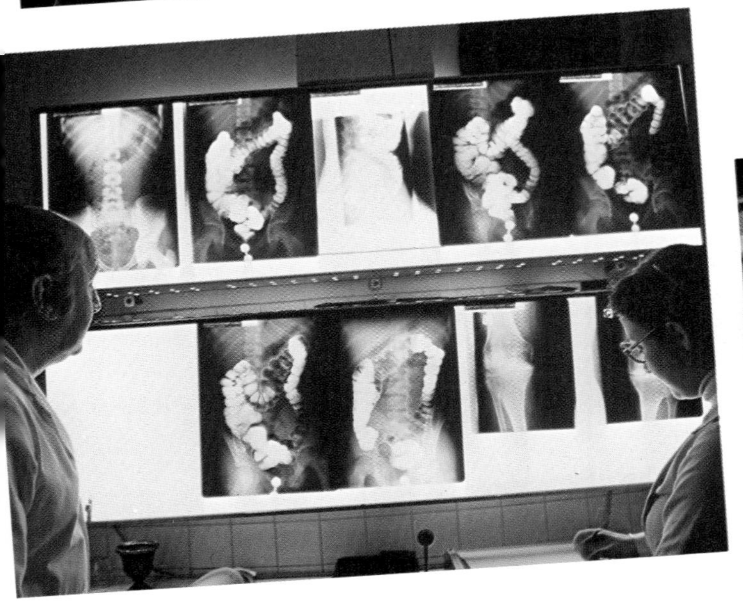

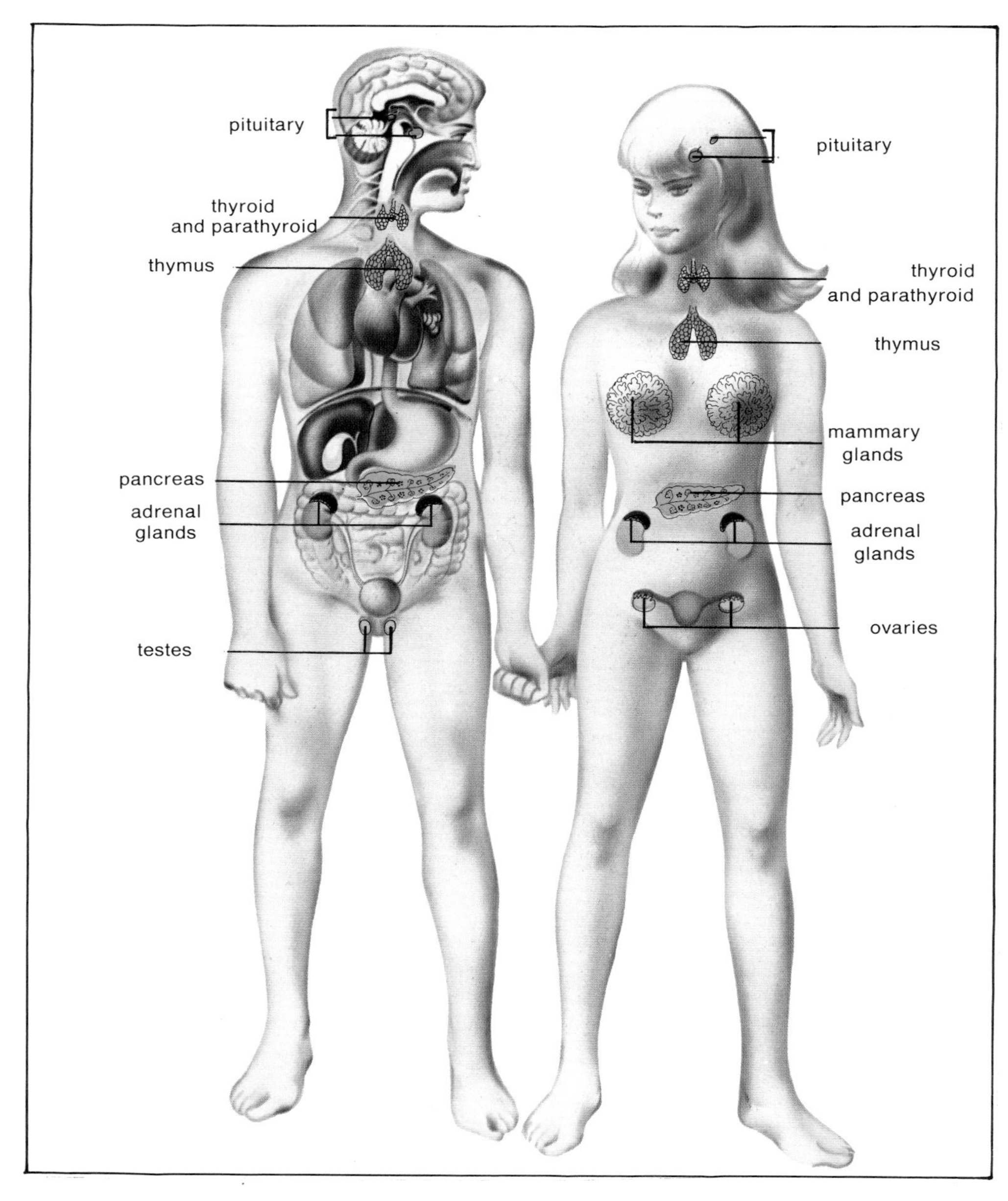

Above: The principal glands of the human male and female. Glands manufacture chemical substances and secrete them for the body to either use or discharge. Exocrine glands secrete substances through a duct, endocrine glands directly into the bloodstream.

What do glands do?

Glands manufacture chemicals and then secrete (or discharge) them. There are two main kinds of gland. "Exocrine" glands discharge their products to the outside of the body or into a body cavity. Examples include sweat glands, the digestive glands of the small intestine, mammary glands (in women) and salivary glands.

"Endocrine" glands release their products into the blood stream. The product of an endocrine gland is known as a hormone.

Which is the body's master gland?

The pituitary is a small, oval gland at the base of the brain and weighs between 13 and 60 g. The pituitary controls all other endocrine glands in the body by producing regulatory hormones. It can therefore be considered the master gland.

What are hormones?

The word "hormone" comes from the Greek *hormon*, which means "urging on". In fact, the purpose of hormones is to stimulate – or inhibit – the function of an organ in the body. In this way hormones act as balancing agents in the principal bodily activities, particularly in growth and development, pregnancy, sex and metabolism.

What does insulin do?

The pancreas gland behind the stomach contains small groups of cells that produce insulin. This hormone lowers the level of sugar in the blood by making it easier for fat and muscle cells to take in sugar and store it. In a person whose pancreas produces little or no insulin, these tissues cannot take in the necessary amounts of sugar, which therefore remains in the blood. This results in the disease known as diabetes.

What is adrenalin?

When the body is under stress, as in situations that cause fear, nerve impulses cause the medulla of the adrenal gland in the kidney to produce the hormone "adrenalin". Its overall effect is to prepare the body for action.

Adrenalin stimulates the heart and causes blood vessels in the skin and gut to become constricted. As a result, blood is pumped at a high rate to the muscles. It also causes the liver to produce more blood sugar and brings the nervous system into a state of readiness.

Facing page.
Top: Preparing for physical activity makes adrenalin flow to stimulate the heart and muscles.
Below: Gymnastics is a sport at which adolescents excel.

What makes people grow?

The gradual growth of a human being is due to the activity of numerous hormones. For example, thyroxin, secreted by the thyroid gland in the neck, accelerates chemical reactions which promote the growth of the body and correct mental development. Another hormone determines the growth of bones in relation to the amount of calcium available. Abnormal secretion of growth hormones leads to stunted or excessive growth, obesity or excessive thinness.

What triggers adolescence?

Adolescence is triggered by hormones which complete the body's development and prepare it for giving birth to new life in the future. This stage differs in males and females and is made evident not only by the appearance of sexual attributes, but also by other characteristics. A boy's voice, for example, becomes gradually deeper, and a first beard appears on his face.

What is an atom?

The word "atom" is of Greek origin and means "indivisible". In about 400 BC, the Greek philosopher Democritus reasoned that substances could in theory be cut into smaller and smaller pieces until finally basic particles that could not be divided further were obtained. These particles are atoms, and Democritus contended that substances are different because they are made of different kinds of atoms. This explanation is now known to be broadly correct, but no one believed Democritus because atoms are much too small to be seen. His ideas were not accepted until the British chemist, John Dalton (1766–1844), put forward his modern atomic theory in 1803.

Individual atoms are very small – typically 0.000,000,01 cm in radius. Atoms could not be seen until extremely powerful microscopes became available recently.

What do atoms look like?

The 105 known elements are different from one another because of the structure of their atoms. Atoms are not "indivisible" and can be divided further. They consist mainly of empty space, but at the centre of the atom is a particle called a "nucleus" which is some 10,000 times smaller than the atom as a whole. Around the atom, and defining its outer boundary, move "electrons", each one-tenth of the size of the nucleus.

The electron is a fundamental particle – it cannot be divided further – but the nucleus is not. It consists of smaller particles, called "protons" and "neutrons", which are bound strongly together. These particles, in turn, are thought to consist of yet smaller, fundamental particles called "quarks". Elements differ from one another simply in the number of protons in their nuclei – for example, hydrogen has one proton, and carbon six.

What is nuclear fission?

"Nuclear fission" is the process by which the nuclei of atoms are split apart. It is carried out by firing a neutron at a nucleus, which absorbs the extra neutron, but becomes violently unstable. In addition to breaking into two smaller nuclei, two or more neutrons are released. These neutrons can then strike more nuclei, causing them to break apart and emit more neutrons that strike more nuclei and so on. A chain reaction occurs which, if it is not controlled, causes nuclear fission to spread rapidly throughout the whole of the fissile material and the immense heat generated blows it apart. It is precisely this type of chain reaction occurring in uranium or plutonium which causes nuclear explosions.

Bottom left: An atom with its nucleus of neutrons and protons. Electrons revolve around the nucleus like satellites.

Below: How nuclear fission works

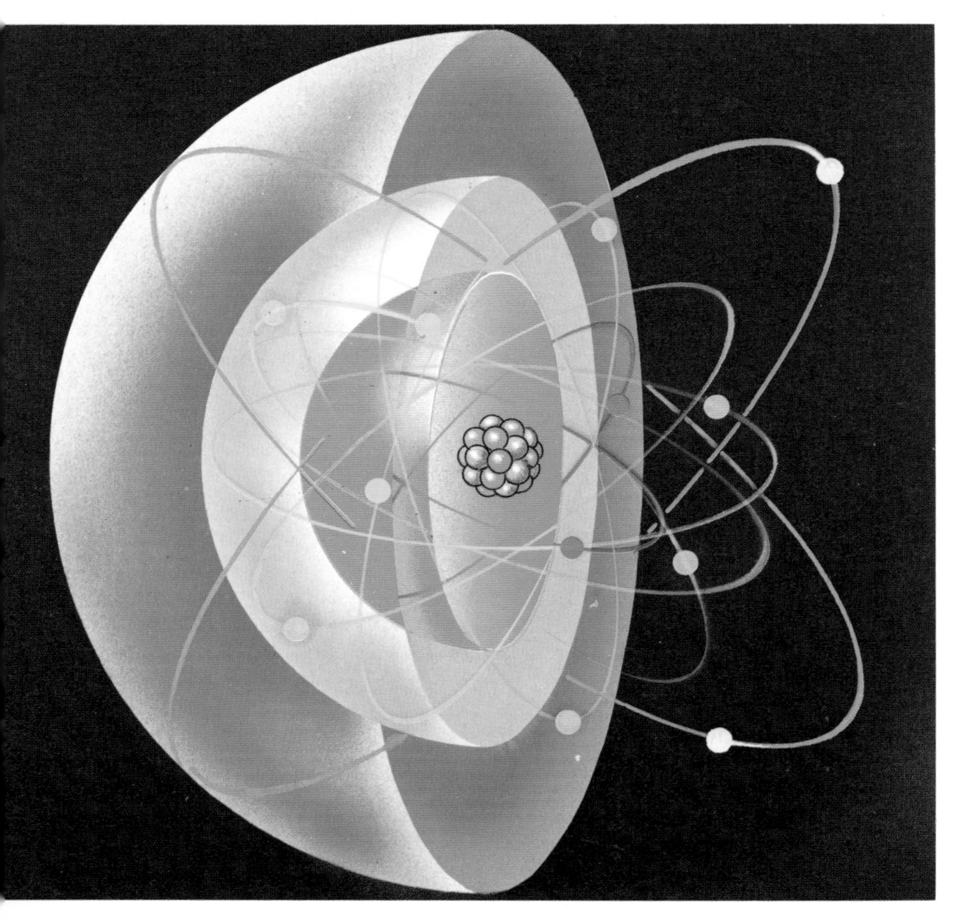

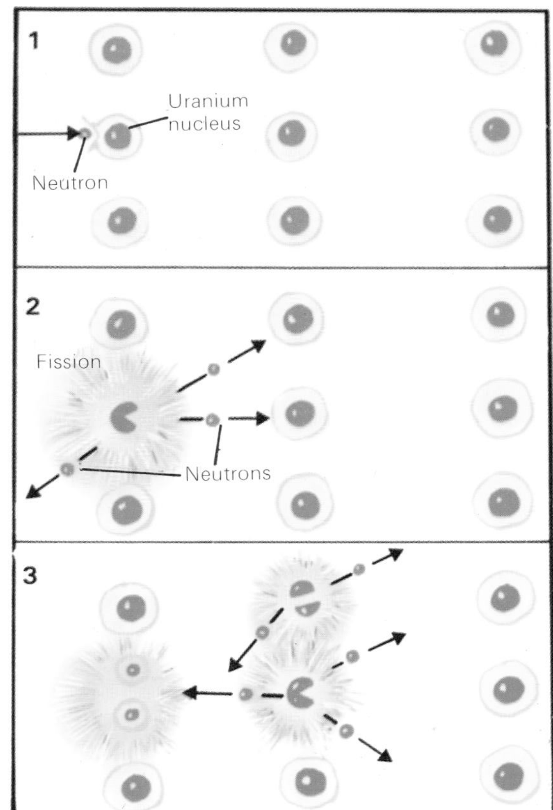

Main picture: A 'mushroom cloud' erupting into the sky following an experimental nuclear explosion in 1952.
Inset: Marie and Pierre Curie, whose discoveries in the field of radioactivity eventually made the production of the atomic bomb possible.

When was the first atomic explosion?

By the time the Second World War began in 1939, most of the world's leading nuclear scientists were well aware that an atomic bomb was a possibility. In the United States, Albert Einstein, Enrico Fermi and their colleagues advised President Roosevelt to start production of an atomic bomb immediately. On 2 December 1942, an American research team headed by Enrico Fermi demonstrated the first controlled release of atomic energy at the University of Chicago. Meanwhile at Oak Ridge, Tennessee, engineers began the construction of a huge factory to obtain relatively large amounts of the element Uranium 235.

On 16 July 1945 at a secret testing ground near Alamagordo in New Mexico, the bomb was exploded. Only three weeks later a bomb was dropped on Hiroshima in Japan, and three days after that a second bomb was dropped on Nagasaki. The results were horrifying but the atomic bombs brought the Second World War to an immediate end.

Who discovered radioactivity?

Antoine Becquerel (1852–1908), a French physicist who worked in Paris, is credited with the discovery of radioactivity. One day in 1896, in the laboratory, he used some old pieces of uranium to weigh down photographic plates. When the plates were developed, they revealed a curious pattern of lines. Becquerel experimented with these "uranium rays" and found them to be in some way rather similar to the X-rays discovered by Wilhelm Röntgen (1845–1923) only a year before.

Fascinated by these "radioactive" rays, Marie Curie, Becquerel's Polish research assistant, devoted her life to the study of natural radioactivity. Together she and her husband Pierre discovered two new elements, polonium (after Poland) and radium (from the Latin *radius* meaning ray). Marie Curie (1867–1934) is now regarded as one of the founders of modern physics.

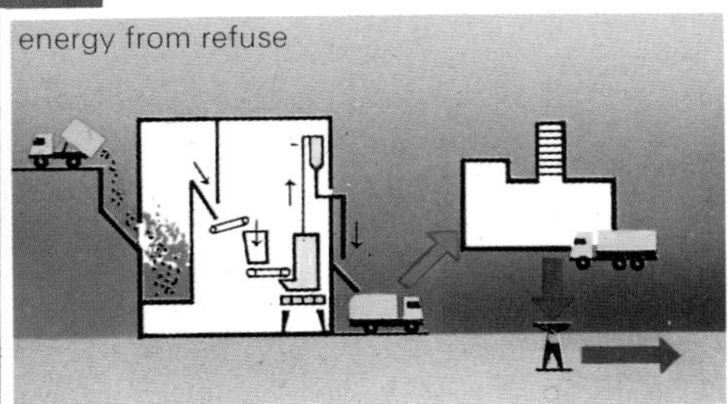

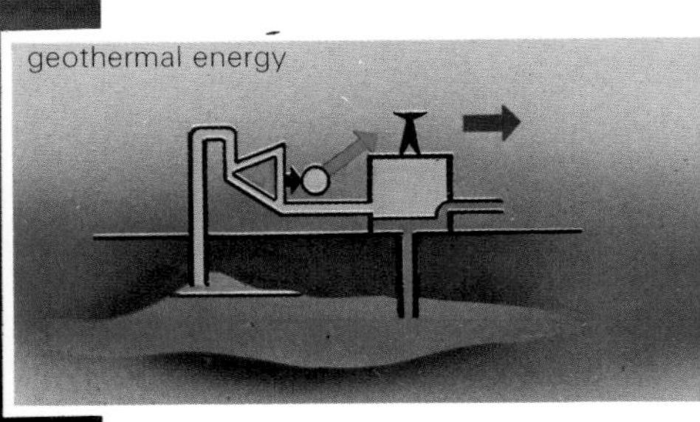

There is also another important kind of energy that everything has. This is "potential" energy, a kind of stored energy that is ready to produce movement. A coiled spring has potential energy, and so too does water held behind a dam. Any object that is raised has potential energy because it is ready to fall. Movement occurs when the spring, water or object is released.

What is heat?

Heat is a form of energy that every object possesses and, when heat is made or used, it flows from one object to another. Heat flows from a fire into a room for warmth, for example, or from a hot iron into clothes to help press them. Cold objects contain heat, too, no matter how cold they may be. An object becomes colder by losing heat, but it cannot lose all its heat.

Everything has heat because everything contains molecules, which vibrate. The hotter an object becomes, the faster its molecules move. Because molecules can never slow to a stop, everything has heat, no matter how cold it is.

Above: The sun, provider of most of the world's energy
Inset: Some of the alternative forms of energy now being researched

Bottom right: When heat is applied to most substances it makes them change their form. Here, platinum is being heated to make it soft.

Where does energy come from?

Scientists say that energy can neither be created nor destroyed, it can only change its form. This is the law of conservation of energy. It is one of the most important laws of science. Energy has to come from somewhere, however, and the Earth gets most of its energy, as radiant energy, in heat rays and light rays from the Sun. The rest comes from chemical energy and nuclear energy in the minerals which make up rocks. The energy then goes through many conversions as the world makes use of it. Finally, it becomes radiant energy again, leaves the Earth and passes out into space.

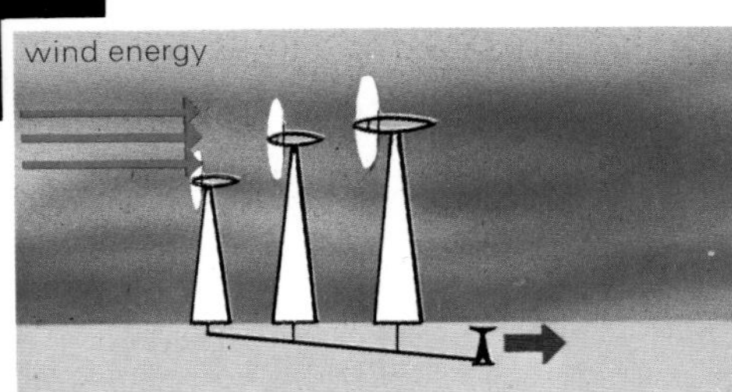

Is there only one kind of energy?

The most obvious kind of energy is "kinetic" energy, the energy of movement. Everything has kinetic energy when it moves, and the faster something moves or the heavier it is, the more kinetic energy it has. An aircraft in flight has an enormous amount of kinetic energy because it travels very fast and is also very heavy.

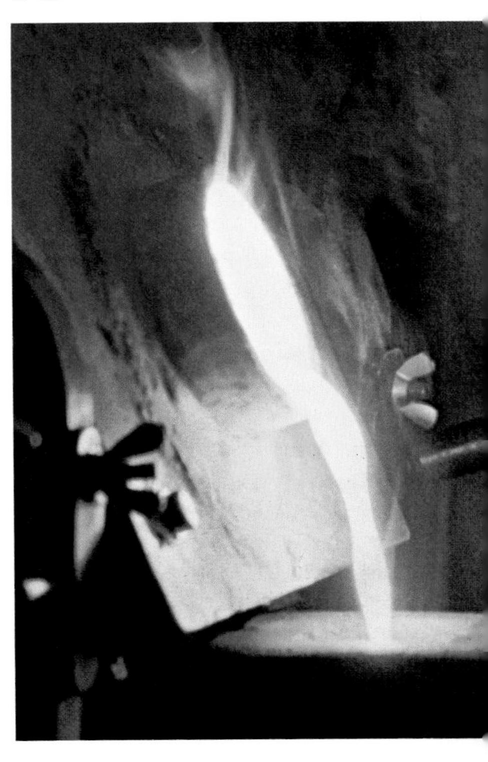

Above: A solar furnace in the Pyrenees, France. Solar energy is becoming increasingly popular as the disadvantages of other types of energy become known and fossil fuel supplies are significantly reduced.

Bottom right: An alcohol thermometer used for measuring low temperatures

How is heat measured?

The temperature of an object is a measure of how hot it is. If one object has a higher temperature than another, then it is hotter, and heat will flow from the hotter object to the colder one.

Temperature is usually measured in degrees on the Celsius (or Centigrade) scale. In this scale, 0°C is the freezing point of water and 100°C is the boiling point. (The Fahrenheit scale is also used, but less frequently. In this scale, water has a freezing point of 32°F and a boiling point of 212°F.) In science, the Kelvin scale is often used. In this scale, OK (zero kelvins) is a fixed temperature called absolute zero, and the kelvin is equal to 1°C.

Absolute zero is the lowest temperature possible. At absolute zero, all heat energy disappears and molecules slow to an absolute stop. It is equal to −273.15°C.

How does heat flow?

Heat flows in three ways: by conduction, convection or radiation. "Conduction" occurs inside a solid object, such as a pan on a hot plate or burner, as the warmed-up molecules vibrate faster and faster, transmitting energy. "Convection" occurs inside liquids, such as the water in the pan. It also occurs in the same way in gases too; a convector heater warms the air next to it and this warm air rises to spread heat throughout the room.

The third method of heat flow is "radiation". Heat can flow from one object to another in the form of heat rays (or infrared rays). The Sun's heat rays cross space to reach the Earth, and fires and radiators in rooms give out heat rays – though they also heat by convection.

How can we tap the Sun's energy?

The energy in the Sun is produced by complicated reactions at its centre. These "thermonuclear" reactions change hydrogen into helium, causing the Sun to lose 4 million tons of hydrogen per second and producing an enormous amount of heat.

We tap the Sun's energy directly in solar heating systems and in the solar cells used in calculators and satellites. But to get a lot of energy from the Sun, it is necessary to have a large collector. Solar power stations have been built in sunny regions to produce electricity. They contain sets of mirrors grouped around a central tower with a boiler. The mirrors are controlled by computers so that they all turn to reflect the Sun's rays on to the boiler, which raises steam to power a generator in the usual way.

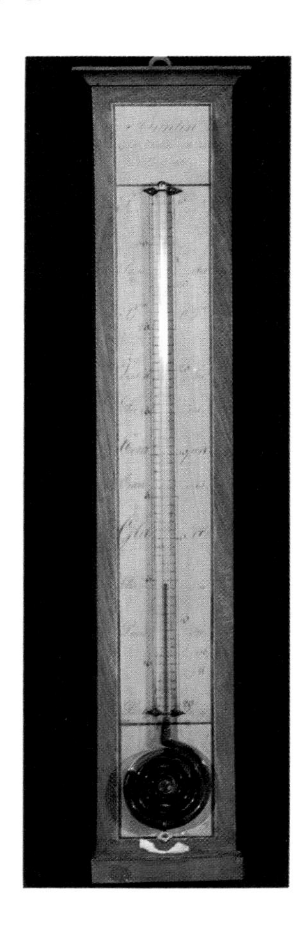

What are molecules?

Molecules are tiny particles that can be seen with very powerful microscopes. They are made of groups of even smaller particles called atoms, and the molecules of some substances consist of single atoms. The way they move depends on whether a substance is a solid, a liquid or a gas.

In a solid, the molecules are held together by strong forces and they vibrate about fixed positions. In a liquid, the molecules are held much more loosely and they can jostle around inside the liquid. However, in a gas, the molecules are completely free to move and they dash about in every direction. The different kinds of molecular movement explain: why solids have a set shape and are hard; why liquids flow to take up the shape of their container; why gases fill any space available to them.

How do atoms bond together?

The illustrations on the right show how the atoms of five elements bond together in molecules. Common salt is a compound of sodium and chlorine, which have one and seven electrons in their outer shells respectively. A sodium atom donates an electron to a chlorine atom, the atoms gaining positive and negative electric charges that hold them together in "electrovalent" bonds. With diamond, each atom shares an electron with the four atoms surrounding it to create a "covalent" bond. In metals, such as sodium, free electrons transmit electricity and heat.

The last two illustrations represent bonds between molecules. With solid hydrogen, as well as other substances, the cohesion between the molecules is due to weak reciprocal attractions of an electrical nature, known as Van der Waals' forces. With ice, the water molecules are linked by bridges consisting of hydrogen atoms.

Right: A diagram of five atoms and some of the ways in which they are linked in molecules

How do chemical compounds get their names?

The names of chemical compounds usually indicate the elements that they contain. For example, hydrogen oxide is the chemical name for water, indicating that it is a compound of hydrogen and oxygen. Salt is sodium chloride, a compound of sodium and chlorine.

The proportions of the elements in a compound are given in its chemical formula, which uses the chemical symbols of the elements together with numbers to show how many atoms of each element are present in a molecule of the compound. For example, the mineral in iron ore is iron oxide. There are two kinds of iron oxide, because iron and oxygen can combine in different proportions. This difference is clear in the formulae of the two compounds: the iron mineral called hematite is Fe_2O_3 and the mineral magnetite is Fe_3O_4, Fe being the chemical symbol for iron and O for oxygen.

What is chemistry?

Chemistry is the study of elements and their compounds, which is why these are also known as chemical elements and chemical compounds. There are two main branches of this science. The study of the elements as a whole is "inorganic" chemistry. The study of the compounds of carbon, with the exception of a few simple carbon compounds, is called "organic" chemistry. The reason for these names is that it was once thought that non-carbon compounds came only from mineral sources and carbon compounds only from living things. Although this is now known to be untrue, the names have remained and are still used.

Expressed simply, chemistry's prime task is to study substances, classify them and identify the properties and characteristics of each, analyze them and study how substances react together to produce other substances.

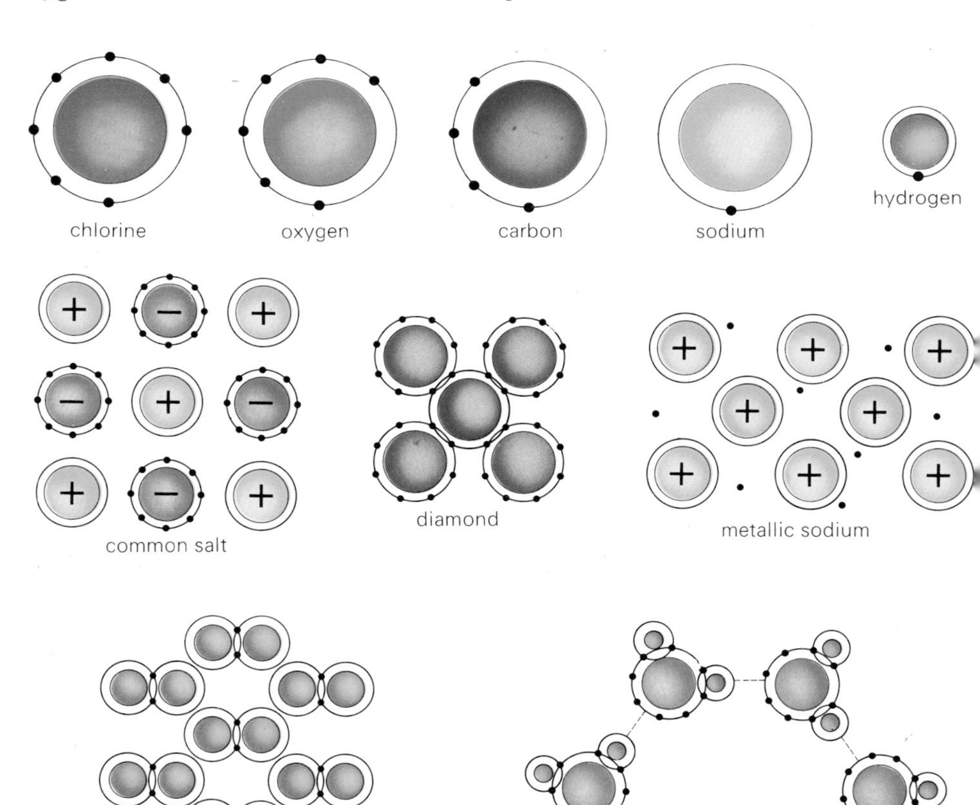

What are elements?

Elements are the basic stuff of which the whole universe is made. These are not the four elements of earth, fire, air and water that the Ancient Greeks believed everything was made of. The Greeks had the right idea, however, in assuming that everything is made from elements.

There are, in fact, ninety-three elements in nature, and twelve artificial elements can be manufactured, making a total of 105. The elements are gases, liquids and solids at ordinary temperatures. Solids predominate, especially metals such as iron, aluminium, nickel and chromium. Only two elements are liquids – bromine and mercury – while the gaseous elements include hydrogen, oxygen and chlorine.

Top: A page of the *Encyclopédie* of Diderot and D'Alembert, written in 1751, showing the complicated symbols for chemical elements then in use

Right: A ground-to-air missile powered by a hydrogen-fuelled rocket

Which is the lightest element?

Hydrogen is the lightest element. It is also the simplest. Because of its lightness, it is used in the balloons that are released to mark important ceremonies. Because hydrogen has a lower density than air, it carries the balloons upwards. Hydrogen is likely to catch fire, however, because it combines explosively with oxygen in the air to form water. In gas balloons and airships, therefore, it is replaced by helium which is a "noble gas" (i.e. it is unreactive).

The chemical reaction between hydrogen and oxygen can, however, serve as an important source of energy. Fuel cells used in spacecraft are designed to consume hydrogen and oxygen to produce electricity, with pure water produced as a by-product. The most powerful rocket engines, which burn liquid fuel, run on liquid hydrogen and liquid oxygen.

Top: A machine for producing plastic articles by injection moulding
Inset: Rolls of transparent plastic sheet

What are plastics?

Plastics are artificial products, made from simple organic chemicals that undergo "polymerization" to form very large molecules. If the molecules are in long, linear chains, the plastic is flexible because the long molecules can bend. Plastics of this type are called "thermoplastics" because they soften when heated. They can therefore be shaped easily by various moulding processes when hot, and they harden as they cool. Thermoplastics are used to make most plastic objects. They include polyethylene (polythene), polyvinyl chloride (PVC), polytetrafluoroethylene (Teflon), polystyrene, acrylic plastics, nylon, polyesters and polycarbonates.

Cross links may be set up between adjacent chains during polymerization to bind the chains firmly together. When formed, they set hard and these plastics are strong. Originally this was done by heating, and so these plastics are known as "thermosetting" plastics. They are used to make artificial resins that are the principal constituents of powerful adhesives, varnishes and many paints.

What is glass made of?

Common glass, such as that used for window panes, is made by heating sand (silicon oxide), soda (sodium carbonate) and lime (calcium oxide). These substances react to produce a complex molecule in which several molecules of sodium, calcium and silicon compounds are associated together. The glass is molten but hardens slowly as it cools so that it can be moulded or blown into shape. The properties can be varied by adding compounds of other elements to the melt. Some metals give colours, for example, while incorporating boron produces glass that resists cracking when heated which can be used for kitchenware.

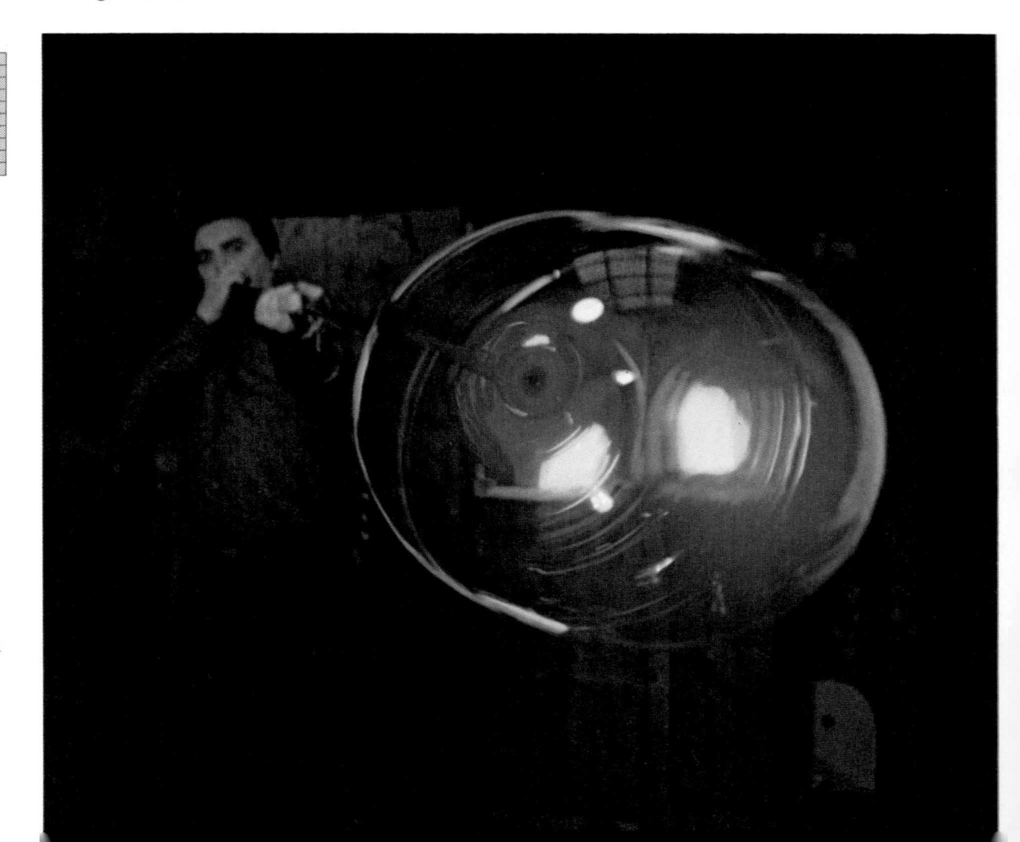

Below: For glass to be moulded into different shapes, it must first be heated to very high temperatures and then blown through a tube.

How is coal mined and used?

Layers of coal, or coal seams, may be near the surface of the ground. Here, the coal can be removed very easily and the soil replaced afterwards. This is done in opencast mines. Other seams are deep underground, so mine shafts and tunnels have to be built to reach the coal.

Coal was the first "fossil fuel" to be used extensively for heating and power generation and made possible the steam age and the Industrial Revolution of the eighteenth and nineteenth centuries. When coal is heated without air it gives coke, coal gas and coal tar. Coke and coal gas are still used as fuels, while coal tar contains many valuable substances which are used to make, for example, soap, medicines, dyes and plastics. Coal is still useful, as a primary fuel in power stations and as a source of valuable by-products.

How is steel produced?

Iron is mainly used as steel, which is basically an alloy of iron and carbon to which other elements may be added.

Iron occurs in iron minerals or as ores that are mainly compounds of iron and oxygen. The iron is extracted in a blast furnace, in which the iron ore is heated with coke and limestone. The resulting "pig iron" is converted to steel in another furnace or converter. Air or oxygen is blown through or over the molten pig iron, and it burns away most of the carbon. Other alloying elements may be added, together with scrap steel which is being recycled.

Steel is a hard, strong metal, and it is cheap to make. It is used to manufacture all kinds of things, from pins and needles to trains and skyscrapers. Ordinary steel corrodes as the iron in it combines with oxygen in the air. In this way rust is formed. "Stainless" steels resist corrosion because they contain large proportions of the metallic elements chromium and nickel.

Above: A large iron and steel works in Northern France

Why is oil important?

Oil is now the world's most important fuel. Every day 5,000 million l of it are used throughout the world to give power to cars, aircraft, heating systems and many other things. Oil is also the main ingredient in the manufacture of plastics and all kinds of other synthetic materials.

The big refineries of oil companies heat up thick crude oil and "crack" it down into different substances. Some become kerosene, gasoline, petrol, lubricating oils and tar and others become ethylenes or "feed-stocks" for factories which produce polythene for bags, vinyl for floor coverings, and nylon for clothing. The list of oil-based products is enormous and keeps growing as research continues. This means that oil companies must also continually search for new oil deposits.

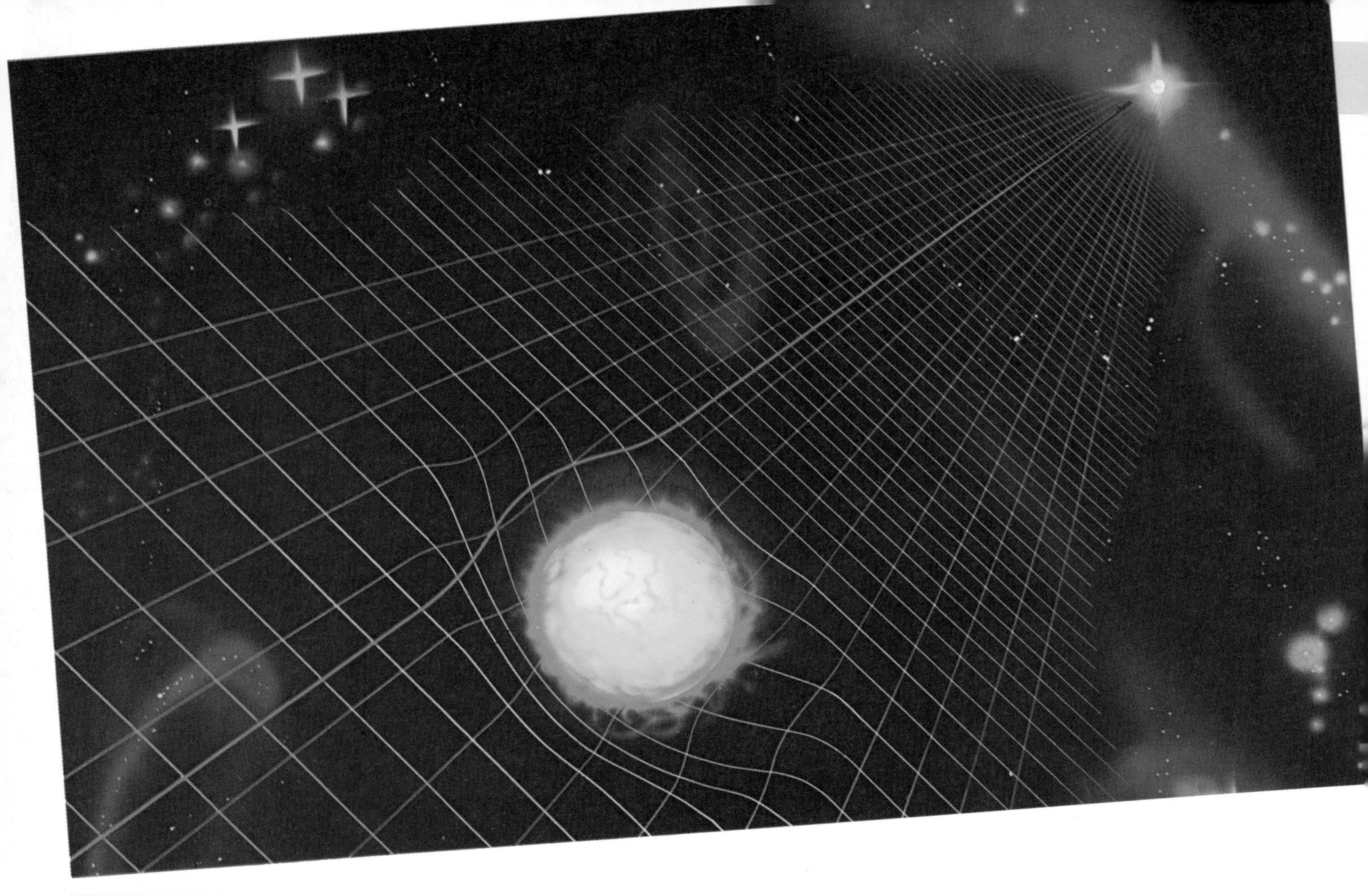

What is the theory of relativity?

A clock on the Earth measures time more slowly than a clock on a spacecraft far away from the Earth. A ray of light does not always travel through space in a straight line, but bends when it passes close to a star such as the Sun.

These effects were predicted by Albert Einstein (1879–1955) at the beginning of this century in his general "theory of relativity". This says that a body moves in a straight line and at a constant speed only as long as it is sufficiently distant from other masses, since it is in a zone where space is unaffected and time passes at a uniform speed. But when the body draws near to a large agglomeration of matter – for example a planet – its motion becomes curved and it accelerates. This is not because the body is subjected to the action of a force of attraction, but because it has entered a zone where the presence of matter has curved space and made time pass at a different speed from before.

How are space and time related?

The American physicist Albert Einstein (1879–1955) constructed a concept examining what happens when the simplest parameter of space is measured, namely that of length. In this operation the measurement of time must necessarily be involved and, as a result, Einstein concluded that space and time are not mutually independent and that physical phenomena always take place in a "space-time" of four dimensions – three of space and one of time.

How did people tell the time before watches?

Up to the beginning of the sixteenth century, sundials, candles, hour-glasses and water clocks were, for most people, the only available means of keeping time. The forerunner of the modern clock was a rather clumsy, weight-driven mechanism used mainly in observatories, churches and public buildings.

The discovery by Galileo Galilei (1564–1642) of the laws governing the motion of a pendulum led the Dutch physicist, Christiaan Huygens (1629–1695) to construct the first pendulum clock, containing a mechanism which could operate at sea. Still powered by weights, it proved unreliable, and it was not until Robert Hooke (1635–1703), English chemist and physicist, had established the laws governing the stretching of springs that the spring-driven clock movement became a possibility.

Below: An Egyptian water clock

Facing page, top: A diagram showing how light travels. When it passes close to a star or planet, it no longer moves in a straight line but in a curved line.

Below: A painting dedicated to Christiaan Huygens who constructed the first pendulum clock

Above: Sky divers falling in formation

Below: An astronomical clock of the fourteenth century

What is terminal velocity?

A feather falling in air shows a small acceleration at the start of the motion, followed by an almost constant speed. The same feather falling in a vacuum drops "like a stone", since it now has only the gravitational pull of the Earth acting on it.

The effect of the air is obvious in the case of the feather, but although less obvious with a heavier falling object, it is still there. If a person falls out of an aeroplane, their speed does not continue to increase. They will, in fact, reach a point where their speed remains constant, called "terminal velocity".

Sky divers are able to use the effect of the atmosphere in this way and can, on reaching their terminal velocity, link hands and all fall together at this same constant velocity. They would all be travelling at well over 45 ml/s.

Above: A track designed to test cars' roadholding on bends.

Right: This diagram of a body (yellow) tied to a string shows how centrifugal force works. The centrifugal force (pink) is an inertia force because the body which is experiencing it is moving in a circle and constantly changing direction. This force is the reaction to the centripetal force (green) in the string which, together with a tangential force (blue), keeps the body in motion. When the string breaks, the centripetal force and therefore the centrifugal force disappear and the body continues to move in the direction of the tangential force.

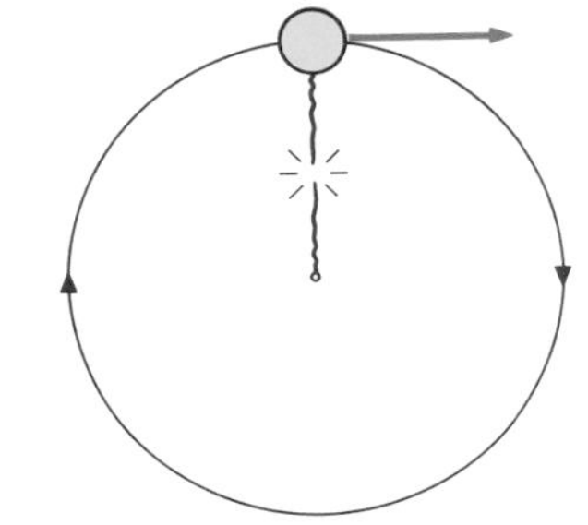

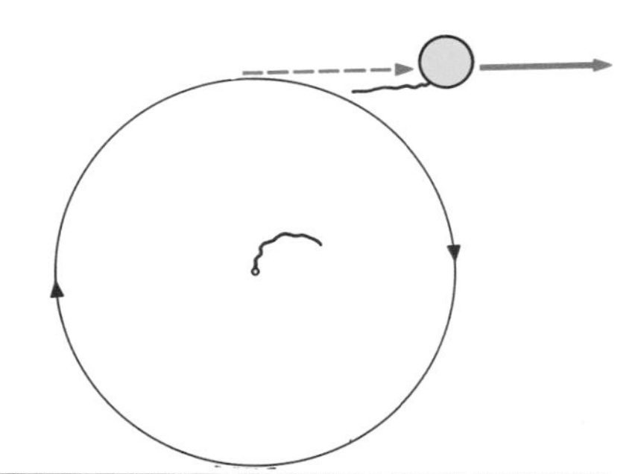

What is centrifugal force?

"Centrifugal force" is experienced whenever someone or something moves in a circle. For example, as a car turns a corner sharply, the people inside the car are pushed to one side.

When any object is made to turn in a circle, its inertia resists the change of direction and the object tries to continue moving straight ahead. The result is that the object tends to move outwards, away from the centre of the circle. As it turns, it experiences an outward-acting force called "centrifugal" force. To keep the object moving in a circle, it is pulled by an equal "centripetal" force acting towards the centre of the circle. In a turning car, the centripetal force is provided by the reaction of the road on the tyres. Because the two forces are equal, the object remains at the same distance from the centre of the circle as it moves.

What are Newton's laws of motion?

When things move, no matter how large or small they are, they obey three laws. These are Newton's laws of motion, which were discovered by the English scientist Isaac Newton (1643–1727) in 1687. The laws explain how all things move.

The first law states that any moving object continues to move at the same speed in a straight line unless a force acts upon it. It explains why a ball continues to roll after you let go of it. Although a force is needed to start it rolling, no force is needed to keep it moving.

The second law explains how forces change motion. It states that a force acting on an object causes it to speed up or slow down in the direction that the force acts; the change in speed depends on the amount of force and the mass of the object. A heavy object needs a stronger force to get it moving or to change its speed.

Newton's third law of motion states that to every action, there is an equal and opposite reaction. This means that when a force acts on an object (the "action"), the object always pushes back with the same force (the "reaction"). This is true whether the object moves or not. For example, when a person stands on a floor, the force of gravity pulls them down with a force equal to their weight. The floor pushes back with the same amount of force so that, overall, no force acts and, therefore, no movement occurs. This is just as well because if the floor did not push back, the person would fall through it.

Below: Isaac Newton, shown in a portrait from the Science Museum in London

What is inertia?

It takes a lot of force to start a heavy object like a car moving. However, once the heavy object is moving, a lot of force is needed to make it stop. This is not because the wheels or brakes of the car are not as good as they should be; it is true of all moving objects and is caused by "inertia". In the same way, if a car stops suddenly, the people inside tend to keep on moving. They fall forwards – because of inertia.

The inertia of an object is simply its tendency to resist a change in its speed or direction. The heavier an object is, the greater are the inertia forces which act on it.

Above: Inertia forces push back passengers and luggage in a vehicle if the driver suddenly accelerates (left) or push them forward when he brakes (right). The forces are not present if the vehicle is at a standstill or travels in a straight line at a constant speed (centre).

Above: A speedway rider using his feet to increase friction

Far right, bottom: Tightrope walkers must keep their centre of gravity directly above the rope.

What is friction?

Braking and drag are examples of a kind of force called "friction". This force occurs in all machines and it always operates to slow a machine. Friction is caused by one part or a material rubbing against another, and it is present in the moving parts of all machines. It produces heat and noise, and wastes energy unless it is used deliberately, as it is in brakes or when a speedway rider uses his feet to increase friction when cornering.

Where is an object's centre of gravity?

When any object is at rest, the force of gravity acts on every part of the object and holds it to the ground. There is one point inside the object at which its total weight – the weight of every part of it added together – appears to act. This point is called its "centre of gravity". In a symmetrical object, such as a sphere, the centre of gravity is at its actual centre. In other objects, it is to one side or may even be at a point outside the object.

The centre of gravity is important because it can make objects unstable if it is in the wrong place. For an object to be stable, its centre of gravity must be directly above its base, otherwise it falls over. In vehicles, the centre of gravity is low. A table lamp has a heavy base to give it a low centre of gravity, while a tightrope walker keeps his centre of gravity directly above the rope.

What is work?

When people and machines use up energy, they often exert a force and push or pull something so that it moves – for example a person might lift a bag, or an engine turn a shaft. Scientists would say that both are doing work. The amount of work that is done is equal to the force exerted multiplied by the distance that an object moves or turns. Use more force, or move an object further, and more work is done.

Work is, in fact, the same as energy; if more energy is used, more work is done. Like energy, work cannot be created or destroyed. This means that the amount of energy or work that a machine gives out is (almost) the same as that which is put into it. If this were not so, machines could create energy as they work. They would get faster and faster, or hotter and hotter, rapidly running out of control. In the same way, if machines lost energy, they would all slow down and stop working.

Above right: An Egyptian well, its huge wheel driven by oxen
Inset: One wheel is attached to a shaft in this early engine

Below: Using a pulley to lift a heavy weight

How does a pulley work?

If an object cannot be lifted directly, it is possible to pass a rope around a wheel, fix the wheel to an overhead beam and pull the rope to raise the object. A wheel used in this way is called a pulley. The force of the effort pulling the rope is equal to the weight of the object, and the object rises the same distance as the rope is pulled.

Systems in which the rope passes around several pulley wheels will lift objects using much less effort. With two wheels, for example, the top wheel is fixed and the bottom wheel is free to move. As the rope is pulled, the bottom wheel moves up to raise the object. However, the length of rope that has to be pulled is double the distance that the object is raised. The effort moves twice the distance of the object, so the effort needed to raise the object is only half the weight of the object.

What happens when a wheel turns?

The wheel and axle is the name of a group of simple machines that include the steering wheel, spanner, screwdriver, brace and bit, winch and capstan, as well as the wheel and axle found in a vehicle like a bicycle. Several of these devices consist of a wheel or a handle that is fixed to a central shaft or axle. Usually the effort is applied to the wheel or handle to turn the shaft. Because the shaft is at the centre, it turns a shorter distance than the effort, but with a greater force. Winding the handle of a winch enables a heavy load to be raised, such as a bucket of water in a well.

In a wheeled vehicle, the effort is applied to the axle and moves the wheel a greater distance with less force. The bigger the wheel, the greater the distance moved and the faster the vehicle goes.

How does a crane lift a load?

Cranes make use of pulley systems to lift heavy objects. The pulley block is at the end of a long arm called a boom (or jib) that is raised above the load. A hook on the end of the bottom set of pulleys is lowered to the load and fixed to it. The other end of the rope is attached to a drum at the base of the crane, and the drum turns to wind the rope in or out and to raise or lower the load. A mobile crane is a crane on wheels with a boom that is raised by hydraulic rams. Tower cranes are built at a site and have a long horizontal jib. A trolley runs along the jib and contains a simple pulley system to raise or lower the load.

How does a lift work?

A lift consists of a box-shaped car that runs up and down guide rails fixed to the sides of a lift shaft. The car is attached to a set of ropes that run over a pulley at the top of the shaft. A counterweight is fixed to the other end of the ropes, which are driven by an electric motor. The counterweight equals the weight of the car so that the motor only lifts the weight of the passengers. A device limiting the speed of the ropes, and a safety device beneath the car, prevent the car from falling if anything goes wrong. Even if these devices should fail, a shock absorber at the bottom of the shaft can bring the car to a safe halt.

How do simple machines work?

Overall, the purpose of a simple machine is to transmit a force from one point to another. The force of a muscle or a motor, called the "effort", is applied to one part of a device, causing it to tilt or to turn. As it moves, the device applies force at another point to produce a useful action – for example, to lift a load. It works so that the effort moves a greater or lesser distance than the load. Because the work done by the effort is the same as that done to the load, the load moves with a greater force than the effort, if it travels a shorter distance. Using a screw jack, for example, the heavy weight of a car can be lifted single-handed. But the handle of the jack has to be moved a great deal to raise the wheel just off the ground.

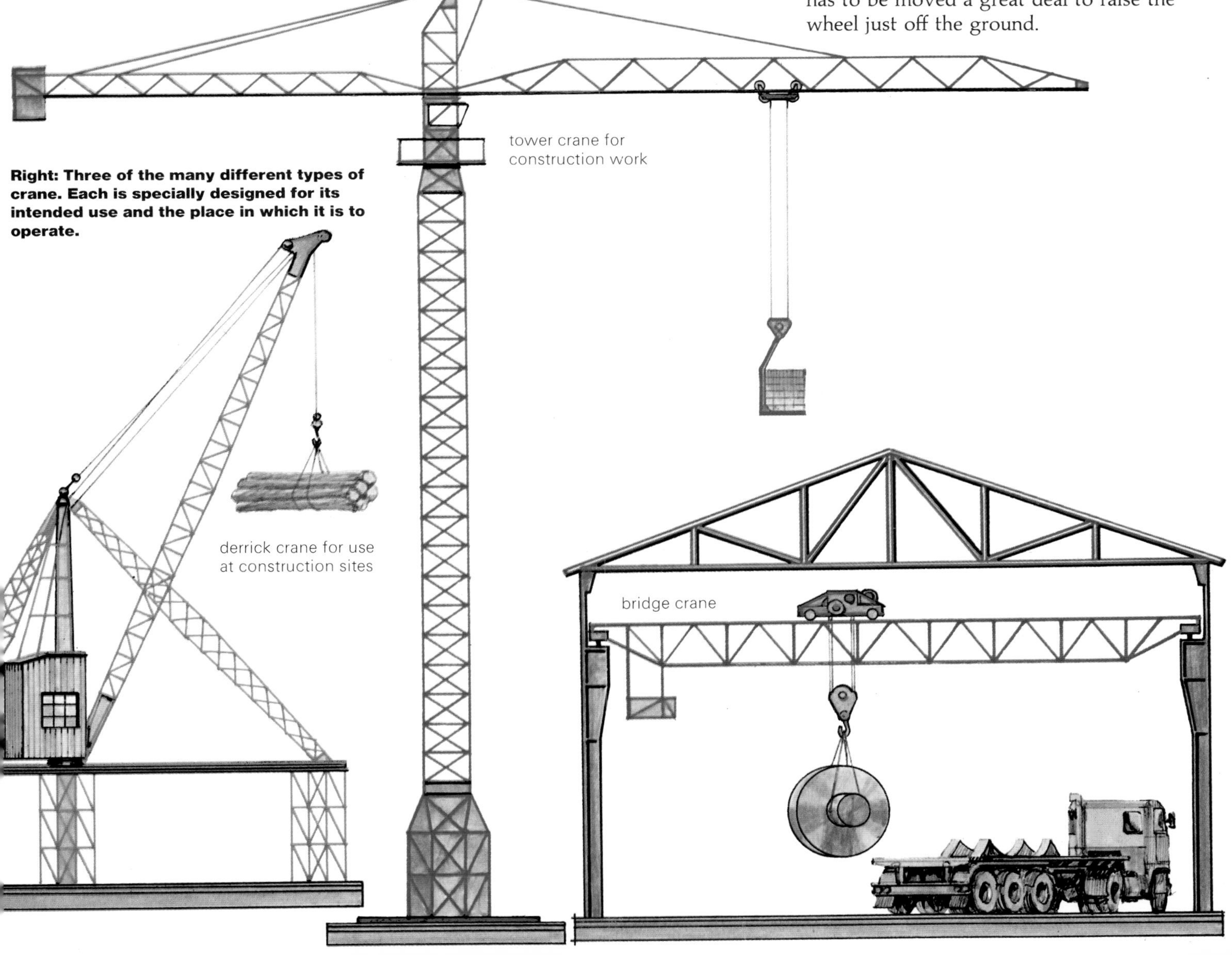

Right: Three of the many different types of crane. Each is specially designed for its intended use and the place in which it is to operate.

What is refraction?

When light rays strike a transparent surface, they usually enter the surface. However, unless the rays meet the surface at right angles, the rays bend as they cross from one material to another, such as from air to glass. This bending of light is called "refraction". The reason for this is that the rays slow down in a denser medium and speed up on entering a less dense medium.

If the rays enter a denser medium, then they bend away from the surface. If they enter a less dense medium, they bend towards it. Refraction explains why an object on the bottom of a pool of water looks closer than it is. The light rays travel up through the water from the object. When they enter the air, they bend towards the surface of the water and then enter the eye. However, the eye believes that the rays have come in a straight line from the object – as if it were higher in the water than it is.

Above left: Light being refracted through a prism

Above right: Rainbows are caused by refraction and reflection of the Sun's rays through rain.

How is a rainbow formed?

When the Sun is shining and it rains at the same time, a beautifully coloured arch is often seen in the sky – it is called a rainbow. This is the result of the reflection and bending of the Sun's rays by the water droplets. The seven colours that the rainbow displays are those of the spectrum – red on the outside, and shading through orange, yellow and green to blue.

What causes reflections?

Reflections seem to come from mirrors, panels of glass or the still surfaces of lakes or ponds. In fact, all opaque (non-transparent) surfaces reflect light rays. Most objects have surfaces that are slightly rough, and the imperfections reflect rays at different angles. But if the surface is smooth, then all the rays that come from an object to the surface are reflected away at the same angle. If these reflected rays enter the eyes, an image of the object is seen in the surface.

Light rays leaving an object, such as a candle, are reflected by a mirror to meet the eye as if they had come directly from a candle behind the mirror. Therefore, the eye sees an image of the candle in the mirror. Two cones of rays come from the base of the candle and the flame. A reversal of the rays occurs as they are reflected, causing the candle to appear reversed in the surface of the mirror.

Why are different objects different colours?

Objects are coloured differently because of the nature of their surfaces. Unless it is white, a surface does not reflect all the light falling on it. A red surface reflects only red light, absorbing light of all the other colours in the white light. Light passing through coloured materials, such as stained glass, is similarly affected. Blue glass absorbs all colours except blue. The energy levels of the atoms in the material determine the amount of energy in the reflected or transmitted light and, therefore, its colour. For example, a black surface absorbs all the light falling on it, and does not reflect any light.

What is a virtual image?

Cameras and projectors all produce a "real image" that falls on a surface such as a film or a screen. The images that are seen in microscopes, binoculars and telescopes are "virtual images" that cannot be projected on to a surface, and they form in a different way.

The lenses in these optical instruments bend the light rays coming from an object as if they were coming directly from the object instead of passing through the lenses. But they do so as if the object were much nearer than it actually is. This is why a magnified view of an object or scene is seen in a microscope or telescope. Binoculars are simply two small telescopes fixed together – the virtual image is considered to be at the position where the object appears to be.

How fast is the speed of light?

Light is a form of energy that can travel over a distance, but it is not the only kind of energy to do so. Sound travels, too, but sound has to move through a material such as air or water. Light can travel across empty space to reach the Earth from the Sun and also from the Moon, the planets, stars, and distant galaxies. These distances are enormous, but light travels very fast. Its speed is almost 300,000 km/s and this is the fastest speed possible. In fact, no object can quite reach the speed of light because it would then have an infinite amount of energy.

Right: Lasers were used as part of the Christmas decorations in Oxford Street, London, in 1981.

Below: Two views through a microscope. The top picture shows a piece of marble, the lower picture a section of human bone in polarized light.

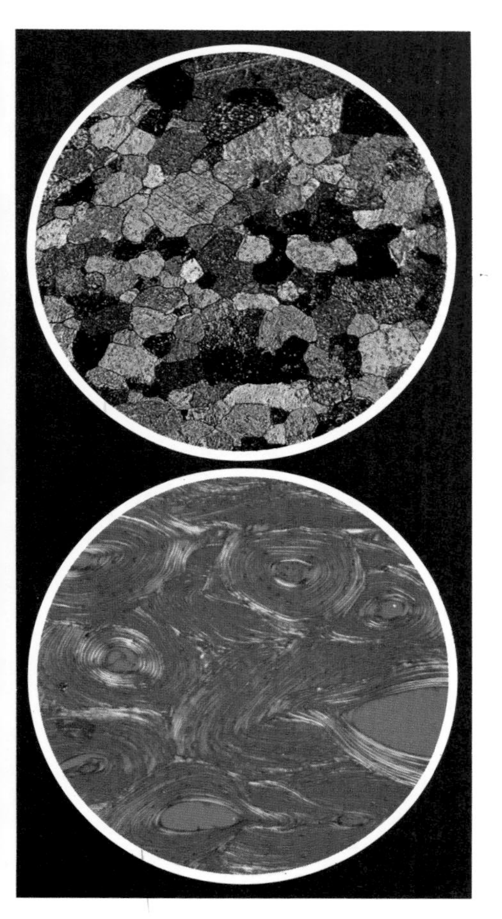

What is a laser?

A laser is a device which emits a very thin, powerful beam of a special kind of light capable of travelling immense distances. The name "laser" stands for "light amplification by stimulated emission of radiation".

There are several kinds of laser, but they all work in basically the same way to amplify light by stimulating a cascade of photon (light particle) emission. Lasers can produce pulsed or continuous beams of different colours, and they can also generate powerful heat beams.

A laser beam can have valuable uses in medicine. For example, the beam can be directed into the eye to repair vision defects without cutting the eyeball open. Lasers are also of great importance in communications because the beam can carry signals with a high density of information. Fibre-optic cables transmit laser signals over distances, for example in telephone networks and can carry a much greater volume of traffic than conventional electric cables. Lasers are also required to handle the recording and reproduction of high-speed digital signals in compact disc and video disc systems.

When was the electric light bulb invented?

The American scientist Thomas Alva Edison (1847–1931) was determined to produce a successful electric light bulb – one which could be manufactured easily and cheaply and which would continue to glow for a long period without burning out. The secret lay in the material to be used for the filament of the lamp and many materials were tried and rejected – some as too expensive, others as too weak. Then, on 21 October 1879, a filament made from a length of carbonized sewing thread, mounted in an evacuated glass bulb, produced a steady glow for over forty hours. Three years later, on 4 September 1882, New York marvelled as Edison switched on the first successful electric light system in the world.

The British scientist, Joseph Swan (1828–1914), also invented a bulb at the same time and both men are now given credit for the invention.

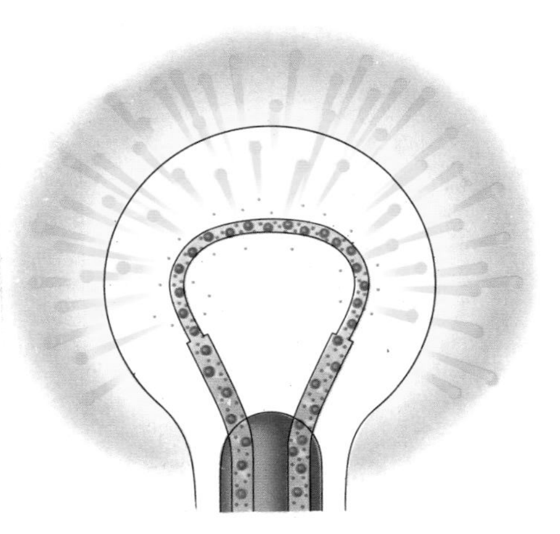

Above: An electric bulb showing the filament emitting photons (light particles)

How does a light bulb work?

Electric light bulbs and electric heaters consist of a wire through which electric current flows from the mains supply. As the current flows through the wire, the electrons jostle the atoms of metal in it. The atoms vibrate faster and the wire gets hotter. If the wire gets very hot, it begins to give out light as well as heat. The bars of an electric fire glow red hot. At higher temperatures, the wire glows white hot and gives out bright light – this is how a light bulb works.

Inside a light bulb is a thin filament of tungsten wire surrounded by an inert or "noble" gas, such as argon, which does not react easily with other substances. Tungsten is a metal with a very high melting point, so it can get very hot and give out a lot of light. The noble gas prevents oxygen in the air from getting to the metal, which would cause it to burn out immediately.

Why do neon lights glow?

Strip lights and street lights work in a different way from light bulbs. They consist of a tube of mercury vapour or sodium vapour (a vapour is a kind of gas). When an electric current passes through the tube, the vapour glows with a bright light. Sodium vapour gives out a bright orange light. Mercury vapour gives out invisible ultraviolet rays, and these make a fluorescent coating inside the tube glow with white light. The bright advertising signs, often called "neon" signs, work in the same way as sodium lamps. Some contain neon, which produces a bright red light, while others contain different gases to give other colours.

Below: Neon lights are often used to illuminate funfair rides (below) and in advertising signs (bottom).

How does a battery make electricity?

The first battery was the simple Volta cell, invented by the Italian scientist Alessandro Volta in 1800. A battery converts chemical energy to electrical energy. It contains chemicals that react together to release electrons from their atoms. This can only happen when the electrons are free to move, which is when the two terminals of the battery are connected to an electrical circuit – for example, the switch and bulb in a torch or flashlight. The current continues to flow until the circuit is broken by switching off.

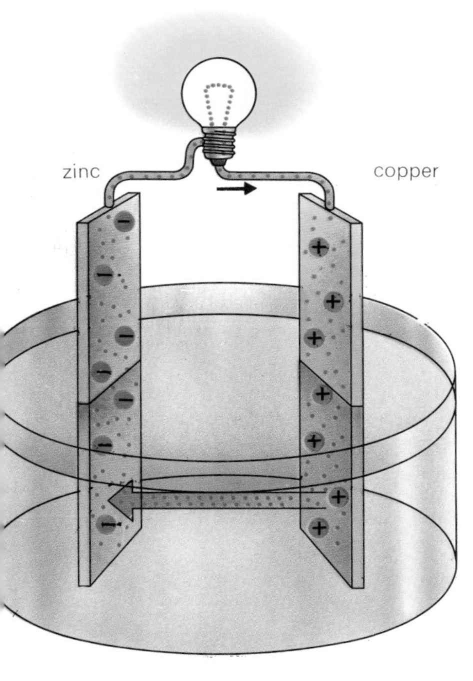

In a primary cell, which is the kind of battery used in a torch or tape player, the chemicals eventually stop reacting and the battery produces no more current – new batteries are needed. A secondary cell, which is the kind of battery used in a car, can be used again. Here, electricity is fed back into the battery from the car's generator and it recharges the battery, changing the used chemicals back into new chemicals. These react to give more electric current. In this way, electricity produced by the generator is stored in the battery, which is always ready to provide current to start the car.

What is an ampere?

In an electrical circuit connected to a battery, millions of electrons are being injected into the wire at the same time as a similar number are being expelled at the other end. On average, the number of electrons passing any part of the wire in one second will be the same and this is the measure of the electric current. As this is likely to be a very large number, a more useful unit of current to use is the "ampere" (or amp, for short). It is named after the French physicist André Marie Ampère (1775–1836). When a current of one ampere is flowing through the wire, 6,240,000 million million electrons pass by any part of the wire every second.

Left: A simple Volta cell, the earliest type of battery. The copper and zinc bars are immersed in a solution of sulphuric acid and water. The zinc transfers atoms into the solution faster than the copper and so becomes negatively charged, causing a current to flow between it and the positively charged copper bar.

What is electric current?

There are two kinds of electric current. Direct current (DC), which comes from batteries, flows right through the circuit from the negative terminal of the battery to the positive terminal. Alternating current (AC), which comes from power points, consists of a flow of electrons that continually changes direction, flowing backwards and forwards alternately. The current changes direction fifty or sixty times a second, and this is known as the "mains frequency". It is easier to generate and supply alternating current for homes. Simple devices such as light bulbs can work on alternating current or direct current, but most electrical machines use alternating current.

Below: A transformer station where electrical energy from power stations is reduced in voltage. The electricity is sent on to consumer centres where it is further transformed to a level suitable for use in homes and factories.

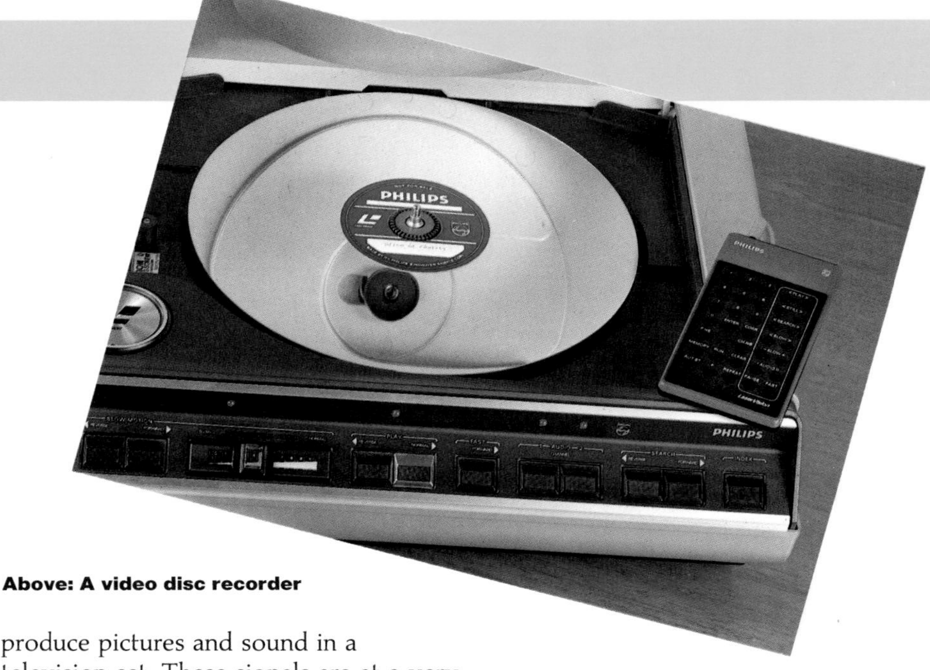

Above: A video disc recorder

How does radio broadcasting work?

The radio (or wireless as it was first called) was invented by Guglielmo Marconi in 1895. The first radios sent messages in Morse code. The first radio programmes for entertainment were broadcast from radio stations in the 1920s.

Radio uses radio waves to carry sound from one place to another. In radio broadcasting, voices, music or other sounds are turned into electric signals in a microphone. These are transmitted in the form of electromagnetic waves by an aerial or a tall mast. They are picked up by another aerial on a receiver – the radio sets in homes are receivers. They change the waves back into sound.

Ground waves travel direct from a transmitter to a receiver in a straight line, and low-frequency waves may then travel along the Earth's surface. Sky waves reach distant receivers after being reflected from the ionosphere (the upper layer of the atmosphere). High-frequency waves, however, penetrate the ionosphere for satellite communications.

Below: A 1934 radio set

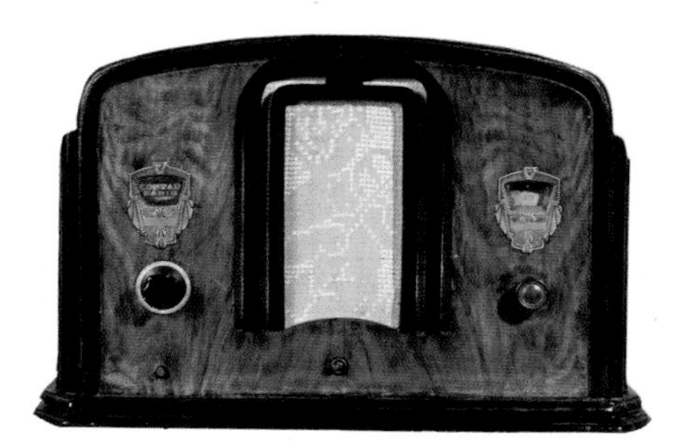

How does a video work?

There are two basic kinds of video system: video cassette recorders and video disc players. Video cassettes are tapes that can be erased and on which new pictures and sound can be recorded. Video discs only replay the pictures and sound.

Video cassettes are analog tapes that record the electrical signals that go to produce pictures and sound in a television set. These signals are at a very high frequency and a high tape-to-head speed is required to record and replay them satisfactorily. This is achieved by making the video (picture) signal in a series of diagonal tracks across the tape. The audio (sound) signal may be recorded in a separate straight track along the edge of the tape, or with the video signal for high-quality sound.

Video discs work in a similar way to compact discs. They are analog, with the lengths of the pits representing the varying wavelength of the signal carrying the pictures and sound.

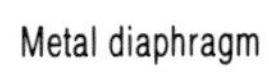
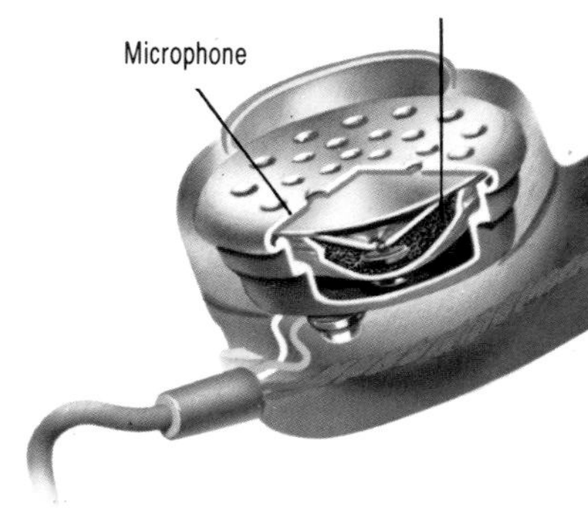

Above: The inside of a telephone showing the metal diaphragms which vibrate to reproduce the sounds spoken into the microphone.

When was the telephone invented?

Three inventors discovered how to generate electric pulses which could transmit and reproduce sounds. The first was Antonio Meucci, an Italian resident in the USA, in 1871. He was followed, five years later, by two Americans – Alexander Graham Bell and Elisha Gray. Only Bell was able to go on to make a practical instrument (in 1876) and he is consequently regarded as the inventor of the telephone.

The modern telephone, although very different in shape from those of the last century, is essentially the same as the instruments of that time. The receiver in the earpiece is similar to one invented by Bell and Meucci, and the microphone in the mouthpiece is a development of Gray's device.

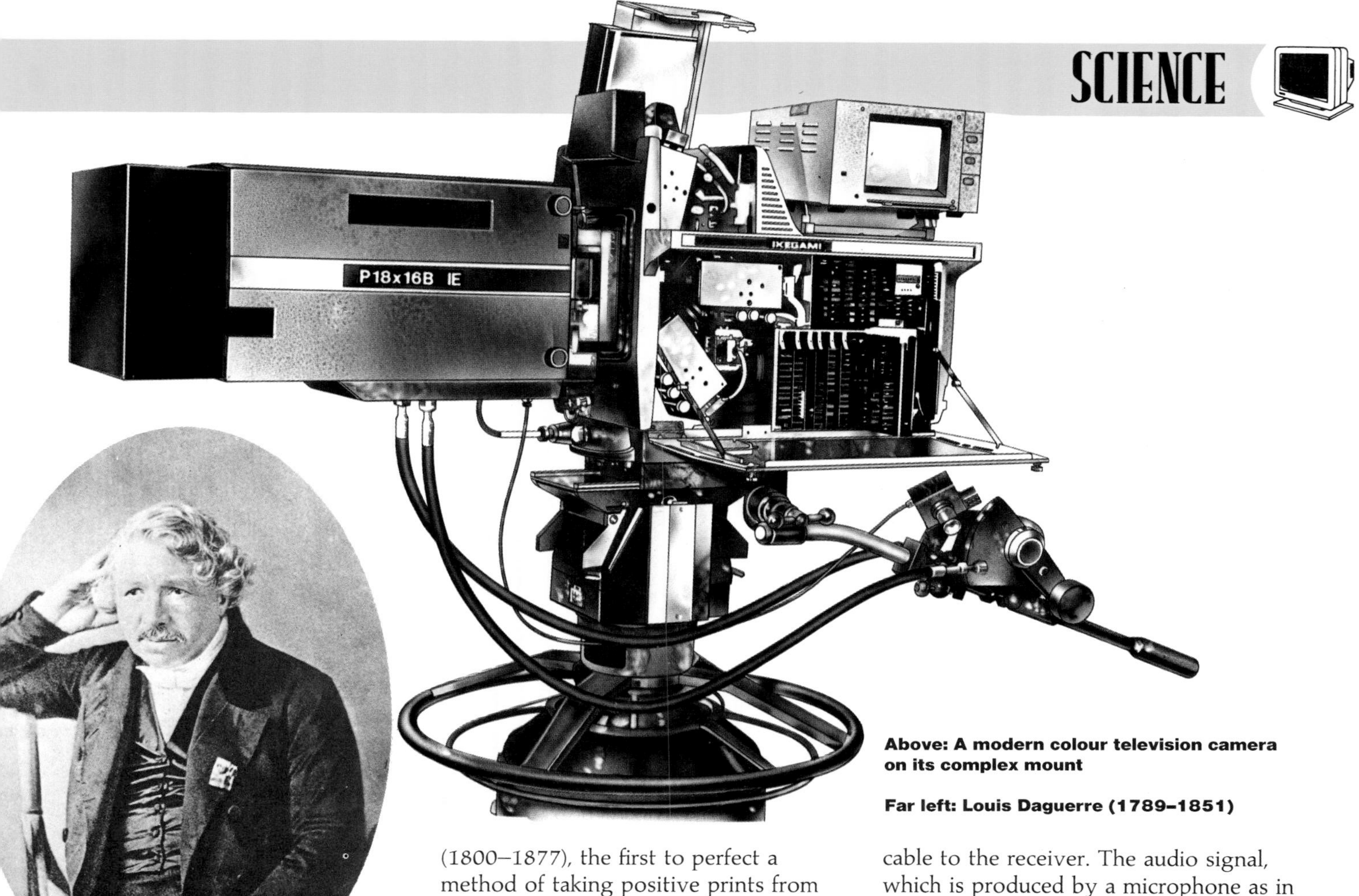

Above: A modern colour television camera on its complex mount

Far left: Louis Daguerre (1789–1851)

Who invented photography?

When a Frenchman, Louis Daguerre (1789–1851), developed a photograph from the inverted image produced by a pin-hole camera in 1837, he had no reason to believe that he was experimenting with electromagnetic waves. Nor did he realize that the reactions of the silver, iodine and mercury vapour he used to develop his first photographic plate were the result of electron movements within atoms. Indeed the early pioneers of photography were mainly amateur investigators with little scientific and certainly no electrical knowledge. Nicéphore Niépce (1765–1833), who developed one of the first box cameras containing a convex lens, was a retired French army officer; Daguerre himself was a decorator, and W. H. Fox Talbot (1800–1877), the first to perfect a method of taking positive prints from negatives formed on glass, was an English gentleman of leisure.

In 1887, an American, George Eastman (1854–1932), was able to fix a layer of sensitive emulsion on to celluloid, making the first roll film and paving the way for the invention of moving pictures.

How does a television camera work?

A television camera contains a lens that forms an image of a scene on a light-sensitive detector. The detector breaks up the image into a series of horizontal lines, and produces a sequence of electrical signals that vary according to the brightness of the picture along each line. This is carried out many times a second to give the video signal. There are two main television standards: in Europe, a television picture is composed of 625 lines formed twenty-five times a second, and in North America, 525 lines are formed thirty times a second.

The video signal from the camera is then transmitted by radio or sent along a cable to the receiver. The audio signal, which is produced by a microphone as in sound radio, travels in the same way. The aerial connected to the receiver picks up the carrier wave, and the receiver demodulates it to produce the video and audio signals. The latter goes first to an amplifier and then to a loudspeaker in the set, while the video signal goes to the television tube.

How is a colour photograph produced?

A colour film contains three layers of emulsion that respond to the amounts of the three primary colours – blue, red and green – in the image formed by the lens. When the film is developed, a silver image forms in each layer but the silver is then replaced by a dye of the secondary colour – yellow, cyan and magenta. The resulting three-colour images combine to form a colour negative – for example, blue in the scene is yellow in the negative. The negative is then printed on to a piece of colour paper similar to colour film, reversing the negative colours to give a full-colour photograph of the original scene.

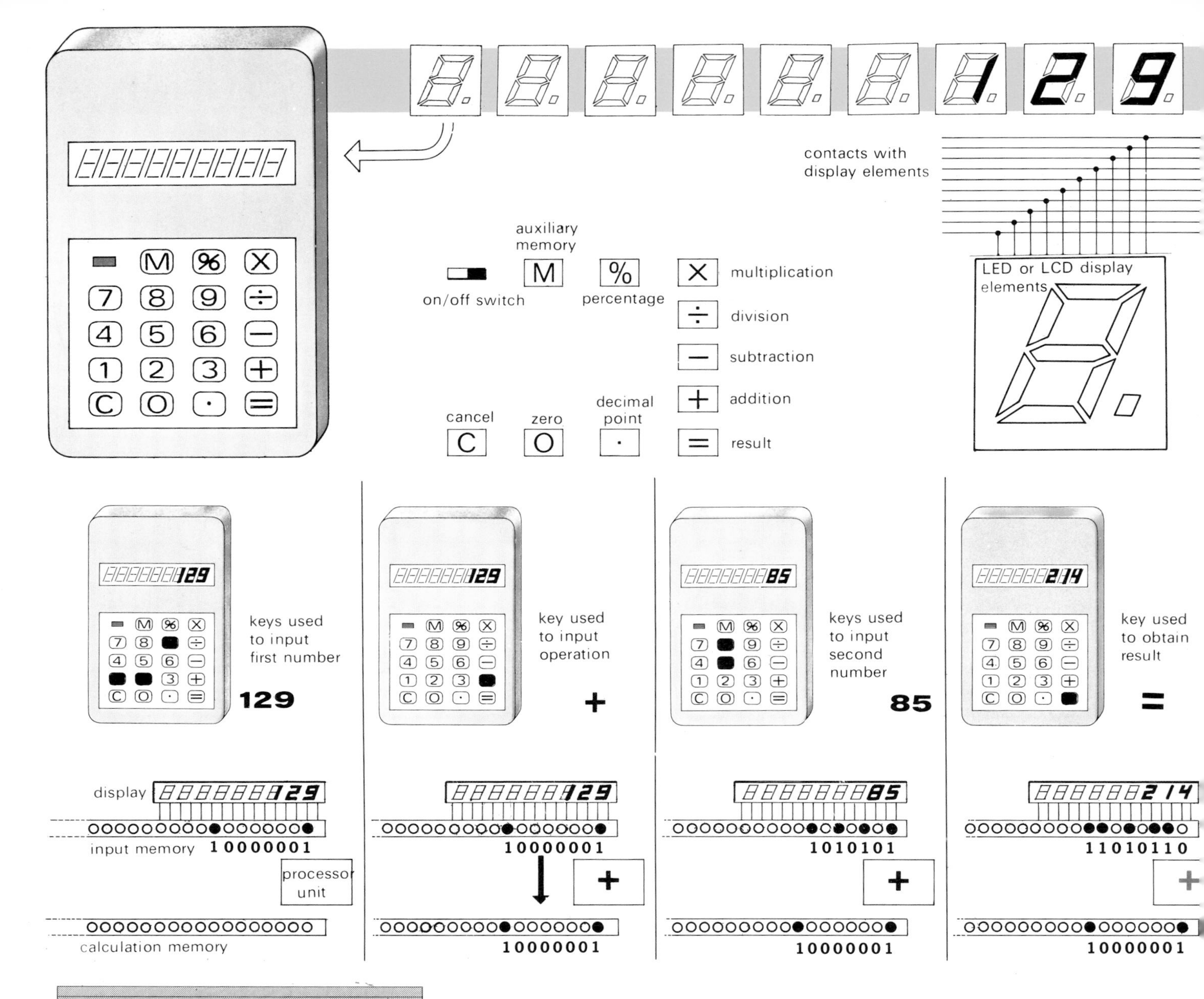

Above: How a sum (129 + 85) is done on an electronic calculator. The numbers appear in decimal form on the display and in binary form in the input memory.

How does a calculator work?

When the keys of a calculator are pressed, the numbers are changed into on-off electric signals – each number has a different signal. Then the "brain" of the calculator adds the signals together to produce another signal, which is then changed back into a number that gives the answer. The brain of the calculator is a microchip, which contains thousands of electric circuits that handle the signals. Because it is very small and the signals travel around the circuits very quickly, the calculator is able to do additions very fast indeed. More difficult calculations are done by making additions one after the other, and the calculator carries them out so fast that it appears to get an instant answer.

Below: An early calculating machine which worked by means of a system of levers and gears. Mechanical devices such as this were the forerunners of today's complex electronic calculators and computers.

When was the first computer built?

No machine, with perhaps the exception of the space station and space shuttle, typifies our age more than the computer. Although the idea of a computer was conceived about 150 years ago by the British scientist Charles Babbage, the construction of one did not become possible until electronics had been developed. The first electronic computer was called "Colossus", and was built in total secrecy in Britain in 1943 to crack enemy code messages. Since then, the arrival of the transistor and the increasing miniaturization of this and other electronic components, resulting in today's microchips, have resulted in ever smaller and more powerful computers.

What is binary code?

Inside a computer, all the information and instructions exist in the form of electrical code signals. The code that is used is "binary code", which represents numbers using only two digits: Ø (meaning zero) and 1 – just as "decimal" numbers use ten digits (0 to 9). In the computer, all the instructions are given different code numbers as are all letters, so that the computer handles only numbers, which is why it is called a "digital" machine.

Binary code is used because it is very simple. In a code signal, 1 in the code number is represented by a pulse of electric current and Ø by the absence of a pulse. Code signals composed of on-off sequences of electrical pulses move rapidly through the many electronic components in the computer as it follows a program and handles information. When results are required, the computer converts the code signals back into letters and decimal numbers or pictures, or anything else that is needed. Millions of pulses pass through a computer every second, which is why these machines are able to work so quickly.

How does a computer know what to do?

A computer has to be programmed, or given a set of instructions, to perform any task. Whenever required, the computer can be given new instructions to perform another task. The set of instructions is called a "program", and programs in general are known as "software". This distinguishes them from "hardware", which is the actual machinery in the computer and any units connected to it.

A computer faithfully follows the program it is given, and it can carry out the instructions in the program at very great speed. Provided the program is correct and any information required by the program is correct, the computer will perform its task faultlessly and rapidly.

How are computer programs stored?

Hard disks and floppy disks record computer programs and data in concentric tracks on their magnetic surface. A computer "reads" the disks by means of an electromagnetic head in the "disk drive". The head can move over the disk to access any section very quickly.

Programs and data may also be held temporarily or permanently in "memory chips". Some chips are erasable, making it possible to replace permanent programs (or data). Small temporary memories called "buffers" handle temporary operations in a computer.

What are modems?

Large computers may have many separate input and output units connected to them. These units are called "terminals", and they usually consist of a keyboard and a VDU. The computer itself may be a long distance away, and the terminals are connected by wires. A combined input and output unit called a "modem" enables any two computers to be connected via the telephone network. The modem converts the computer code signals into sound signals; these then travel over the telephone wires to another modem that converts them back into computer code signals. In this way a network of computers can exchange information.

Can computers recognize speech?

Some computers have voice units that speak words – code signals drive a speech synthesizer that forms the words by stringing together basic speech sounds called "phonemes". It is also possible for computers to recognize spoken words by having a voice recognition unit as the input unit. The user speaks into a microphone and the computer converts the words into code signals; it then compares them with codes for a set of words in its memory. If a code matches, then the computer recognizes the word. However, the user must first speak the words into the computer so that they can be stored in its memory.

Below: A modern newspaper office, showing journalists writing their stories directly into a computer typesetting machine

Left: A *draisienne* or dandy horse, an early type of bicycle propelled by the rider pushing his feet against the ground

Below: A penny farthing

What is a dandy horse?

The first two-wheeled conveyance that enjoyed any popularity was invented in Germany by Baron von Drais de Sauerbrun, and was exhibited in Paris in 1819. Called the *draisienne*, it was propelled by the rider pushing his feet against the ground. Similar machines were built in England and came to be called "hobby horses" or "dandy horses", but they were clumsy and crude and uncomfortable to ride.

What is a penny-farthing?

In 1870 the "penny-farthing" (or "ordinary bicycle") appeared on the scene. Designed by James Starley, it was driven by pedals and cranks on the huge front wheel, which measured up to 1.5 m in diameter. It had spoked wheels – a feature of all bicycles ever since.

The name of this new type of vehicle came from two British coins: one large and one small. The rider sat above the large front wheel (the "penny"), while the tiny rear wheel was the "farthing". There were no gears.

When did the modern bicycle appear?

Of all the methods of transport so far devised, the bicycle is the cheapest and most efficient. It requires no fuel to keep it running and needs little maintenance, yet it can propel people many times faster than they can run. Indeed, the world record speed for a bicycle is no less than 94 km/h.

Not until 1839 did a practical bicycle appear. It was designed by a Scottish blacksmith, Kirkpatrick Macmillan, who used a system of swinging cranks and levers to turn the rear wheel.

In the 1860s, a French father and son, Pierre and Ernest Michaux, built a bicycle propelled by cranks on the hub of the front wheel. It came to be called a "velocipede", although it was more commonly nicknamed the "boneshaker".

In 1888, the comfort of the bicycle rider was greatly improved by the invention of the air-filled (pneumatic) tyre by John Boyd Dunlop. Just after the turn of the century, J.J.H. Sturmey and J. Archer introduced variable speed hub gears.

How has bicycle design changed?

In the last fifty years the basic design of the bicycle has altered little, although there have been improvements in materials, styling and braking efficiency. The standard bike has a diamond frame, so called because of its shape. It is made of brazed steel tubing. The brakes are usually of the calliper type, working by scissors action. Bikes for commuting and general town use generally have horizontal handlebars and hub gears.

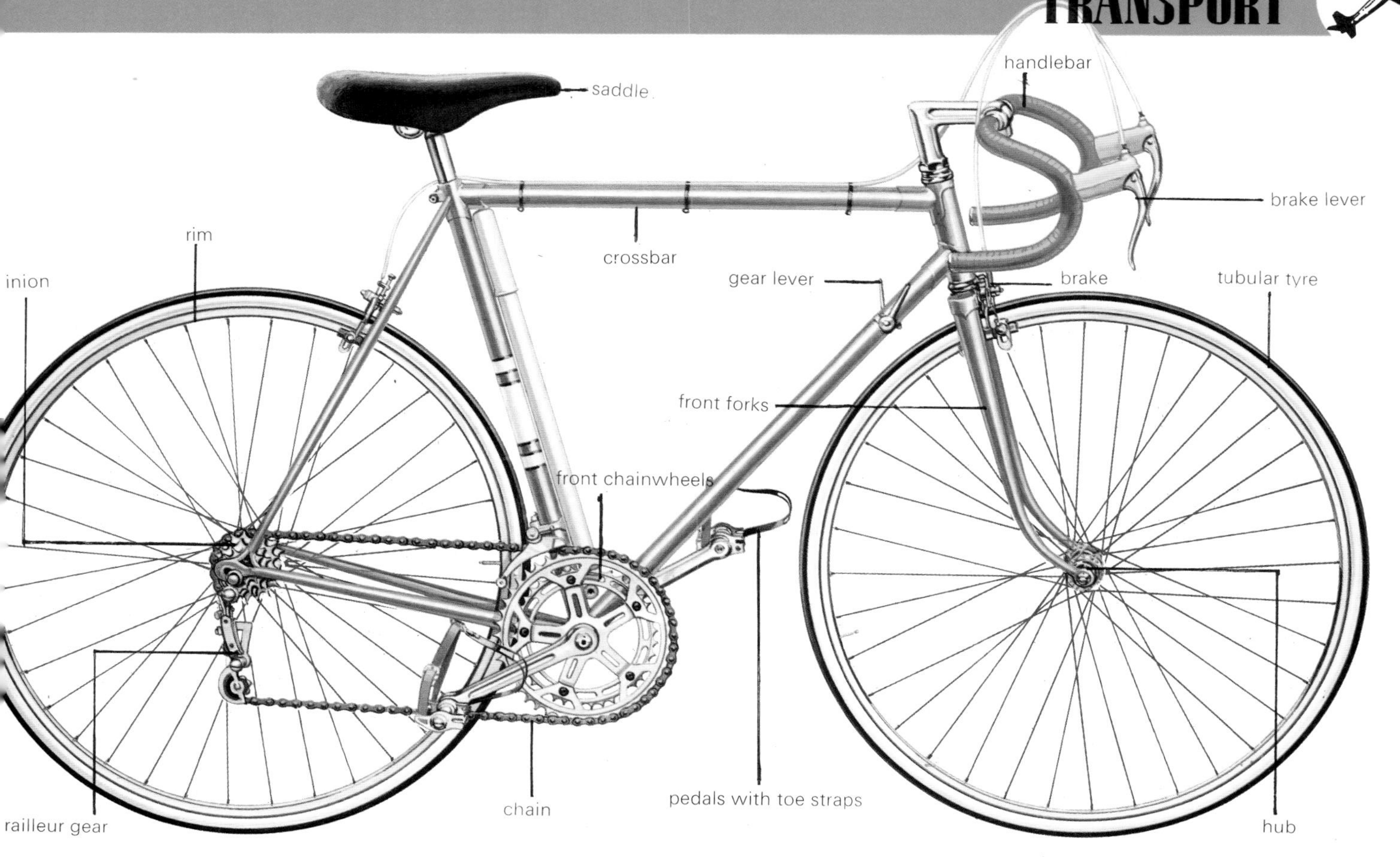

Racing and touring bikes are much lighter in weight. They usually have alloy wheels and fittings, curved drop handlebars and derailleur gears. High-performance bikes are ultra-lightweight, with very narrow tyres.

The cross-frame design, which has a unique suspension and smaller wheels, was developed by Alex Moulton in the 1960s.

Why does a bicycle need gears?

A bicycle's gears enable the cyclist to extract the maximum motion with the minimum of effort by altering the distance that the bicycle moves as the pedals are turned. In a high gear, a bike can be ridden on the level at speed. The wheels move a long distance as a person's feet turn the pedals once around. Little force is applied to the wheels, because little is needed under such conditions. But when a person starts off or has to climb a hill, more force is needed to turn the wheels of the bicycle. Using a low gear, so that the wheels move a shorter distance as the pedals are turned once, allows more force to be transmitted to the wheels.

Some bicycles have gears inside a hub unit. Others have derailleur gears. These consist of a number of different-sized gearwheels or sprockets on the rear wheel hub. A spring mechanism moves the chain from one to the other to change gear. Some racing bicycles have a two-sprocket chain wheel and a five sprocket hub unit to give ten gears.

Top: A racing bicycle

Below: A group of racing cyclists labouring up a hill in the 1979 *Giro d'Italia* competition

Who invented the motorcycle?

It was not until the development of a lightweight petrol engine in the 1880s that the motorcycle developed into a practical vehicle. The German engineer, Gottlieb Daimler, led the way with his machine of 1885, but he soon lost interest in two wheels and went on to pioneer development of the motor car.

Other engineers tried their luck, with variable success, with both bicycles and tricycles. The breakthrough finally came at the turn of the nineteenth century in France. Two Parisian journalists, Michael and Eugene Werner, improved their already popular motor-assisted bicycle by placing the engine low down in the frame between the wheels. The engine has remained there ever since.

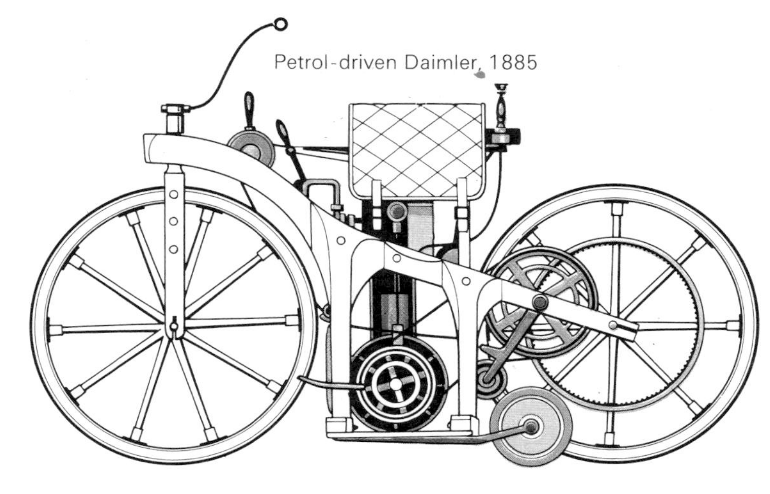
Petrol-driven Daimler, 1885

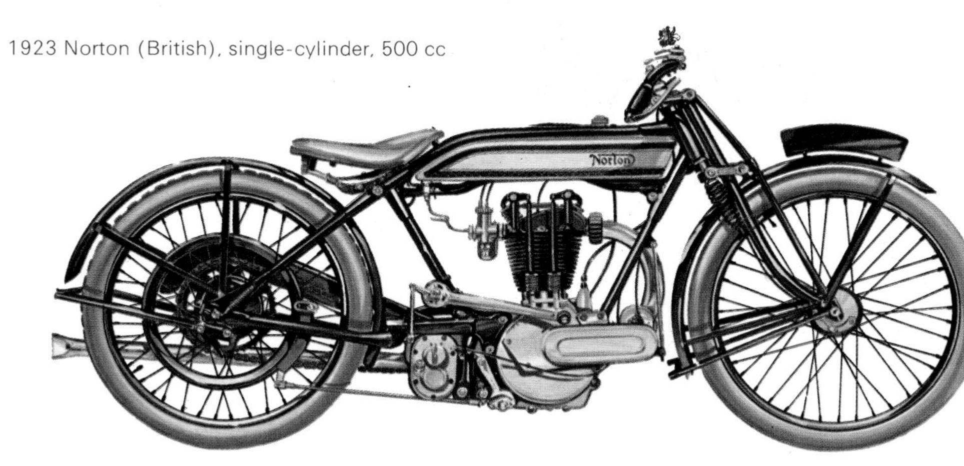
1923 Norton (British), single-cylinder, 500 cc

Right: These three motorcycles show the great advances made in design in less than fifty years. The introduction of a clutch and gears in particular made the machine a much faster and more reliable method of transport.

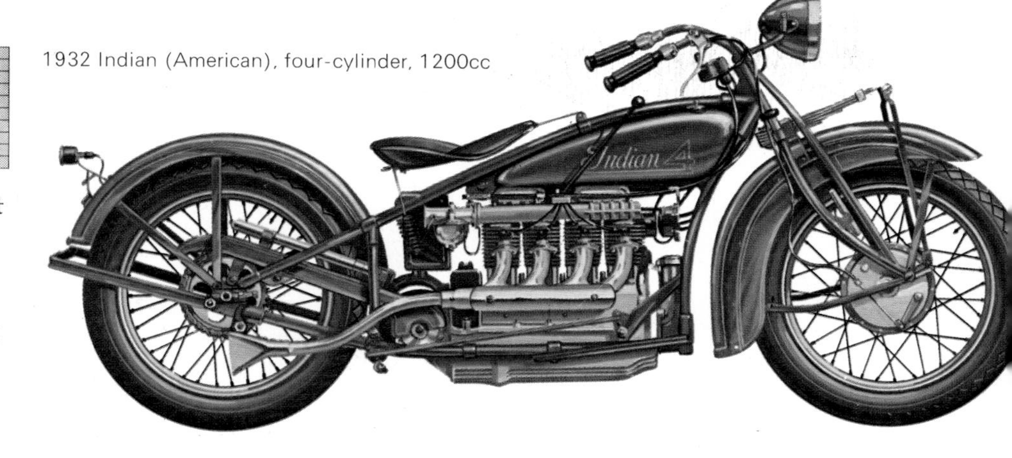
1932 Indian (American), four-cylinder, 1200cc

How is a motorcycle powered?

Smaller-engined mopeds and lightweight motorcycles are generally powered by a two-stroke petrol engine with a single cylinder. "Two-stroke" means that the petrol engine goes through its operating cycle on just two movements (or "strokes") of the piston inside the engine's cylinder. The engines of larger machines work on a four-stroke cycle, like a car engine. They have from one to as many as six cylinders, with a capacity of up to 1300 cc or more.

The motorcycle engine works in much the same way as a car engine. It has coil ignition, powered by a battery or an engine-driven generator, but it is usually air-cooled, not liquid-cooled like a car. Only a few motorcycle engines use liquid cooling by radiator.

How has motorcycle design changed?

From 1905 onwards, motorcycle technology began to make rapid strides. With the introduction of the clutch, the engine could be started when the machine was stationary; with the addition of gears, hills could be taken without the need to use the pedals (which, until then, the rider had made use of to assist the engine when climbing); with the removal of the pedals the frame could be made lower; and finally the addition of gears meant that a chain could be fitted. A chain was far more reliable than a belt, which in wet weather and on muddy roads often slipped.

Below: One of the first motor scooters to be manufactured was the Vespa, made in Italy by Piaggio in 1946.

When did the motor scooter first appear?

The motor scooter, an original and very practical vehicle, was first thought of as far back as the 1920s, but was not produced in any numbers until after the Second World War. The first models to be brought out were the Vespa, manufactured in Italy by Piaggio in 1946 (shown in the illustration above), and the Lambretta, introduced by Innocenti in 1947. They enjoyed an enormous success, being known as the "poor man's car", and were soon in widespread use all over the world. Scooters enjoyed a peak of popularity with riders in Britain in the 1960s during the era of "Mods" and "Rockers", two rival teenage gangs.

How did the modern motorcycle industry emerge?

After the Second World War, especially at the beginning of the 1960s, a great change came over the motorcycle world. The increase in the use of cars at first led to a serious crisis in the market for two-wheelers. Scooters and motorcycles had been the chief means of motor transport in the immediate post-war years, but they now decreased in popularity. While European motorcycle manufacturers came close to bankruptcy (many did go out of business), Japanese manufacturers began to prosper.

Japanese companies (Honda, Suzuki, Yamaha and Kawasaki) now dominate the market. They produce a wide variety of machines from 50 cc mopeds suitable for learners, to streamlined "superbikes" capable of speeds approaching 250 km/h. Competing with them, mainly in the touring bike category, are long-established European manufacturers such as Germany's BMW, Italy's Ducati, Laverda and Moto Guzzi, and Harley Davidson in the USA.

Below: A powerful modern motorcycle made by the Japanese manufacturer, Yamaha

Who invented the petrol engine?

Steam was the driving force of engines in the nineteenth century. Yet the demand for a simple, but efficient, lightweight engine which could be operated by an unskilled driver and be switched on at will, without the need for a head of steam, led scientists to investigate other sources of energy. They experimented with inflammable gas, hot air, and finally petrol vapour.

The Otto four-stroke gas engine, named after its Bavarian inventor, Dr Nikolaus Otto (1832–1891), adapted many earlier ideas. Its invention made possible the modern car. In 1875, petrol gas was tried for the first time in the Otto engine by the Viennese engineer Siegfried Markus (1831–1899) and the stage was set for the appearance of the "horseless carriage".

Above: One of the first four-stroke internal combustion engines, which was built in about 1876 by the German inventor Nikolaus August Otto

Below: A prototype of the diesel engine, built in 1897

What are the advantages of diesel engines?

The petrol engine was a marked improvement on the steam engine and it achieved its greater efficiency of 28 per cent by working at a higher temperature. In the same way, the diesel engine, with an increased efficiency of up to 35 per cent, obtained this figure by working at even higher temperatures.

The German engineer, Rudolf Diesel (1858–1913), perfected the engine named after him in 1897. Diesel engines do not require a carburettor or electrical ignition system. Fuel is injected directly into the cylinder, where air is compressed to the point where it is very hot. The fuel ignites because of this "compression-ignition" effect. Because of their high efficiency, they are used to drive trucks and buses, ships and trains, electric power plants and submarines. An increasing number of cars are now driven by diesel engines.

When was the car invented?

In 1885, the German engineer Gottlieb Daimler developed a practical, lightweight petrol engine, with which he created the first true motorcycle. Without his knowledge, Daimler's countryman, Karl Benz, had been working on similar lines. In the autumn of 1885, Benz installed a petrol engine in a three-wheeled vehicle to create the first motor car.

The Benz car pioneered many features of the modern car engine – battery spark ignition, mushroom valves, and water cooling. The engine drove the rear wheels by belt through a differential (a mechanism that allows the two wheels of a car to travel at different speeds around a corner without slipping).

Daimler produced the first four-wheeled car in 1886, fitting one of his engines to an existing "horse-carriage". The term "horseless carriage" then came into use to describe this new form of transport.

Below: The first motor car – a three-wheeled vehicle with a petrol engine attached. It was built by Karl Benz.

Fiat 'Zero' 1912

Austin 'Seven' 1922

Fiat 'Topolino' 1936

Volkswagen 'Beetle' 1940

Citroën '2 CV' 1948

BMC/BL 'Mini' 1959

Fiat 'Panda' 1980

Above: A series of family cars dating from 1912 to 1980 (the dates given indicate the first year of manufacture).

How has the car body developed?

The original purpose of a car body was simply to protect the passengers from rain, sun and dust. For this, no finer inspiration was needed than that provided by the horse-drawn carriage, whose luxurious interior fittings were often reproduced in the early motor cars. These early cars had leather divan seats, carpets, velvet covers and even window curtains. The body was bolted to a wooden (or metal) frame called the "chassis". The first stage in the development of the car body occurred when, instead of functioning merely as a "lid", it became an integral part and support of the whole car.

Modern bodywork must be resistant to rust and normal wear, for which it is specially treated before being painted. It must be robust in some places, such as the passenger compartment, but capable of collapse in certain other parts, such as the bonnet and rear, so that in case of a crash the impact can be partly absorbed.

Which is the world's most popular car?

Family cars that are economical and practical to run – that are low in cost, modest in fuel consumption, and require minimum servicing – have been responsible for the great increase in car use. Today the Japanese dominate the world car market, but the model that still holds the record for mass production is West Germany's Volkswagen "Beetle", of which over 21 million were built between 1938 and 1987.

Why are car bodies streamlined?

Modern cars are sleek, efficient and comfortable machines. Engines have undergone many changes in recent years to improve fuel consumption and to reduce the pollution caused by the exhaust fumes. The car body too has been changed.

Gradually the shape of the body has progressed from square and angular to more streamlined, aerodynamic forms, in order to make cars faster and more efficient. To maximise this effect, a car's profile is now dictated by computer. The final design is tested in a wind tunnel, which reproduces the conditions of air resistance that will be encountered at different speeds.

What will the cars of the future be like?

Designers are working hard to produce more efficient cars with engines that use very little fuel and do not pollute the air with their exhaust fumes. Cars will become safer to drive and more streamlined in order to save fuel without sacrificing speed. They will be more durable and capable of being serviced easily and economically, and also more comfortable, with automatic, computerized devices to make driving in traffic and following road maps easier.

The major change in the car design of the future will be the use of new fuels to replace petrol. These might be synthetic hydrocarbon fuels, or fuels with a high alcohol content extracted from sugar cane or sugar beet, or hydrogen, possibly in liquid form. But perhaps the answer lies in the use of electricity, already tried but so far impractical because of the range limitation imposed by current battery technology. However, small electric cars, highly manoeuvrable and pollution-free, could be taken on a bus or train and then used just for short journeys in a city. A more practicable system might be the provision of coin-operated cars – small, self-drive taxis for everyone to use.

Why are Rolls-Royces so prized?

In contrast to the mass-produced cars of most vehicle manufacturers, the Rolls-Royce has long been considered one of the most exclusive and perfectly engineered of all cars. The first Rolls-Royce, the legendary Silver Ghost, came out in 1906. The Phantom (shown in the illustration on the right) was produced in 1931.

Charles Rolls and Henry Royce did not follow the production-line system of the American car manufacturing pioneer Henry Ford. Instead they built small numbers of superbly engineered cars for the few (and wealthy). Ford and Rolls-Royce cars have survived, both fulfilling an important role in modern car production.

How does a car engine work?

The modern "piston-in-cylinder" car engine works on the same operating principle as those developed 100 years ago by Daimler and Benz on a four-stroke cycle. A mixture of petrol and air is drawn into an engine cylinder as the piston moves down ("induction stroke"). The piston compresses the mixture as it comes back up ("compression stroke"). Then an electric spark ignites the mixture, and the expanding gases produced force the piston down on its "power stroke". When the piston next rises, it forces the burnt gases out of the cylinder ("exhaust stroke"). Then the cycle begins again. The piston is linked through a crankshaft to the driveshaft which powers the car's wheels.

Below: Three Ferrari sports cars show Newton's laws of motion in operation.

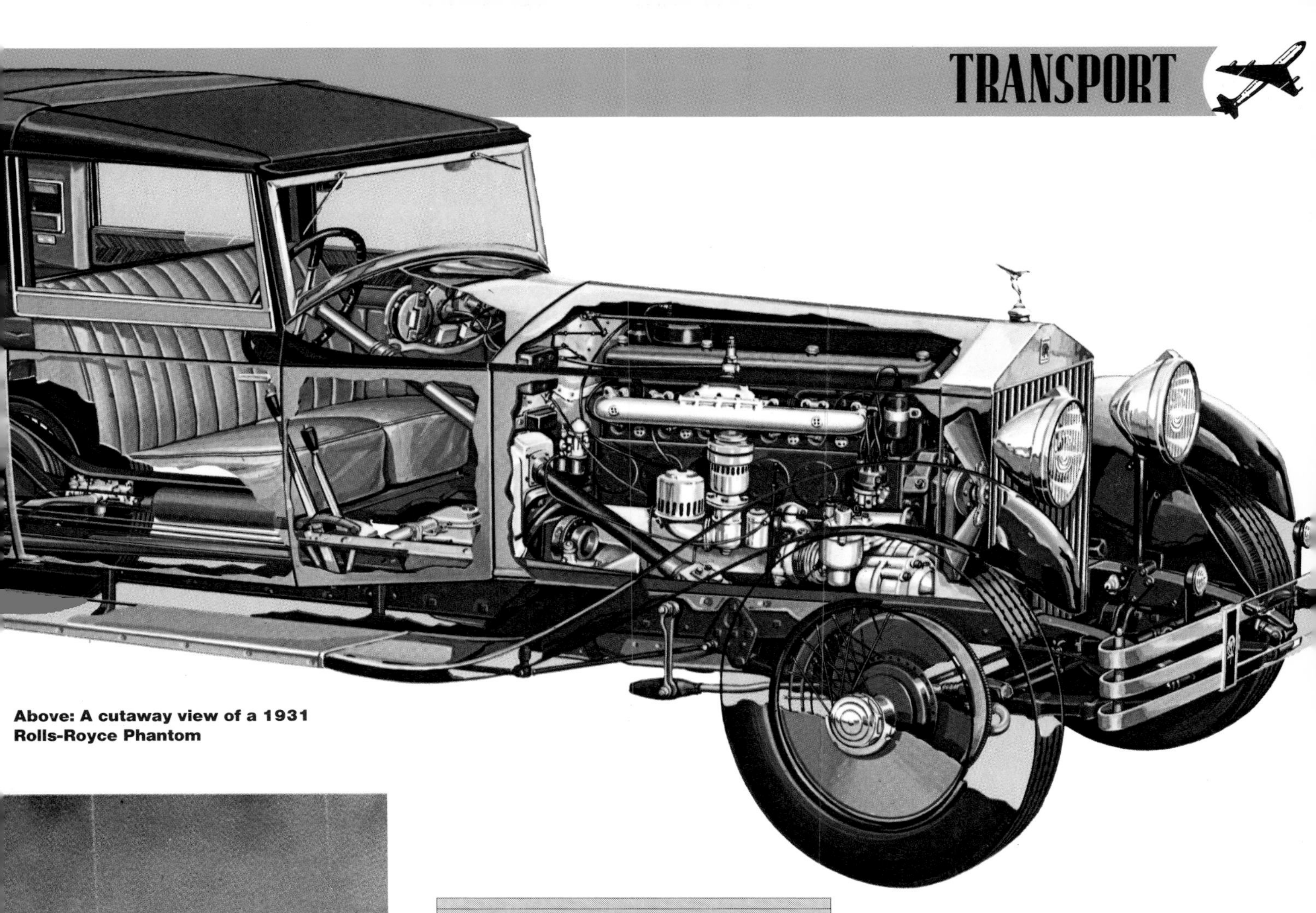

Above: A cutaway view of a 1931 Rolls-Royce Phantom

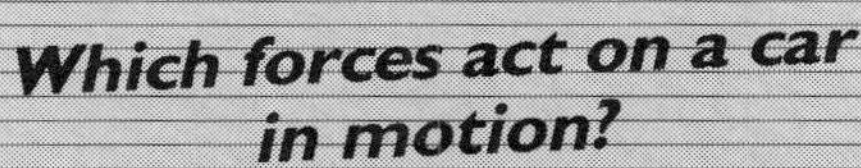

Which forces act on a car in motion?

When an object is set in motion, Newton's three laws of motion (see page 106) operate in reverse order. The third law comes into action first – to produce a force that acts on the object. When a car starts, for example, the tyres on the wheels push back against the road surface. The reaction of the road pushes the car forward and it begins to move. The second law now comes into operation – the force moving the car makes it get faster and it accelerates. If the car has a powerful engine, and if it is not heavy or loaded up, it will accelerate rapidly. However, as the car moves, it pushes into the air. The air exerts a force ("drag") in the opposite direction. The drag gets stronger as the car gets faster until it equals the force driving the car forward. Now the two forces cancel each other out and no force acts on the car. It obeys the first law of motion and continues to move forward at a constant speed.

What does a car gearbox do?

Car drivers use the gears to accelerate from start to a high speed and to climb hills. The gears operate to drive the wheels at different speeds while the engine speed (the "revs") does not change greatly. Most cars have four or five forward gears and, because the engine can turn only in one direction, a reverse gear that enables the car to move backwards.

Pre-selection gear changes and increasingly efficient gearboxes and clutches make it easy to change gear correctly and smoothly. In the past, drivers had to "double-declutch", that is, go into neutral, press the accelerator, and then engage the gear. In the modern automatic gearbox, the right gear is automatically selected according to the engine speed.

Which is the world's longest railway line?

Railways represented a real revolution to which the development of motor transport in the twentieth century can in no way be compared. Various lines became famous, for example the Trans-Siberian Railway which totalled more than 9,300 km. It is today still the longest railway line in the world and crosses the whole of the USSR.

The most famous line, and the setting for a number of films and novels, was the original Orient Express which was opened in June 1883. The trains began from Paris, passed through Strasbourg, Stuttgart, Munich, Salzburg, Vienna, Budapest, Bucharest and went as far as Varna on the Black Sea in Bulgaria. From there passengers could continue to Constantinople (now Istanbul) by steamer. The journey lasted a total of eighty-three hours, in conditions of luxurious comfort.

Who built the first railroad across the USA?

In 1848, the discovery of gold in California gave a new boost to railroad construction in the fast-growing USA. Severe competition existed between firms to obtain concessions for lands considered richer and more profitable. The competition between two well-known companies – Union Pacific and Central Pacific – has now become a legend. Each of these two companies set out to built a railroad across the continent. Rivalry was intense and a few days before the two lines met in 1869 to complete the first transcontinental line, there were fights, arguments and even killings. The "winner" was Union Pacific which succeeded in building 1,748 km of the railway line against the 1,110 km of Central Pacific.

Top left: An American steam engine of about 1840

Below: A cross section of the famous British A4 *Mallard* steam engine which set the world speed record in 1938 by travelling at a speed of 203 km/h.

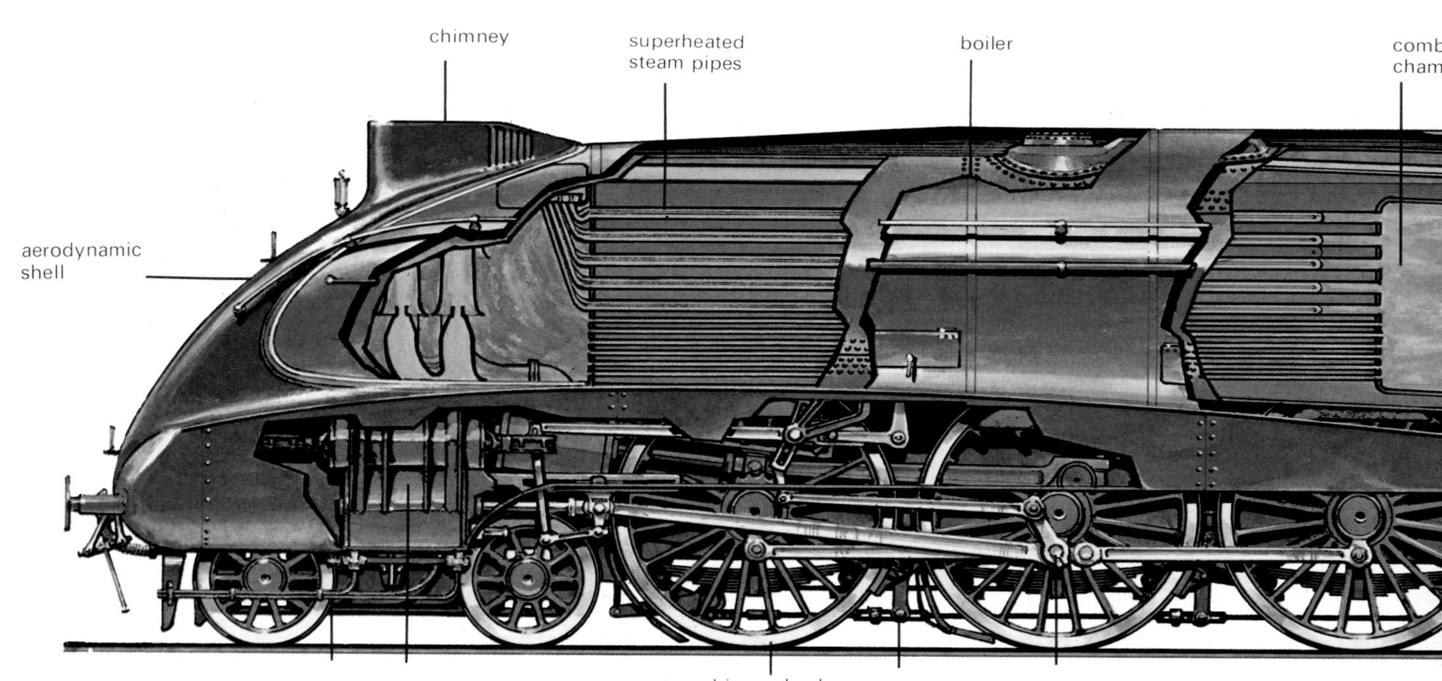

Left: A freight train travelling along the Trans-Siberian Railway in the USSR. The railway was built between 1891 and 1916 and extends from the Ural Mountains in the centre of the country to Vladivostok on the Pacific coast.

How does a steam locomotive work?

Stephenson's *Rocket* pioneered features which were adopted by steam locomotives for many decades, notably a fire-tube boiler. In a steam locomotive, coal (or sometimes wood) is burned in a furnace. The hot flames and gases are drawn through a number of tubes (the "fire" tubes), which run through a boiler containing water. The water heats up and turns to steam. The steam is led into the driving cylinders, where it forces the pistons back and forth. The motion of the pistons is carried by rods to cranks on the wheels and drives them round.

The famous locomotive *Mallard* (shown in the illustration below) represented the peak of steam locomotive design. In 1938, the *Mallard* set a world speed record for steam of 203 km/h on British track.

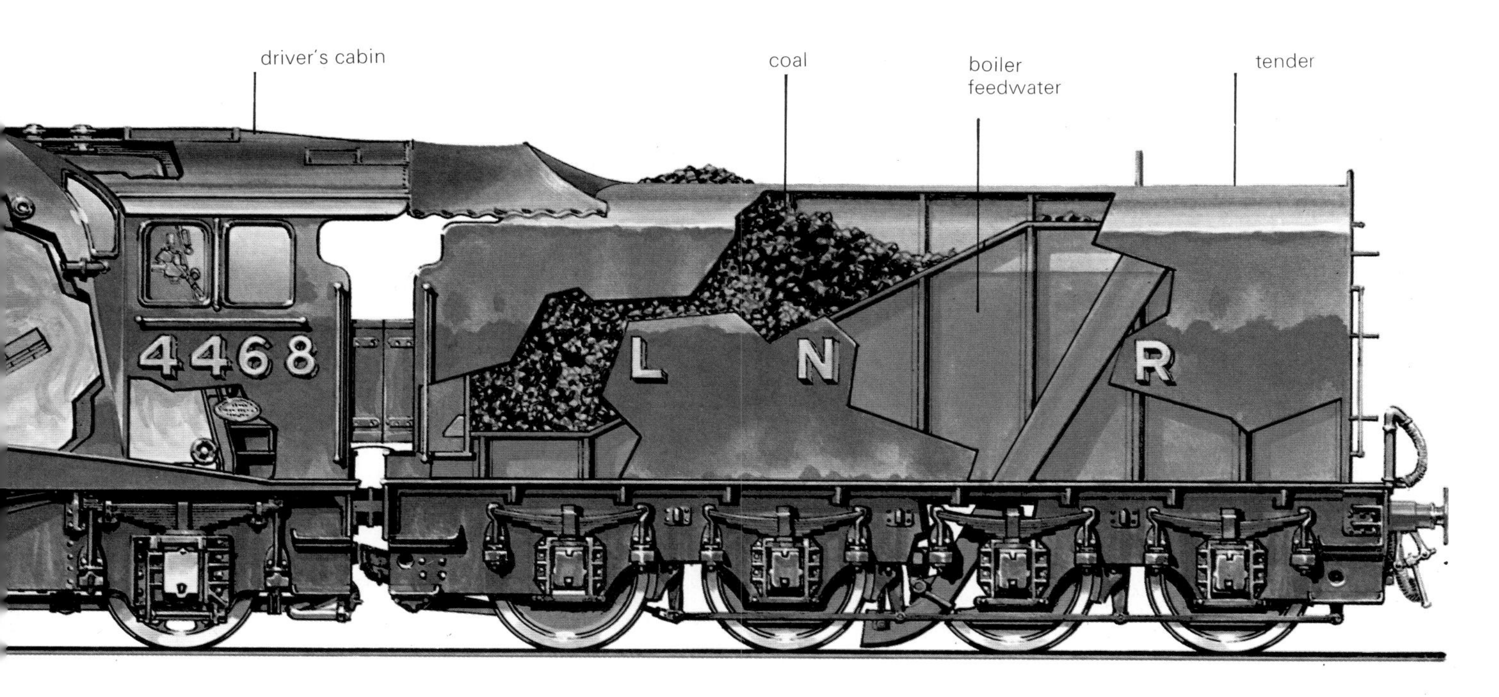

When was the first underground railway built?

It took three years to build the first $6\frac{1}{2}$ km of the London underground railway line which opened on 10 January 1863. The new stretch was supposed to be just an extension of the normal railway line into the centre of the city, but the 30,000 people who used the new line that first day declared it an unexpected success. London's underground was born – the first underground railway in the world. Even then, although there were no automobiles around, the horse-drawn traffic in the crowded capital made it very difficult to get about, so a train that travelled quickly *under* the ground was just what was needed. However, the smoke of the steam locomotives in the tunnels made the air very unpleasant to breathe!

Which is the world's largest underground railway?

The London "Underground" was the first of its kind and still boasts the world's largest network, comprising 404 km of track. This is just a few kilometres more than New York's underground system (the "Subway") which carries over 1,000 million passengers a year (only about half the number of passengers using the Moscow "Metro").

The term "underground" is not entirely appropriate for most networks. More than half of the track length of the London Underground, for example, runs on the surface. In recent years, therefore, other terms have been adopted. The Hong Kong system is called MTR (Mass Transit Railway), while in San Francisco it is known as BART (Bay Area Rapid Transit).

How does a diesel locomotive work?

Diesel locomotives first made their appearance in Germany in the 1930s. They are powered by a diesel engine, similar to that used in buses and trucks, which burns a light oil. The engine may drive the wheels of the locomotive in a number of ways. Some small diesels use a mechanical transmission system similar to that found in buses. Others use "hydraulic" (or "liquid") transmission, where power is conveyed by a kind of turbine device. Most locomotives, however, have diesel-electric transmission. The engine spins a generator to produce electricity, which is then fed to electric motors that turn the wheels. The diesel-electric locomotive is basically an electric locomotive with its own power plant, able to run on any kind of track.

Top left: A section of a London underground tunnel at Baker Street station as it was in the nineteenth century

Above: Two types of diesel locomotive used on railways in the USA

Left: A modern underground station in Milan, Italy

How does an electric locomotive work?

Electric locomotives are faster, quieter and more efficient than all other types. They also cause no pollution. They power the world's fastest trains, such as the French "*TGVs*" (*Trains à Grande Vitesse* – High Speed Trains) and the Japanese "Bullet" trains.

Most electric locomotives pick up the electricity they require from an overhead wire. They carry a hinged, sprung arm called a "pantograph" on top, which presses against the wire. In most systems, alternating current is used at a high voltage of, for example, 25,000 volts. But some systems use direct current at a much lower voltage, such as 1,500 volts. While diesels are still the most common type of locomotive in the USA, in Europe electric locomotives predominate. Overhead electric pick-up by pantograph is the most common system.

Which are the world's fastest trains?

The fastest train running on the world's railways is the French "*TGV*" (*Train à Grande Vitesse* – High Speed Train). In early tests, a *TGV* travelled at a speed of 380 km/h. The maximum speed of the operational *TGV*, however, is slower – 270 km/h. The *TGV* averages a speed of some 210 km/h on its two-hour journey between Paris and Lyon. To achieve such high speeds, it has to be very well streamlined. It also runs on specially laid track.

In Japan another very fast service operates on the super-rail network known as the "Shinkansen". This, too, is worked by highly streamlined "Bullet" trains. The first section of the system, between Tokyo and Osaka, opened in 1964. It is known as the New Tokaido line. Today, the line has been extended to Hakata to the west and Niigata and Morioka to the north.

Can turbines drive trains?

Several countries began experimenting with gas-turbine locomotives in the 1950s, when jet aeroplanes, which work on similar principles, were taking to the air. Gas-turbine locomotives have been operated most successfully in North America, the USSR and France. In the USA, the famous railroad company, Union Pacific, has for some time operated powerful units for long-haul freight duty. They use propane gas as fuel and develop over 6,000 hp.

The French national railway company, *SNCF* (*Société Nationale des Chemins de Fer*), has developed efficient compact turbine units for passenger duty, which have been in service since 1970.

Below left: A French *TGV* speeding between Paris and Lyon

Below: The driver's cabin in a *TGV*

Bottom: A Japanese high-speed train

Who made the first ocean-going ships?

The first known sailing boats were used by the ancient Egyptians to sail on the Nile at least 6,000 years ago. Pictures, and even models, of these boats have been found in tombs. The Phoenicians, and later the Romans, developed the boats into thoroughly seaworthy ships. They were tub-like craft with square sails, and were known as "round" ships. They were up to about 30 m long and made of long planks, strengthened by ribs, and supported by a stout keel. The Viking longships of about AD 1000 were similarly built but were slimmer and speedier. Oars as well as sails were used for propulsion.

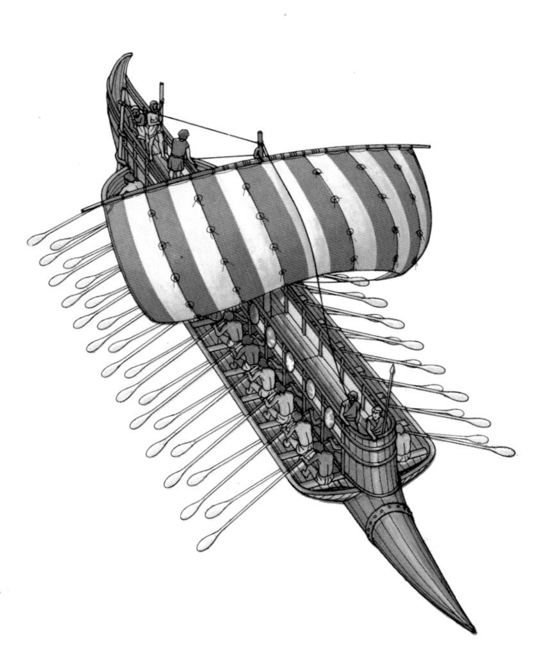

Which developments made the "Age of Sail" possible?

During the Middle Ages, several developments led to better and more manageable ships. Among the most important were the rudder, extra masts, and the adoption of the triangular ("lateen") sail. Using a lateen sail, sailors could sail their ships close to the wind. This is why modern yachts have triangular sails. The magnetic compass also came into use, enabling sailors to sail out of sight of land without losing their sense of direction.

By the end of the fifteenth century, the stage was set for the great "Age of Sail". This resulted, for example, in the discovery of the "New World" of America by the Italian navigator Christopher Columbus in 1492, and the first circumnavigation of the globe by the Portuguese Ferdinand Magellan, between 1519 and 1521.

What were clippers?

By the mid-1800s, continuous improvements in the design of sailing ships led to the fastest and most graceful ships ever – the "clippers". The clippers were so called because they "clipped" time off existing schedules. They operated on the long-distance routes between the Far East and Europe or America, usually carrying tea or wool. The clippers were about 60 m long, carried up to 3,000 sq m of sail on three masts, and were capable of speeds up to 20 kn (31 km/h).

Far left: A Phoenician war bireme (galley with two banks of oars)

Left: Ferdinand Magellan (1480–1521)

Below: The four-masted galleon *Henry Grâce à Dieu* was built by the English king Henry VIII in 1514. It was considered the best ship of the sixteenth century.

Above: The English clipper *Cutty Sark*, which was launched in 1869. It sailed for more than fifty years, but is now kept as a museum-ship at Greenwich, London.

Below: The English steamship *SS Great Britain*, which in July 1845 crossed the Atlantic in fourteen days. It was built by Isambard Kingdom Brunel.

Which were the first steam-powered ships?

As early as 1819, the American ship *Savannah* made a transatlantic crossing partly under steam, driven by paddle wheels turned by a steam engine. In 1845, the British engineer, Isambard Kingdom Brunel, built the first modern steamship, *Great Britain*, with an iron hull and driven by the new screw propeller.

Brunel designed another great ship, *Great Eastern* (1858), which was nearly 215 m long, a staggering size for the period. It foreshadowed the great transatlantic passenger liners of the next century, such as the *Mauretania* (1907), the ill-fated *Titanic* (1912), and the biggest of them all, the *Queen Mary* (1934). The *Mauretania* was one of the first passenger ships to be fitted with steam turbines. Britain's Charles Parsons had developed the marine steam turbine ten years earlier, demonstrating how superior it was to the steam engines of the day.

How are modern ships built?

Practically all modern ships are built of steel. Their hull is constructed by welding together steel plates. This is a much stronger method of construction than riveting – the method once used to join the plates. In practice, the ship is usually built in small sections (subassemblies) which are then welded together in position. Each subassembly would probably consist of a part of the outer hull, horizontal deck plates and vertical "bulkheads".

The bulkheads stiffen the hull and also provide watertight compartments which can be sealed off if the ship is holed in a collision. The ship is also given a double bottom for a similar reason. This is often used for storing fuel (or water ballast) to make the vessel more stable.

Which is the world's longest cruise liner?

The *Norway* is the world's longest cruise liner with a length of 316 m. She (ships are traditionally referred to as "she") was originally named *France* when she was launched in 1961.

Majestic cruise liners such as the *Norway* are easy to recognize because they look like luxurious floating hotels. These great ships have every conceivable facility – restaurants, swimming pools, sundecks, shops, banks, hairdressers, theatres, bars, and so on. Another noticeable feature of these passenger ships is the row of lifeboats that line each side.

What keeps a ship steady?

The designers of ships which carry passengers, such as liners and ferries, are particularly concerned to keep the vessels steady in all weathers. For this reason, they fit "stabilizers". Stabilizers are huge vanes (or paddles) that project from the hull underwater. They operate under the control of gyroscopes. When the ship rolls in one direction, the gyroscopes sense this movement and move the vanes so that they push against the water to counteract the rolling.

Below: The *Queen Elizabeth 2*, one of the great transatlantic liners

Why are hydrofoils so fast?

Conventional ships waste most of their power in overcoming the resistance ("drag") of the water on the hull. The higher the speed, the greater the drag.

To overcome this problem, some craft are designed so that their hulls lift out of the water as they speed up. They do this by means of devices called "hydrofoils", which can be thought of as underwater wings. Just as an aeroplane's wing provides lift when it travels through the air, so a hydrofoil lifts the boat when it travels through the water. The faster it travels, the more it lifts. Eventually, it lifts the boat's hull out of the water. Only the struts carrying the hydrofoils and the shaft carrying the propeller remain in the water. Freed from drag on the hull, the hydrofoil can reach speeds up to about 50 kn (92 km/h).

How does a hovercraft hover?

Hovercraft (air-cushion vehicles) skim over the surface of water or land on a cushion of air. The English inventor, Christopher Cockerell, worked out the principle of the hovercraft in 1955, and the first craft was tested four years later.

The hovercraft is propelled by air propellers, while a fan provides the air to maintain the air cushion underneath. A flexible "skirt" runs around the bottom edge of the hovercraft to help keep air in. Large hovercraft use gas turbine engines to spin the fan and the propellers. The craft are steered by rudders on tail fins in the slipstream from the propellers, which face backwards.

The British SR-N4 has been in cross-Channel service since 1968. It is 56 m long, with a beam of 28 m. It can carry a maximum of 412 passengers and sixty cars at a speed of 65 kn (120 km/h).

How are boats propelled?

The sails of a sailing vessel such as a yacht function as aerofoils to propel the craft into the wind. The air blows over the curved surfaces of the sails, producing a lift force that acts horizontally to push the craft forward into the wind. Yachts cannot sail directly into the wind, however, but usually are able to sail at about a 45° angle to the wind's direction.

The screws (propellers) on powered boats and on some aircraft are shaped as aerofoils to produce horizontal lift as they rotate and force the boat or aircraft forward. They also work to move water or air backwards, producing an additional forward force by action and reaction.

Below: A hydrofoil surging through the sea. The foils themselves are clearly visible at the front of the vessel.

How big is a supertanker?

Supertankers have a capacity of more than 75,000 t. One of the first to be built was the *Globtik London*, which was launched in 1973. It has a capacity of 491,700 t, is 379 m long and 62 m wide, and its hull goes down over 28 m under water. It is 75 m from keel to masthead (as high as a twenty-five storey skyscraper) and the crew get around on motorbikes on the upper deck of 20,700 sq m (equal to about eighty tennis courts in area). It takes 400 t of paint to cover the tanker, and the welded joints of the vessel have a combined length of 1,100 km. The rudder weighs 250 t (as much as a jumbo jet), the anchor 30 t, and the propeller 61 t.

A supertanker's inertia is such that "braking" takes a long time. The *Globtik London* needs 5 km of clear water in front of its colossal bulging prow to come to a stop.

When was the submarine invented?

In 1776, the American engineer David Bushnell built a wooden submarine called the *Turtle*, which was propelled by a hand-cranked propeller. Its weapon was an explosive charge that could be screwed into the hull of an enemy vessel. It saw service in the American War of Independence but failed to attach its explosive because the English ship it attacked, the *Eagle*, had its hull sheathed in copper.

Another American engineer, Robert Fulton, was commissioned by Napoleon in 1800 to build a submarine for attacking English ships. The result was the *Nautilus*, a sausage-shaped craft built of copper and iron. It too was driven by a hand-cranked propeller underwater, but had a sail for surface propulsion. For control over diving and surfacing, it had diving planes – "vanes" at the sides that could be angled up or down.

One of the first successful submarines

Left: A supertanker viewed from above

was the American *Holland* of 1900, which had dual propulsion. On the surface it used a petrol engine, under water, battery-powered electric motors. It was armed with a bow torpedo tube and carried three torpedoes. It also had guns mounted on top of the hull for use on the surface.

Right: The *Leonardo da Vinci*, an American-built submarine serving in the Italian navy. It carries ten missiles and displaces 2,425 t of water when immersed.

Bottom: Robert Fulton, who invented an early type of submarine

Which are the fastest and biggest submarines?

The fastest submarines are believed to be Soviet vessels of the "Alpha" class which can travel at speeds in excess of 40 kn (75 km/h) under water. These same submarines are also believed to be constructed of strong, lightweight titanium alloy, which gives them an operating depth of perhaps as much as 1,000 m.

The latest Soviet submarines of the "Typhoon" class (code-named "Oscar") are the biggest submarines ever built. Some 170 m long, they have a displacement of 30,000 t, which is over three times that of Britain's "Polaris" submarines. They are armed with twenty long-range missiles, each carrying seven nuclear warheads which can be directed at separate targets.

Who invented the hot-air balloon?

Two French brothers, Joseph and Étienne Montgolfier, started the modern age of aviation in June 1783, when they built and launched a hot-air balloon. It was a large, open-ended fabric bag, with a fire slung beneath. The fire heated the air inside, making it expand and therefore, lighter than the air outside. Thus, the balloon rose into the air.

The following October, the noted French physicist, J.A.C. Charles, devised another kind of balloon by filling a bag with hydrogen, lightest of all the gases. Rivalry soon arose between the followers of the Montgolfiers and of Charles – the *Montgolfières* and the *Charlières* as they became known. During 1783 both balloons carried people into the air, pioneering human flight. Today, people still fly hot-air balloons – for the enjoyment of silent, floating flight.

Above: The Montgolfier hot-air balloon, whose first manned flight took place on 21 November 1783

Top right: A hang-glider in flight. Hang-gliding is becoming increasingly popular, but bad weather conditions often make it unsafe to fly.

Right: The Wright brothers' "Flyer", the first aeroplane ever built

Who pioneered gliding?

In the 1800s, some aviation pioneers experimented with flying in airships. Other people were approaching the question of flying in a different way and began experimenting with gliders. The English scientist George Cayley designed a man-carrying glider in the 1850s, but the gliding craze did not catch on until the 1890s.

The foremost glider pilot of that period was the German, Otto Lilienthal. He was killed in 1896 after making more than 2,000 successful flights. Lilienthal flew in what we would today call a "hang-glider". It was of two-wing (biplane) design, whereas modern hang-gliders are monoplanes, with a single wing.

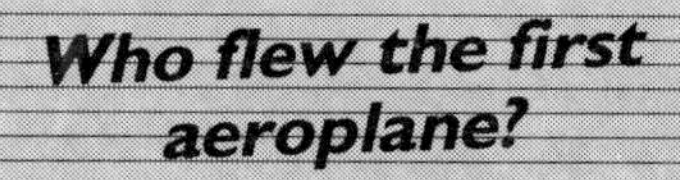

Who flew the first aeroplane?

Two American brothers, Wilbur and Orville Wright, owned a cycle shop in Dayton, Ohio, but their main interest lay in flying machines. By 1903 they had built a large biplane glider and made many successful glides, some for more than 180 m. Then they decided to power the glider. They built a lightweight petrol engine which drove two "pusher" propellers.

On 17 December 1903, at Kitty Hawk in North Carolina, the Wrights' machine flew under its own power. Their "Flyer" had become the world's first aeroplane. On their best flight that day, the machine was airborne for less than a minute and travelled no further than 260 m. But it pointed the way ahead.

How quickly did aeroplanes develop?

Soon after the historic first aeroplane flight in 1903 by Wilbur and Orville Wright, much-improved aircraft began to attract attention. By 1908, these craft could remain airborne for more than two hours, and turn and circle with ease. The Wrights demonstrated their new aeroplanes in Europe, and flying soon developed into the latest craze, especially in France.

In 1909, the French pilot Louis Blériot made the first crossing of the English Channel in a monoplane of his own design. He took 36 min 30 sec and averaged a speed of some 65 km/h. Politicians took note and began to recognize the military potential of the "plane". In the First World War (1914–1918), both the Allies and the Germans developed powerful air forces, using aeroplanes for reconnaissance and bombing missions. Most aeroplanes were biplanes, built of wood and fabric, but a few were monoplanes, the shape of the future.

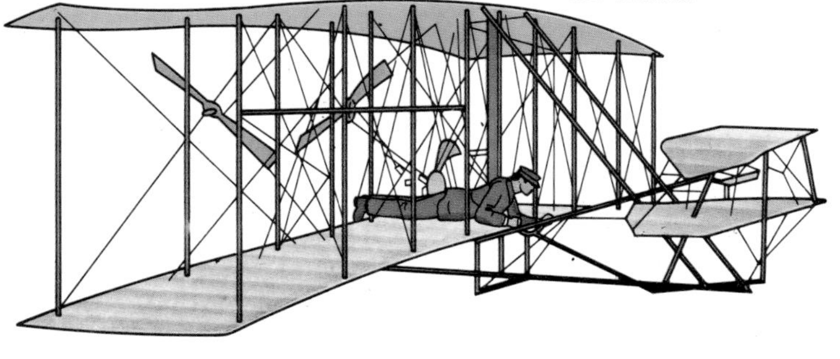

Above: The airship *Hindenburg*, which burst into flames as it was about to land in the USA in 1937. Thirty-five people were killed.

When did transatlantic flights begin?

After the First World War, aviators took to the skies in force, looking for new challenges. John Alcock and Arthur Whitten Brown made the first non-stop flight across the Atlantic in 1919. That same year the British airship *R34* made the first two-way transatlantic crossing. In 1927 the American pilot Charles Lindbergh made the first solo transatlantic flight in the monoplane *Spirit of St Louis*.

What was a Zeppelin?

Balloons cannot be steered – they travel only in the direction the wind blows them. So, in the mid-1800s, inventors began experimenting with balloons that could be steered – that is with "dirigibles" (airships). The French engineer Henri Giffard first achieved success in 1852 with a steam-engined craft.

However, the airship era did not dawn until the turn of the twentieth century, following the development of an efficient lightweight petrol engine and the availability of supplies of the new lightweight metal – aluminium – for construction. The German Count Ferdinand von Zeppelin pioneered the practical airship in 1900. His first "Zeppelin" was a machine measuring 128 m long and 11.5 m in diameter. It was of rigid construction, consisting of a fabric "envelope" over an aluminium frame. The hydrogen that provided the lift was carried inside in a number of gas-filled bags.

When did the "Jet Age" begin?

In 1939 an entirely new type of plane was tested in Germany. It had no propellers but was propelled by a stream of gases. This plane – the Heinkel He-178 – ushered in the "Jet Age". It was followed by other German jets, including the formidable Messerschmitt Me-262. In 1944, the British Gloster Meteor became the only Allied jet to see action in the Second World War. Two years later, a Meteor raised the world air-speed record to over 985 km/h.

985 km/h was approaching the speed of sound. When an aircraft nears this speed, it becomes buffeted by shock waves that threaten to tear it apart. It was thought that the speed of sound might prove a speed limit to flight through the air, and the term "sound barrier" came into use. In 1947, however, the US pilot Chuck Yeager broke through the "barrier" for the first time, flying in a Bell X-1 rocket plane at a speed of 1,078 km/h. The way was open for the first jet transports – the Comet and Boeing 707 of the 1950s.

Below: Inside the jet engine of an airliner, burning fuel heats air passing through the engine. This makes the air expand, raising the air pressure inside the engine. The hot high pressure air forces the engine forward as it streaks from the exhaust.

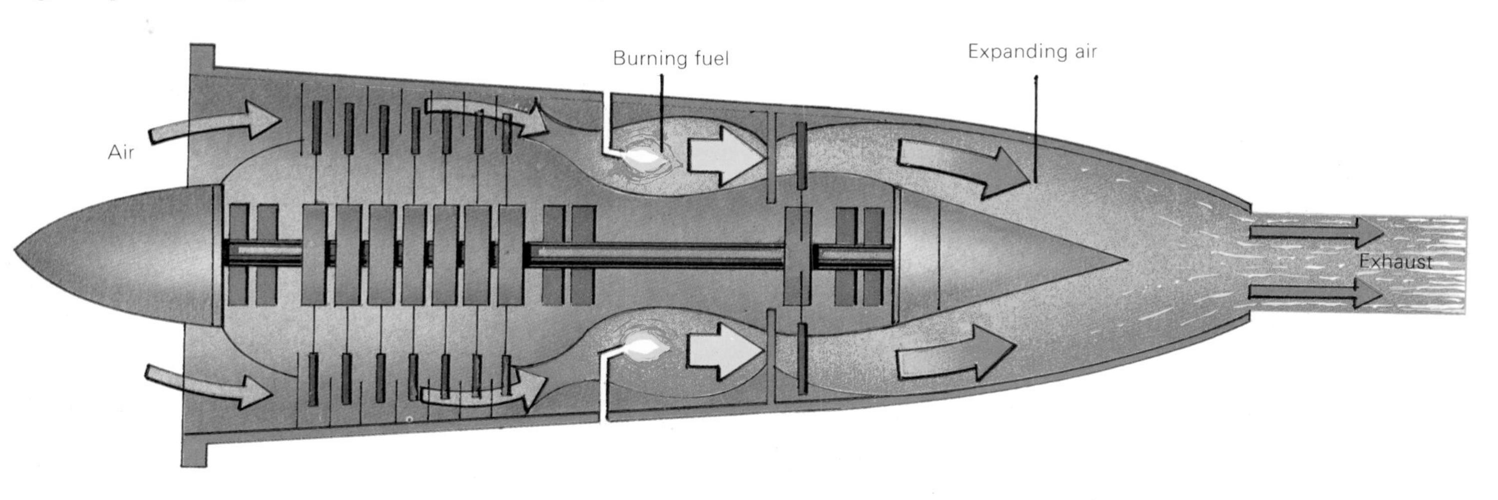

How does an aeroplane fly?

Hot-air balloons achieve flight because of convection (hot air rises), and gas balloons contain light gases that are less dense than air. However, most air transport makes use of wings for flight and does not depend on flotation.

Wings enable an aeroplane to fly through the air because they have a specially-shaped surface called an "aerofoil". The upper and lower surfaces of the aerofoil are curved differently. This causes air to flow faster over the top of the wing. The pressure of air falls as it moves faster, and so the air pressure beneath the wing (where the air is moving more slowly) is greater than the pressure above it. The air under the wing pushes it upwards, creating a force called "lift". Provided the engine's thrust moves them forward fast enough, the wings carry the aircraft up into the air and support its weight during flight.

How does radar work?

Radar works by sending out pulses of very short radio waves (microwaves). When they hit something in their path, they are reflected. The reflections (called echoes) are received and displayed on a fluorescent screen as "blips" (flashes of light). Usually, the transmitting and receiving aerial (antenna) rotates and produces echoes on a circular screen, which shows the range (distance) and direction of the objects making the echoes.

Radars are installed at airports and in most airliners and warplanes. At airports, radar is vital for safety. Air-traffic controllers use it to pinpoint the position of every aeroplane on the ground and in the air. Each aircraft automatically sends out an identification signal which shows up with the echo on the radar screen. The controllers then guide the pilot down by radio to make a landing. Radar systems are continually being improved to make air travel even safer.

Left: Modern airports depend to a very great extent on the latest technology to ensure the safety of the hundreds of flights which pass through them each day. Here air-traffic controllers use radar to pinpoint the position of aircraft. They also maintain radio contact with pilots and controllers in other centres to keep themselves informed of any delays or other problems.

What are STOL and VTOL aeroplanes?

A conventional aircraft needs a long runway from which to operate. International airports operating jumbo jets have runways 3 km or more long. Some aircraft are designed for a short take-off and landing (STOL). The Harrier can take off and land vertically. It is the most successful vertical take-off and landing (VTOL), fixed-wing aeroplane in the world. It also excels in combat because it is so manoeuvrable. It achieves vertical movement by means of swivelling nozzles, which can deflect the exhaust from its jet engine downwards.

Bottom: A vertical take-off aircraft. "VTOLS" as they are known are particularly useful in places where runways are short or non-existent.

Which is the world's fastest plane?

In the 1960s, the American X-15 rocket planes achieved speeds of over 6,000 km/h and heights above 100 km. X-15 pilots who flew over 80 km high were awarded astronauts' "wings".

In 1969, the Anglo-French airliner Concorde introduced the supersonic era for passenger flight. Able to cruise at more than twice the speed of sound, at some 2,300 km/h, Concorde entered airliner service in 1976.

The current world air-speed record is held by a Lockheed SR-71A reconnaissance aircraft with a speed of nearly 3,530 km/h – 3.3 times the speed of sound.

Above: A United States X-15, the fastest aircraft ever to fly, docked under the wing of a B-52, which carries it up to high altitude. Inset: A Supersabre, the type of jet which controls such flights

Bottom right: The Sikorsky S-61L helicopter, which is used for transporting passengers

How does a helicopter fly?

The German aircraft designer Heinrich Focke built the first practical helicopter in 1936. It had twin rotors. Russian-born Igor Sikorsky built the first successful single-rotor helicopter in the USA three years later.

In the helicopter, the rotor is driven round by the engine to provide lift. The blades of the rotor have the aerofoil shape of an aeroplane's wing and develop lift in the same way. The rotor also serves to propel the helicopter horizontally. The blades are angled in such a way that they sweep the air backwards, with the result that the helicopter moves forwards.

Why did a great civilization develop in Egypt?

The annual flooding of the River Nile in Egypt washes a fertile alluvial silt over the surrounding land, which provides a rich soil ideal for farming. Although the Nile valley occupies only one-thirtieth of Egypt's total territory, this fertile strip was (and continues to be) the home of nearly all Egyptians. Farms, villages and then towns and temples arose on the banks of the Nile, giving birth to one of the world's greatest civilizations.

Because of the River Nile and the fertile soils in its valley, Hamitic peoples began to farm the region some 6,500 years ago. The empires of ancient Egypt were ruled by a pharaoh (divine king) and thirty-one dynasties were recorded between 3100 and 332 BC. The first ten dynasties were based on the city of Memphis, on the west bank of the Nile.

Above: The huge statue of a sphinx near the pyramids at El Giza in Egypt.

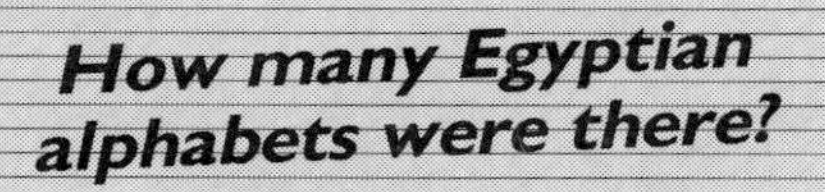

How many Egyptian alphabets were there?

Three alphabets were used by the ancient Egyptians. The hieroglyphic alphabet was composed of over 3,000 ideograms and phonetic symbols. The hieratic alphabet was an abridged form of hieroglyphics used by the priests. The popular alphabet developed as a simpler version of the other alphabets and was used in private communications.

When was the first pyramid built?

The pyramids of Egypt are among the world's most famous ancient monuments. The earliest was built at Saqqara in about 2680 BC by Imhotep, adviser to King Zoser of the Third Dynasty. The finest are to be seen at El Giza, on the outskirts of modern Cairo. These are the royal tombs of Cheops (Khufu), Chefren (Khafre) and Mycerinos (Menkaure). The highest is that of Cheops. Originally 144 m high, it took twenty years to build. Large groups of slaves were used, carrying blocks of stone on heavy sledges, which were hauled along on rollers. Close to the pyramids at El Giza rises the Sphinx, a colossal monster sculpted out of stone, with the head of a human and the body of a lion.

Below: Elephantine Island in the River Nile at Aswan, Egypt.

Above: In 1922, Howard Carter uncovered the treasure of Tutankhamen, who was king of Egypt from 1361–1352 BC.
Inset: The funeral mask of the king

Why were the pyramids built?

The pyramids, most of which were built during the period 2700–2300 BC, were royal tombs in which the bodies of dead kings were preserved. Queens and high officials were sometimes also buried there. In order to keep the corpses life-like, they were mummified by spreading oils, spices and salts on them and wrapping them in bandages.
Preservation of a body was not enough – a lengthy ritual also had to be observed to ensure the continued life of the person in the next world.

Also in the pyramids are inscribed the Pyramid Texts, collections of stories which were recited as part of the ritual. In these texts the dead king is identified with Osiris, the god who ruled the land of the dead. As Osiris once rose from the dead, so did the pharaoh – his body and many of his belongings preserved and placed in the tomb would receive new life after death.

How were mummies preserved?

In ancient Egypt the bodies of important people were embalmed ("mummified") to protect them against decay. Internal organs were removed, and the corpse was filled with aromatic disinfectants, then wrapped with bandages soaked in scented oils, and finally laid to rest in a painted sarcophagus (coffin). Prepared in this careful way, many mummies have remained intact to this day.

Why were the Phoenicians famous?

Phoenician civilization developed after 3000 BC along the eastern shore of the Mediterranean, between the sea and the Lebanese mountains. The Phoenician homeland was bordered to the north by the land of the Hittites (Anatolia and Syria) and to the south by Palestine.

The Phoenicians were great sailors and traders. Their name comes from the Greek *phoinos* (meaning purple), which describes the colour of the cloth they produced. The trees which grew on the slopes of the Lebanese mountains were another resource in which they traded. These included pines, cypresses and the famous Cedar of Lebanon.

When did the ancient Persian civilization flourish?

The ancient civilization of Persia began in the sixth century BC, with the founding of the Achaemenid Dynasty of Cyrus I. The empire rapidly expanded to take in Babylonia, Egypt and Asia Minor. A great flowering of civilization accompanied the conquests, and fine cities and roads were built. Persepolis, the capital founded by Darius I, contained magnificent palaces and sculptures. But the Greeks proved harder to conquer. Xerxes I of Persia was the victor at Thermopylae in 480 BC, but was later defeated in a naval battle at Salamis. The Persian Empire finally fell to the Macedonian-Greek army of Alexander the Great, who defeated Darius III at Issus in 333 BC.

Top left: The palace of the Persian king Darius I, in the ancient city of Persepolis
Inset: A bas-relief of Darius on his throne

Above: A Phoenician sculpture of a winged sphinx
Inset: A Phoenician gold ring carrying the picture of a male deity

Above: Part of the ruins of the palace of King Minos at Knossos in Crete

Far right: The golden mask discovered at Mycenae, Greece by Heinrich Schliemann. It is known as the "Mask of Agamemnon" although it almost certainly did not belong to this Greek king.

Where was the palace of King Minos?

After 2500 BC a rich civilization flourished in the Mediterranean island of Crete. It is called Minoan, taking its name from the king, Minos.

The evidence of archaeology reveals that around 2000 BC, great buildings called "palaces" sprang up in various Cretan centres like Knossos and Mallia. Knossos, believed to be the palace of Minos, was discovered by the English archaeologist Sir Arthur Evans at the beginning of the twentieth century.

What was the myth of the Minotaur?

A dramatic Cretan myth is the story of the Minotaur – a prince who was half bull and half man. He was a shameful secret and was hidden in a maze of underground rooms built by the inventor Daedalus beneath the palace of King Minos. The name labyrinth, given to this part of the palace, comes from *labrys*, a double-bladed axe, "two-horned" like the bull, which was used for sacrifice. It is thought that sacrifice of real bulls may have formed part of Minoan religion. The horn motif is found everywhere in Crete and the decoration of the palace battlements takes this form.

The monster in the underground palace made itself heard, roaring and banging against the walls – in this way the myth explained the low rumbles and shocks of earthquakes, the terror of the islanders.

What is the "Mask of Agamemnon"?

Links between the Minoan civilization in Crete and mainland Greece resulted in the continuation of this civilization in Greece itself. This, the Mycenean civilization, took its name from Mycenae, one of its most famous centres. The Mycenean centres were already flourishing in the seventeenth century BC, while the Minoan civilization was at its height.

In 1874–1876, the German archaeologist Heinrich Schliemann excavated tombs at Mycenae and discovered the golden mask which he called the "Mask of Agamemnon". Agamemnon was king of Mycenae and a hero of the Trojan War. Today the mask is dated to around 1600 BC, whereas the war between Greece and Troy is most likely to have taken place in the thirteenth century BC.

How did the legend of the Trojan War begin?

Among the sea peoples who raided and sacked Egypt towards the end of the second millennium BC were the Myceneans. They also fought wars against nearer mainland peoples, especially in western Anatolia, and these wars were the basis of the legends of the Trojan War, as recounted by the Greek poet Homer in *The Iliad* and *The Odyssey*.

Who were the Greeks?

From about 2000 BC onwards waves of invaders moved down into the land that was to become Greece. They were an Indo-European people, using a language similar to that of the invaders of other parts of Europe, India and Persia. Gradually they built up one of the world's greatest civilizations.

How were Greek city-states governed?

The city-states of Classical Greece, which began to form after 850 BC, evolved a number of systems of government. Some were ruled by "tyrants". Others tried experimenting with "democracy" (rule by the people), although this did not extend to slaves. Others were "oligarchies", ruled by an elite. Sparta remained a monarchy, famous for its harsh military discipline. The chief states of ancient Greece were Athens, Sparta, Thebes and Corinth. The city-states were always at war with each other, but despite the strife, this was a golden age. Ancient Greece was a centre of learning and scientific enquiry. Its architecture, literature, philosophy, sculpture and social innovations have survived for more than 2,500 years.

Who built the Parthenon?

Ancient Greek architects favoured a simple, graceful style, building tall columns to hold up heavy marble beams. These columns had various names, according to their decoration. The three most important are Doric, Ionic and Corinthian. The Greek "Classical" style has been copied ever since, especially by the Romans. Perhaps the most famous Greek building is the Parthenon in Athens, which was built under the direction of the sculptor Pheidias and is a perfect example of Doric architecture.

Right: The remains of the Temple of Apollo at Delphi in Greece

Above: The Parthenon on the Acropolis in Athens, Greece. A perfect example of the Doric style of architecture, it was constructed between 447 and 438 BC at the time when Pericles, the renowned statesman, was in power.

What was the religion of ancient Greece?

The gods of Mount Olympus formed the basis of the official ancient Greek religion. Sacrifices were offered to them in order to ensure the welfare of the state. The gods were all-powerful, and the worst sin for mortals was *hubris* (the arrogance of putting oneself on a level with the gods). Since the gods held the future in their hands, they were able to reveal what it held. To know the future, people consulted the oracles. The most famous of these was at Delphi, where the god Apollo was supposed to speak. In the centre of the temple at Delphi, there was a vent in the Earth from which the fumes of volcanic activity sometimes emerged. Any words uttered by a priestess seated amid the fumes were thought to be the words of the god.

Who was Plato?

The Greek philosophers discarded the old picture of the gods of Olympus and tried to discover some universal principle which was behind all things. Plato (427–347 BC) was, together with his teacher Socrates and his pupil Aristotle, one of the most influential of these thinkers. He believed in a creator who was identified with the good and the true and the beautiful and thought that man's soul needed to grow towards the supreme good, which his creator had set before him. Philosophers such as Aristotle and Plato laid the foundations for later European ideas of the world.

When was Rome founded?

According to tradition, the first settlement on the hills around Rome grew up in 753 BC. Some time in the sixth century BC, Rome was properly established as a city and from then on its power grew until the Roman Empire covered the whole of the Mediterranean world.

Romulus was the legendary founder of Rome and its first king. According to the story, Romulus and Remus were twin sons of the god Mars who were abandoned and set afloat on the River Tiber. The twins survived because, after coming ashore, they were suckled by a she-wolf. Later they were found and brought up by a shepherd and his wife. After the founding of Rome, Romulus is said to have murdered Remus. Romulus was later worshipped by the Romans as a god under the name Quirinus.

Why were the Romans famous?

In cultural matters, the Romans borrowed from the Greeks, but their own achievements in literature, philosophy and the arts were extraordinary. Their military supremacy was the result of brilliant strategy and tactics, of technological innovation and of ruthless efficiency. The empire was held together by the rule of law. Roman skill at engineering resulted in a network of towns linked by roads spreading across Europe for the first time. Many magnificent examples of Roman architecture survive to this day.

Below: The Roman Empire was protected and enlarged by a vast and disciplined army. The illustration shows some of the different uniforms worn and equipment used over the centuries. The ordinary soldiers were led by officers.

lancer (third century BC)

legionary of the Roman consul Marius (second century BC)

mounted soldier

How big was the Roman Empire?

By AD 117, under Emperor Trajan, the Roman Empire had expanded to include much of the known world: Britain, Gaul (an ancient region of western Europe), Spain, western Germany, south-central Europe and the Balkans, the Black Sea coast, Asia Minor, the Middle East and the Levant, Egypt and the North African coast – a truly remarkable achievement that was to determine the course of European civilization.

When did the Romans rule Britain?

The Roman Emperor Julius Caesar carried out two raids upon Britain, in 55 and 54 BC. On both occasions, his fleet was hampered by stormy crossings. It was not until AD 43 that Britain was successfully invaded and nearly four centuries of Roman rule followed. After several revolts, the British Celts settled down to life under the Romans. To the north, however, the Scots and Picts were never really subdued. In the second century, the Emperor Hadrian built a wall of defence against them. Hadrian's Wall ran from the Solway Firth to the mouth of the River Tyne. Its ruins still stand today. The Roman presence in Britain lasted until about AD 426 when the last of the Roman legions departed to help defend Rome from barbarian attacks.

When did Rome fall?

Roman dominance of the known world was assured by their final defeat of the rival Mediterranean power of Carthage in 146 BC. But at home, the early ideals of the republic soon gave way to a society dominated by a wealthy elite. Dictators came to power, and after the murder of the brilliant conqueror of Europe Julius Caesar (100–44 BC), a succession of emperors ruled over Rome. Most were ruthless intriguers. Some were enlightened and just, and a few, such as Caligula (AD 12–41), were insane. Christianity became established in Rome under the reign of Constantine I in 313 AD. In 330 AD he founded an empire in the east at Constantinople (now Istanbul). Rome itself was sacked by barbarian Vandals in AD 455, and the last Roman emperor in the west, a boy called Romulus Augustus, had lost all power in Italy by AD 476.

...dard bearer

soldier of the Roman Emperor Augustus (first century AD)

soldier of the Roman Emperor Constantine (fourth century AD)

tribune

Above: A Viking longship

Who was the great king of the Franks?

In the fourth and fifth centuries AD, successive waves of peoples from central and eastern Europe profited from the decline of Rome and established themselves by force in the territory of the romanized Gauls, and intermixed with them. To the north were the Franks, to the east, the Alemanni and Burgundians, and to the south and west, the Visigoths. In the ninth century, the Normans, of Scandinavian origin, settled in the region which later took their name – Normandy. Of the early invaders, the Franks soon asserted their supremacy. The greatest of their kings, Charlemagne (AD 742–814), united central and eastern Europe in one vast dominion which covered about one-quarter of the area of the old Roman Empire. The kingdom of France was created when Charlemagne's Empire broke up, after his death. It was there that the history of modern France began.

Who were the Vikings?

Between the seventh and tenth centuries AD, sailors from Scandinavia crossed the sea in light longships, with a single sail and two teams of oarsmen. These were the famous Vikings, who spread terror through northern Europe. They sailed the oceans of the known world and their raids were feared from Britain to France, from Russia to Constantinople. They established a trade with the Arabs in slaves and precious metals.

In about AD 1000, Russian civilization first became established with the state of Kiyev (Kiev), founded in the Ukraine by a group of Swedish Vikings with a view to monopolizing commerce between northern Europe and the Byzantine Empire. From the name of *Rossiy* by which these warrior-merchants were known, came that of Russia. It was because of them that the Byzantine civilization and the Greek Orthodox religion penetrated the Slav world, leaving a legacy which survives today. The first European settlers of North America were probably also Norsemen, who arrived there from Greenland nearly 1,000 years ago.

Below: Charlemagne crossing the Alps on his way to conquer Italy
Inset: The first meeting between Charlemagne and the English monk Alcuin who became his friend and adviser

Above: A section of the Bayeux Tapestry, an eleventh century embroidery showing a scene from the Battle of Hastings in 1066

When was the last successful invasion of England?

From 1017 until 1042, England was ruled by Danish kings. Independence, restored by Edward the Confessor, was short-lived. In 1066, after the Confessor's death, Duke William of Normandy landed near Hastings in Sussex with 50,000 men. Edward's successor, King Harold, was killed, and William "the Conqueror" was crowned King of England. England has not been successfully invaded since 1066. The Normans built strongholds all over the country, and Norman power spread beyond England's borders into Wales and Ireland.

Why is Henry II's reign famous?

The principle that an accused person is innocent until proved guilty – a very important one in a democratic society – had its beginnings in England during the reign of Henry II (1133–1189). In 1166, Henry II set up a court known as the Assize of Clarendon to which people came for justice if their land had been stolen from them. Decisions were given by judges who heard evidence from a panel of twelve local men who had taken a solemn oath to tell the truth. In this twelve-man panel lay the origins of the modern trial by jury.

Henry II's reign is also famous for the murder of Thomas à Becket, Archbishop of Canterbury. The archbishop clashed with Henry II over the amount of power the Pope should have in England and was murdered in 1170. In 1172 he was canonized as St Thomas à Becket and his shrine became the object of pilgrimages.

What were the Wars of the Roses?

From 1455 until 1485, England was torn apart by the Wars of the Roses. Two branches of the royal family – that of York (whose symbol was a white rose), and that of Lancaster (whose symbol was a red rose) – fought for control of the country. The final victor was Henry Tudor, a Lancastrian who defeated King Richard III and then married a Yorkist princess. Henry VII (as Henry Tudor became) was a Welshman, and finally united the lands of England and Wales. The house of Tudor laid the foundations of the country's power.

Above: Richard III (1452–1485)

What caused the Reformation in England?

The Reformation was a religious and political movement which swept through Europe in the sixteenth century. One of its results was the formation of the Protestant churches.

In England, the Reformation at first took hold for political rather than religious reasons. King Henry VIII (1491–1547) was for twenty years married to his first wife, Catherine of Aragon. However, she gave birth to only one child, a daughter called Mary. As he was desperate to have a male heir to succeed him, Henry VIII decided to divorce his wife and marry a younger woman, Anne Boleyn. However, the Pope refused to annul the existing marriage. Finally, the king felt he had no alternative but to break with the church in Rome and refuse to acknowledge the authority of the Pope. This was formally carried out in the Act of Supremacy (1534), which made Henry VIII supreme head of the church in England. Once separated from Rome, the English church was also more open to the new religious ideas arriving from the Continent.

How did America get its name?

Although the explorer Christopher Columbus reached America in 1492, he was convinced he had arrived in Asia, basing his belief on the descriptions of Marco Polo. Columbus died in 1506 without realizing how important his discovery was, still believing that he had done no more than show his contemporaries a better sea route to the Indies. After him, however, the exploration of America became more organized. Reports made by Amerigo Vespucci, an Italian navigator, on his expeditions after 1500, showed that Columbus had found a previously unknown continent. In honour of Vespucci, a German geographer proposed to name the new continent "Land of Amerigo" – in other words, America.

Right: Christopher Columbus (1451–1506)

Below: An illustration depicting the death of James Cook in the Hawaiian islands in 1779

Who was the first to sail around the world?

Columbus's discoveries encouraged other navigators to attempt voyages of exploration. The Portuguese, Ferdinand Magellan, obtained from King Charles I of Spain both ships and men (denied him in his own country) to circumnavigate the globe by sailing along the Atlantic coast of South America and then thrusting out into the unknown Pacific Ocean until at last he reached the Philippines. He sailed from Spain on 20 September 1519, and had to contend with storms, mutinies by his crews, scurvy, hunger, massacres and cannibals.

Of the 265 men who left with him, only eighteen returned – "weaker than men have ever been before". He himself was killed in an ambush by the natives of the island of Mactan on 27 April 1521. Only one of his ships, *Victoria*, captained by Sebastian del Cano, returned to Spain in 1522, so becoming the first ship to sail round the world.

Who was the most famous explorer of the eighteenth century?

The most famous of the explorers of the eighteenth century was an Englishman, James Cook. He was born in 1728, the son of a farm labourer, and was a cabin-boy on a merchant ship by the time he was fifteen. He led three important expeditions. In the first (1768–1771), Cook explored Tahiti and its neighbouring islands, made the first proper charts of New Zealand and discovered the east coast of Australia. In the summer of 1771, he returned to England. On his second voyage (1772–1775) Cook became the first European to sail south of the Antarctic Circle, then made a wide search of the southern Pacific. On his third voyage (1776–1779), Cook explored the northern Pacific up to the Bering Strait. He was seeking the Northwest Passage, by which it was thought ships could travel along the Arctic coast of North America to Asia. Cook did not find it. Later, he sailed to Hawaii but was killed by natives there on 14 February 1779.

One of the purposes of Cook's voyages was to find "Terra Australis Incognita" (Unknown Southern Land), which geographers believed existed in the southern hemisphere to balance the lands in the north. Cook proved, however, that it did not exist.

Who was the first to reach the South Pole?

In 1773, the British captain James Cook became the first explorer to cross the Antarctic Circle (latitude $66\frac{1}{2}°$ South), and took his sailing ship into the ice pack. A Russian expedition circumnavigated Antarctica in 1819–1821. The first certain landing did not take place until 1831, although bold seal hunters may have landed long before then.

At the start of the twentieth century, one of the main objectives of explorers was to reach the South Pole. In 1901–1904, the British explorer Robert Falcon Scott got within 925 km of the Pole and in 1908, an Irishman, Ernest Shackleton, got within 156 km.

The final "race" for the South Pole took place in 1911. On 14 December, Roald Amundsen, a Norwegian explorer, reached the South Pole and planted his country's flag. He beat by only a month his friend and rival Scott, whose party perished on the return from the Pole early in 1912, overcome by fatigue, hunger and cold. In 1958 a Commonwealth expedition made the first overland crossing of Antarctica.

Who was the first to reach the North Pole?

In 1909, the American explorer Robert Peary succeeded in reaching the North Pole and in 1926 another American, Richard Byrd, flew over the Pole in an aeroplane, as the Norwegian Roald Amundsen and the Italian Umberto Nobile were to do a little later in an airship. In 1958 the American atomic submarine *Nautilus* was actually able to sail beneath the ice of the North Pole.

Below: Nineteenth-century explorers of the Antarctic took their sailing ships into the ice packs.

Who were the conquistadores?

The Spaniards who arrived on the coast of Mexico in 1519 are referred to as *conquistadores* (conquerors) because they went on to rule much of South America. Having fought a battle with the Tlaxcalan people, the Spanish leader Hernando Cortés made them his allies. Proceeding to Tenochtitlán, the Aztec capital, the Spaniards extracted a ransom and an oath of fealty from Montezuma, the Aztec king. But gradually they provoked the Aztec population into desperate resistance. The Spanish force was small, eventually consisting of about 1,000 foot soldiers and forty-six horses. In the early hours of 1 July 1520, this force had to flee Tenochtitlán, and was almost exterminated in this *noche triste* ("sad night"). Cortés escaped, however, and regrouped his forces. A year later, supported by 10,000 Amerindian allies, Cortés captured the city and razed it to the ground – the modern capital, Mexico City, stands on its ruins.

The last Aztec leader, the young Cuahtemoc, is today a national hero of Mexico. In the capital, where there are many relics of Spanish rule, there are no monuments to Cortés.

Top left: The arrival of Hernando Cortés in Mexico in 1519

Top right: A ritual dance of the Pellerosa Indians of Illinois

Above: The arrival of European settlers in America led to much lawlessness and fighting between "cowboys" and the resident Indians.

When did settlers arrive in America?

In the seventeenth century, European colonies grew up along the eastern seaboard of North America. Religious refugees from England, known as the "Pilgrim Fathers", settled in New England in 1620. Slaves from Africa were sold into the plantations of Virginia and the West Indies. At first the original inhabitants – the Indians – tolerated the newcomers. But gradually they found themselves being driven off their ancestral lands. Throughout North and South America, the settlers stole the lands of the Amerindians, who were cheated, harassed, enslaved, murdered and deprived of their rights. European settlement expanded westwards across North America – at the expense of such nations as the Sioux, the Ojibwa, the Nez Percés, the Cheyenne, the Iroquois, the Navajo and the Apache. By 1886, the surviving Amerindians of the USA were confined to reservations. The "Wild West" era had ended.

Top right: George Washington, first president of the USA

Below: American troops marching up to the city of Yorktown where they defeated the British in 1781

How did the USA gain independence?

By 1760, the thirteen British colonies in North America (New Hampshire, Massachusetts, Rhode Island, Connecticut, New Jersey, New York, Pennsylvania, Delaware, Maryland, Virginia, North Carolina, South Carolina and Georgia) formed a continuous strip of land in the east with a population of about $1\frac{1}{2}$ million. The colonists increasingly resented British interference in their affairs, especially "taxation without representation", that is by their own members in the British Parliament. The Boston Tea Party, when colonists threw tea cargoes into Boston harbour in protest against taxes in 1773, heralded the American War of Independence (1775–1781). At first, the colonists' struggle was based on righting specific grievances, but on 2 July 1776 the Continental Congress (which had been founded by the colonies in 1774 to resist British laws called the Intolerable Acts) voted for independence. On 4 July, it went further and adopted the Declaration of Independence. A new nation had been created. In the war that followed, the colonists, with the help of their French allies, defeated the British at Yorktown in 1781.

Who was the first president of the USA?

Under General George Washington, a small army of American colonists, helped by the French, defeated the British forces during the American War of Independence (1775–1781). As a result, the new United States of America, whose Constitution was drafted in 1787, was created. This Constitution, which is still substantially in force today, was promulgated in the name of the people and is based on the principle of equality and sovereignty of the people.

George Washington, whose leadership had helped win the revolutionary war, became the first president in 1789. His name was later given to the United States capital founded on the banks of the Potomac River in 1800 – the original capital had been New York City.

When was the California gold rush?

In California in the USA, on 24 January 1848, a certain James W. Marshall, working on the construction of a sawmill not far from San Francisco (which was then a small settlement of a few hundred inhabitants), found gold in the gravel of a tributary to the Sacramento River. This set off the so-called "gold-rush" (or "gold fever"), an important moment in the history of the USA, which brought repercussions throughout the world. In only eighteen months, the hunt for gold attracted about 100,000 men to California and soon San Francisco became one of the most important cities in America.

Top right: Gold prospectors rushed to both the USA and Canada in the nineteenth century.

Right: A wooden hut used by gold prospectors

Bottom right: Abraham Lincoln with two officers from the army of the Northern States during the American Civil War

What caused the American Civil War?

In the nineteenth century, the population and the economy of the USA expanded, but serious political divisions appeared between the states, especially between North and South. One of the main differences was over slavery, which was favoured in the South but not in the North. When the candidate of the anti-slavery Republican party, Abraham Lincoln, was elected president, the Southern states decided to withdraw from the Union. This resulted in the Civil War, which raged from 1861 to 1865.

The North had more soldiers, money and machinery, but the South, with fine commanders and great spirit, held on for four years. Lincoln's Emancipation Proclamation in 1863 finally abolished slavery. Lincoln himself was assassinated in 1865, but the USA came out of the war as a single country and ready to advance to new power and prosperity.

Above: Napoleon commanding his troops during the Battle of the Pyramids in Egypt

When did the French Revolution take place?

The French Revolution took place in 1789 and was initially aimed at modernizing a nation in which the monarchy and nobility still enjoyed medieval privileges. The middle classes sought constitutional change, but reform turned to violent revolution. The monarchy was overthrown, Louis XVI and his queen, Marie Antoinette, were sent to the guillotine, together with many aristocrats and churchmen. From the ruins of the past arose a republic, governed by a Constitution based on the rights of man and guaranteeing liberty. The new ideas spread through Europe like wildfire, and were to form an inspiration for all the democratic movements of the nineteenth century.

What was Napoleon's greatest achievement?

Napoleon Bonaparte, the great French general, was appointed Consul of France for life in 1802 and Emperor in 1804. Napoleon's military campaigns heralded new times for the whole continent. The true greatness of Napoleon, who placed France at the centre of an empire greater than that of Charlemagne, did not arise so much from his spectacular victories as from his putting an end to the remains of feudalism throughout Europe. Perhaps his greatest achievement was the introduction of a progressive and more rational legal system, the *Code Napoléon*. Napoleon's rule ended in defeat by the British and Prussian armies at the Battle of Waterloo in 1815. After his fall, France was torn for many decades between attempts to restore the old monarchy and the tremors of fresh revolution.

What was the Industrial Revolution?

The Industrial Revolution which began in the north of England in about 1760 was probably the most important economic change in human society since the beginning of farming about 9,000 years ago. With Britain leading the way, trade, industry and population all expanded at a tremendous rate. The introduction of steam-driven factory machinery and the building of railways stimulated even faster growth.

In less than a century, life for many people changed dramatically. Small market towns, unchanged for centuries, turned into smoky, industrial cities (complete with slums).

Employers grew rich while a new class of industrial workers, working in shocking conditions, earned very low wages and lived in terrible poverty. Finally, laws were passed by Parliament in the nineteenth century which limited working hours and made it illegal for very young children to work at all. In addition, the workers themselves formed trades unions to improve their conditions.

Below: The Industrial Revolution led to the rapid development of new machinery and factories throughout Europe. This nineteenth-century French sawmill is a typical example.

Above: A scene from the Battle of Piave fought between the Italians and the Austrians in the First World War

When was the First World War?

The rise of the German empire after the unification of the German states in 1871 destroyed the old balance of power among the European nations. Europe became divided into two armed camps, with Britain, France and Russia on one side and Germany and Austria-Hungary on the other.

The First World War, mainly a European war in spite of its name, was waged from 1914–1918. On the Western Front, in France, a stalemate soon developed with both sides dug into trenches, and thousands of men sacrificed for a few yards' advance.

In 1917 the USA entered the war against Germany, helping to force a German surrender. Europe was left in a bad way – poor, battered and unstable. Both the Ottoman Empire and the Austrian Empire had disappeared, and German ambitions were checked. The only true victor in the war was the USA which, after 1918, was the most powerful country in the world.

Why was the Treaty of Versailles a failure?

The Treaty of Versailles, which ended the First World War in 1919, pleased almost no one. The Germans were especially angry. They were unwilling to accept the verdict that they were responsible for the war and ought to pay for it. The Versailles meeting also set up the League of Nations – the forerunner of the United Nations – but this organization had little influence on big international conflicts.

On paper, the Treaty of Versailles seemed to be a victory for nationalism and democracy. An independent republic of Czechoslovakia was one result. Yugoslavia, Poland, Hungary and Albania also became independent. Elsewhere, however, brutal dictatorships took power. In the USSR, the Communist system under Stalin became a totalitarian state, in which all opposition was crushed. In Italy the reaction took the form of fascism – a crude, power-loving, racist system which worshipped force and disdained justice. Aggressive fascist dictators also arose in Hungary, Spain and, above all, in Germany, where the Nazis, under Adolf Hitler, came to power in 1933.

What caused the Russian Revolution?

Nineteenth-century Russia was a backward land controlled by tsars. Until 1861, when they were emancipated, peasant serfs could be bought and sold along with the land they worked. Intellectuals and socialists were cruelly persecuted and most Russians lived in terrible poverty.

Among those who were planning to overthrow tsarist rule was Vladimir Ilyich Ulyanov, known as Lenin. While in exile in Switzerland, he plotted to bring the Communist ideas of Karl Marx to Russia. He got his chance to do so after the sufferings of the Russians in the First World War (1914–1918) led to a liberal revolution and the overthrow of Tsar Nicholas II in 1917.

Lenin returned to Russia and seized power from the liberal leader, Alexander Kerensky. In 1918, the Tsar and his family were murdered, and there followed a bloody civil war. At the same time, Russia was invaded by British, American and other foreign armies seeking to overcome the new Communist regime. However, the Communists prevailed and by 1920 the whole of Russia was under their control.

What caused the Second World War?

The immediate cause of the Second World War was the aggressive actions of fascist dictators, including a Japanese attack on China (1931), an Italian attack on Ethiopia (1935) and German attacks on Czechoslovakia and Poland (1939). It was Hitler's invasion of Poland that finally provoked Britain and France to declare war.

By 1941, Hitler had conquered most of Europe, and Britain, supported by the Commonwealth, was his last serious opponent. But then on 22 June 1941, Hitler attacked the USSR despite a no-war pact, and on 7 December 1942 Japan attacked (without warning) the main US naval base in the Pacific at Pearl Harbour in Hawaii.

With the USSR and the USA entering the war, the Nazis and their allies were bound for defeat, and at great cost in terms of lives lost. The Germans surrendered on 8 May 1945. The Japanese surrendered on 15 August 1945 but only after atomic bombs had blasted the cities of Hiroshima and Nagasaki.

When was the United Nations founded?

The United Nations was created mainly in the hope of preventing future wars. It was founded in 1945 by the nations which had defeated Germany, Italy and Japan, that is Britain, France, China, the USSR and the USA. Today, almost every country in the world is a member of the United Nations.

There has been no world war since 1945, and perhaps the UN has been partly responsible. However, there have been a great many smaller wars, such as the Korean War, the Vietnam War and various wars in the Middle East, Africa and Central America. The UN has sometimes played a part in limiting the fighting, but has rarely, if ever, stopped it. However, the UN includes some bodies, such as the World Health Organisation (WHO), which have achieved a great deal.

What was the cold war?

After the Second World War, the former allies soon fell out. The Soviets and the Americans distrusted and feared each other. Each side – East and West – formed military alliances and developed terrifying nuclear weapons. What British wartime Prime Minister Winston Churchill called an "iron curtain" descended on Europe, dividing the Communist Eastern countries from the non-Communist Western nations. During this "cold war", a third world war, which would be fought with nuclear weapons, often looked probable. There were many crises, but gradually the prospects of peaceful co-existence improved as both superpowers recognized that in the next war, if it happened, there could be no winners.

The late 1980s saw a "thawing" of the cold war between East and West. This process was hastened by the appointment in 1985 of a Soviet leader, Mikhail Gorbachev, who actively sought more friendly relations between the two blocs.

What was Japan's economic miracle?

The rebirth of Japan from the ashes of the Second World War (1939–1945) began with the support of the USA, who saw the country as the most effective bulwark against the Communist regime in China. The importance of Japan to the USA was confirmed during the Korean War (1950–1953). When the American forces withdrew in 1952, Japan's "economic miracle" was already under way.

Today Japan shares third place with West Germany in the world economic league, after the USA and the USSR. It is the most industrialized and successful country in Asia, despite a scarcity of natural resources. Industrial success has been based principally upon initiative, an initial supply of cheap labour, and technical mastery of modern manufacturing processes. In Japan, the large companies are powerful, paternalistic organizations which the individual is expected to serve with complete loyalty.

Below: The Japanese city of Hiroshima was destroyed by an atomic bomb in 1945 and subsequently completely rebuilt.

Bottom: Some customs from before the Second World War still remain in Japan. Here two rickshaw drivers wait for clients.

What is Hinduism?

"Hinduism" is a western term – it is the name which the people of the West use to describe the main religion of India. Indians call it the *sanatana dharma* (the eternal faith).

Hinduism, which today has over 250 million followers, has no set doctrine or creeds. It is simply the religion of the people of India, and there are no truths which one must believe in order to be a Hindu. The variety of teachings within the religion of Hinduism is expressed by the Hindu conviction that all beliefs and practices are ways of reaching the supreme goal of nirvana.

Far right: A bronze statuette of Siva, one of the three principal gods of Hinduism

Below: Hindu pilgrims bathing in the holy waters of the River Ganges at Benares

Which gods do Hindus follow?

Most Hindus today are followers of one of the personal gods – Vishnu or Siva. A third god who is sometimes worshipped is the wife of Siva, known as Kali. The centres of worship are the temples in which there are statues of the deity or objects representing him or her. Daily rituals are carried out in the temple by the priests – waking, dressing, feeding and entertaining. The ordinary worshippers are not present at these rituals, but come at other times to the temple to offer their gifts to the god and to make their requests.

In addition to the temple worship there is worship in the home which is still practised by many Hindus. Somewhere in the home is a small shrine where an image of the god is placed. At certain times of the day the head of the family will make offerings and say prayers before the image.

Right: Muslim pilgrims in the Ka'abah, the most sacred Muslim shrine, in Mecca, Saudi Arabia

What is yoga?

The yoga system is a set of physical and mental exercises practised in Hinduism. It aims to enable a person to achieve absolute mastery of him- or herself – both of mind and body. In Europe particularly, yoga has become popular and is practised also as a form of healthy exercise.

It is not easy to become a "yogin". First of all, a person has to study and meditate, follow special diets and observe a series of practical devotions; then, the student starts on various stages which lead to the achievement of salvation. These stages are: to obey the five commandments (non-violence, truthfulness, honesty, chastity and poverty); to follow the five observances (purity, sobriety, the so-called "ascetic heat", reciting of sacred texts and worship of the Lord of the universe); to learn the positions of the body which lead to concentration and control of breathing; to learn to divert attention away from objects; concentration; meditation; and, lastly, the perfect union of one's self with the cosmos.

Above: A follower of the Hindu god Vishnu in meditation. He is sitting in an advanced yoga posture.

Who was the Buddha?

The legends concerning the life of Siddhartha Gautama, founder of Buddhism, date from long after the period when he lived, but there is little doubt that they refer to an historical figure, born probably about 560 BC. The legends say that he was the son of the chief of a small tribe living near the River Ganges on the borders of what is now Nepal. Brought up by his father in great luxury, Gautama was trained as the future ruler of his tribe. At the age of twenty-nine he saw four signs which caused him to rethink the meaning of life. The first three of these were an old man, a diseased man and a corpse. These sights brought home to Gautama the truth that life was not the luxury to which he had been accustomed but was marked by old age, suffering and death. The fourth sign, a wandering hermit, made him realize that a way of escape from this life might possibly be found, by ridding oneself of worldly possessions, like the hermit.

What does Islam mean?

The word Islam means "submission", and the followers of the religion of Islam are known as Muslims (or those who submit to the power of God). The religion of Arabia in the sixth century AD was a simple belief in a family of gods. Islam was founded as a reaction against this Arabian paganism. It is 600 years younger than Christianity, but includes many of the ideas of both Christianity and Judaism. The founder of Islam was the Arabian, Muhammad.

How was Islam established?

Muhammad, the founder of Islam, was born in AD 570 in Mecca, Arabia. He was orphaned at an early age and was brought up by his relatives. At the age of about forty, Muhammad saw in a vision the messenger of God, who told him that he was to be God's prophet. He began to preach in the name of God, whom he called Allah, calling men to repentance and warning them of the day of judgement to come. His following in Mecca was very small and finally he left for the nearby city of Medina. Here he became the leader of the city and established the new religion. The first mosque was built and Friday became the day of community prayer. When war broke out between Medina and Mecca, Muhammad led the Medinan army and captured Mecca. He made it the centre of the new religion and its shrine – the Ka'abah – became the most holy spot in the Muslim world. In 632, two years after taking Mecca, Muhammad died.

Who were the Hebrews?

Hebrew means "one from the other side (of the river)". This name was given to a small group of Semitic people originating from Mesopotamia, where they established themselves on the western side of the River Jordan in Palestine about 1,800 years before the birth of Christ. They preferred, however, to be called Israelites in memory of their patriarch Jacob, who was also known as Israel. They were also later called Judeans from the name of one of their main tribes, Judah. Today, their descendants are known as Jews.

The history of these people from their origin to the Roman conquest is narrated in the most famous sacred book in the world, the Bible. It is a fascinating story, full of adventures and miracles and it occupies most of the Old Testament, the first part of the Bible, beginning with the creation of the world and its first people – Adam and Eve.

Right: The vast statue of Jesus Christ which dominates the city of Rio de Janeiro in Brazil. Much of South America was converted to Christianity following European colonization in the sixteenth century.

Below: Jews praying at the "Wailing Wall" in Jerusalem

To which people is Jerusalem a holy city?

Jerusalem is the holy city of three faiths – Judaism, Christianity and Islam. To many people, the region in which it is situated has been known variously as the "Promised Land" and the "Holy Land". It has always been held in special respect, and its religious significance has, over the ages, resulted in a history of strife and bloodshed, as well as in the fruits of civilization.

The Western Wall of the city, sometimes known as the "Wailing Wall", a supporting wall of the Temple destroyed by the Romans in AD 70, is visited by Jews on Saturday, the Jewish Sabbath, and on other holy days in accordance with a custom that goes back to the first century AD.

What does the name Christ mean?

Christianity takes its name from Christ, a Greek word which means "the anointed one". The Hebrew equivalent is the word "Messiah" which also means "anointed" or, more generally, "the man anointed by the Lord". When they used the term "Messiah", the Jews had in mind a future king, appointed by God, who would make them a great nation. In the New Testament, however, the words "Messiah" and "Christ" are used only for Jesus, the son of Mary, whom Christians believe to be divine. Jesus was born at Bethlehem and lived at Nazareth, a village in Galilee, in the north of Palestine. Palestine lay almost exactly where the state of Israel is today; its capital was Jerusalem.

Why were the early Christians persecuted?

Christ's followers (apostles) spread the aith taught by their Master. They eached Greece, Italy, northern Africa ınd the regions of the East. In Rome, at irst, they were treated like other Jews, vith whom they shared a stern moral tandard and fear of being affected by he pagan practices carried on around hem. However, their belief in Jesus as he Messiah – a person infinitely greater han the Roman Emperor – led the Romans to doubt their loyalty to the tate. As a result, the Christians came to e persecuted and were compelled to neet in caves called "catacombs". If liscovered, they were tortured or killed or fed to the lions during the bloody ublic spectacles at the Colosseum in Rome.

Why was a basilica built in Rome?

The most notorious persecution of Christians was that by the Roman Emperor Nero, which took place in AD 64. The Emperor was believed, wrongly, to have set fire to Rome, and he tried to shift the blame on to the Christians. At that time the apostles Peter and Paul were killed. Nearly three centuries later, the Roman Emperor Constantine built a basilica to honour the shrine of St. Peter. It is the place where today the Basilica of St. Peter stands, in the Vatican. Before the reign of Constantine, between the rule of Nero and that of Diocletian, the Christians underwent ten great persecutions and many more minor ones, which caused thousands of deaths.

Who led the Protestant movement?

In the sixteenth century, many people were not satisfied with the state of the Christian church. The authority of the Pope was used to establish taxation and the selling of pardons. A widespread demand grew for change, led by the German, Martin Luther (1483–1546). As he studied the New Testament, Luther came to believe that true Christianity was not a matter of belonging to the church but of inward repentance and trust in Jesus Christ. Many followed Luther in protesting against the Pope and his church and for this reason they were called Protestants. Finally, Lutheran churches were formed which rejected the Pope's authority.

Other Protestant churches were also founded. In Switzerland John Calvin (1509–1564) formulated his ideas on the sovereignty of God which led to the founding of the Calvinist churches. Rejection of the Pope's authority also led to the formation of the Church of England.

bove: The nave of the Basilica of St. Peter nside the Vatican in Rome. The Basilica was uilt between 1506 and 1615 and, at a ength of 188 m, is the largest church in the vorld.

ight: The Diet of Worms, a meeting held in 521 at which Luther defended his ideas in ront of Charles V, the Holy Roman Emperor

Who were the first artists?

The first painters were at work over 20,000 years ago. They were Stone Age cave painters and they painted pictures of animals on the rock walls of caves. Particularly fine examples can be seen in the caves of Lascaux in France. They had no written language, and so they had no books – instead they painted pictures. Possibly they thought that painting a deer or wild ox would give a hunter power to kill those animals for food.

Much primitive art has a magical or religious meaning. Australian aboriginal people still decorate their secret magical places with paintings that tell a hidden story. As well as painting (using coloured earth, clays and vegetable oils for paint), ancient peoples also carved figures in wood, ivory and bone and made figures from wet clay. The civilizations of ancient Egypt, China, India, Greece and Rome were rich in art. Wealthy rulers wished to live in luxury and paid painters to decorate their palaces. The Egyptian pharaohs were buried in tombs decorated with beautiful wall paintings.

How did the Greeks change art?

Around 600 BC Greek civilization settled down; temples and other buildings were made of stone, and cities like Athens were built. Gradually, there began the amazing changes which the Greeks made to the course of art.

Instead of copying the old symbolic or religious way of representing the human body, the Greeks represented what they saw, so making art more realistic. This was the birth of the artist as an individual, making his own personal contribution to society. Greek artists also introduced a new realism to sculpture. The human body was now shown standing naturally, almost coming to life.

Right: A statue of the god Apollo by the famous Greek sculptor Praxiteles

Which artist founded modern painting?

Medieval paintings of six or seven centuries ago generally strike the modern observer as unnatural and stiff – figures appear flat and have no expression; faces with the same features are sometimes repeated indefinitely; perspective, the three-dimensional effect of height, width and depth seen in real life, does not exist: the size of the characters does not depend on their position in the painting, but on their importance.

Giotto, who lived from approximately 1267–1337, was the son of Florentine peasants. He created a new type of painting which shocked scholars, turning away from the stereotyped forms of the medieval tradition and creating instead in his paintings, scenes of dramatic reality with solid, natural figures. Painters of the late fourteenth and fifteenth centuries were influenced by him and he is generally regarded as the founder of modern painting.

Above: The first artists drew animals on the rock walls of caves.

Below: Giotto's masterpiece, the *Maestà*

Above: A beautiful fresco on the ceiling of the Pitti palace in Florence. The soft, luminous colours are typical of fresco painting.

What is a fresco?

From about the fourteenth century, fresco painting was very popular. Workers prepared a wall or ceiling by applying a layer of lime and covering this with plaster. The artist then painted onto the wet plaster, so that the colours were mixed with the plaster and dried with it. The effect was soft, luminous and durable. There were special problems – once the plaster was dry, it was almost impossible to correct the work. If a mistake was made, the plaster had to be cut out and the work done again.

During the Middle Ages, drawings to be incorporated in a fresco were made directly onto the wet plaster. Later, in the middle of the fifteenth century, a cartoon (that is a careful preliminary drawing) was used. This consisted of a set of paper sheets on which the picture was traced with a charcoal pencil. It was then marked on the wall by "dusting" (that is by making a number of very small holes along the lines of the pictures and filling them with carbon dust which deposited on the plaster). The picture was later coloured.

Above left: Leonardo da Vinci (1452—1519)
Inset: His famous painting, the *Mona Lisa*

Above right: Rembrandt (1606–1669)

Who was Leonardo da Vinci?

Leonardo da Vinci (1452–1519) was an Italian painter, sculptor, architect, engineer and musician. Born in Vinci in Italy, he studied painting with Verrocchio and worked as an artist under the patronage of Lorenzo the Magnificent, ruler of Florence. He painted the *Last Supper*, a fresco in a church in Milan, in 1498 and the *Mona Lisa*, probably the most famous portrait in the world, in 1503.

Leonardo represents the highest achievement of Renaissance culture. He accomplished more than any other person in history in a wide range of arts and sciences. His understanding and knowledge of most of the sciences was far beyond that of his age. His original thoughts, which included a plan for an aircraft, were contained in a series of notebooks and drawings.

Who was Michelangelo?

Michelangelo (1475–1564) was, with Leonardo and Raphael, one of the three greatest artists of the Italian Renaissance. Even as a child, Michelangelo wanted to be a sculptor. Unfortunately, his father, the chief magistrate of a small town near Florence, did not agree. But Michelangelo was determined, so at last his father gave way and apprenticed him to the painter Domenico Ghirlandaio (1449–1494) for three years.

Although his greatest love was sculpture, Michelangelo won everlasting fame with his magnificent paintings on the ceiling of the Sistine Chapel in Rome. Against his wishes, he was forced to do the paintings by Pope Julius II. Michelangelo undertook the enormous task alone. He worked in secret for four years, and astounded everyone with his almost superhuman achievement.

Michelangelo also worked as an architect, and in 1546 took over the great task of designing St Peter's in Rome. This was still not completed when he died in 1564.

Who is the greatest Dutch painter?

The greatest Dutch painter is Rembrandt (1606–1669). Born in Leyden, in Holland, the son of a miller, Harmenszoon van Rijn Rembrandt became famous when he was still a young man. His style rejected classical themes and gained powerful original effects by his use of light and shade (chiaroscuro). His output was enormous – he produced about 650 paintings as well as about 300 etchings and nearly 2,000 drawings.

What did Bruegel paint?

Pieter Bruegel, who lived from about 1520–1569, was a Flemish painter who took Italian ideas and used them in a completely different way. The scenes in Bruegel's paintings are those of rural life. Peasants are seen going about their normal business – working, hunting, feasting or celebrating a wedding. There is nothing sophisticated or elegant about these paintings; they swarm with hearty, boisterous life. But Bruegel himself was not a peasant, and he observed these rustic activities with the cool eye of a townsman. It was the custom at that time to regard the country "yokel" as a sort of clown, and there is also a trace of this mockery in Bruegel's work.

What is Baroque?

In the late sixteenth and early seventeenth centuries, a confident spirit grew up throughout western Europe. It was an age of contrasts. While the Catholic church was bringing back a medieval intensity of faith in its opposition to the Reformation, the French philosopher René Descartes (1596–1650) was challenging medieval faith with the arguments of reason.

It is not surprising that the art of the time was varied and complicated too. The word "Baroque", which is used to describe it, may have come from the Portuguese *barocco* (meaning a pearl of irregular shape). It is a fitting description for an art which was rich, lavish and full of contrast.

One effect of the religious tussle was a revival of interest in church building and decoration. The more the Protestants preached against outward show, the more eager were the Catholics for the kind of lavishness and ornate style seen in the work of artists and sculptors such as Giovanni Bernini (1598–1680).

Right: Pieter Bruegel's famous painting *The Numbering at Bethlehem*

Why were the Impressionists so named?

The Impressionist movement was born at an exhibition in Paris in 1863. Edouard Manet (1832–1883), along with Claude Monet (1840–1926) and Pierre Renoir (1841–1919), had been refused permission to show his paintings in the Salon exhibition. Because the artists protested so loudly, the Emperor Napoleon III insisted that they should be allowed to exhibit in another room. This room became known as the *Salon des Refusés* (meaning the "Hall of the Rejected"). The name Impressionist was coined by a critic who jeered at a painting by Claude Monet in this exhibition called *Impression, Sunrise.*

The Impressionists worked on the principle of simultaneous vision. This means that the human eye will focus only on one small part of any scene at any time, and detail within that part will be sharp. Over the rest of the scene, detail will be less clear. Impressionists tried to reproduce this effect in their work, showing how light plays on the surface of objects, constantly changing the way they appear.

What are Cubist paintings?

"Cubist" is the name given to the paintings which Pablo Picasso (1881–1973) and Georges Braque (1882–1963) made between 1908 and 1914. These painters tried to show their subjects as though they could be seen from several points of view at the same time. All the different planes shown made them look as though they were composed of little cubes. The Cubist painters also rejected the Impressionist colours and worked mainly in browns and greys.

Picasso's painting continued to change and develop after his Cubist phase. His mural *Guernica,* painted in 1936 on the theme of the Spanish Civil War, was a combination of the Cubist and Surrealist styles.

Above: Picasso's famous *Portrait of a Woman*

Why did modern artists invent new forms of painting?

The growing science of psychology was largely responsible for the movement in art called "Surrealism". The work of Sigmund Freud at the beginning of the twentieth century was echoed in the paintings of Max Ernst, Giorgio de Chirico and René Magritte, who presented bizarre images with a nightmare-like quality.

The Expressionist painters, beginning with Van Gogh, needed to express their personal reactions to the confusing world around them. The pioneer of this new movement was Georges Rouault (1871–1958), and others who have followed in it are Chaim Soutine, Francis Bacon, Graham Sutherland and Oscar Kokoschka.

Two individual painters of fantastic works, quite different from those of the Surrealists, are Marc Chagall and Paul Klee. Chagall's fantasies are dream-like, while Klee's are intellectual and witty.

What are the principal movements in modern sculpture?

Most of the movements in twentieth-century painting have their counterparts in sculpture. Jacob Epstein (1880–1959), who settled in England in 1906, certainly worked in the language of the Expressionists. His portrait busts show an intense, nervous energy in the way he handled the clay.

The Rumanian sculptor, Constantin Brancusi (1876–1957), on the other hand, carried Abstraction almost as far as it would go. His very simplified forms get the maximum effect from the materials he used – whether it was marble, metal or wood.

Sculptors such as the Russian Naum Gabo, have made much use of modern materials such as transparent plastics and nylon. Gabo, Jean Tinguely and Alexander Calder have also introduced real, rather than suggested, movement into their works.

Among the sculptors whose subject is still the human figure are Henry Moore (1898–1986) and Alberto Giacometti (1901–1966). Moore is famous for his many different versions of the reclining figure, and Giacometti for his elongated, wistful forms.

Above: *Musa metafisica* by Carlo Carrà, one of the great Italian painters of this century

Right: Two examples of modern sculpture: *Bookmaker* (1894) by Medardo Rosso (left), *Rocking Chair* (1950) by Henry Moore (right)

What is abstract art?

The first "abstract" painter, in the 1890s, was Vassily Kandinsky (1866–1944), and he was soon joined by others, including Piet Mondrian (1872–1944) and Joan Mirò. Their idea was to abstract (or take out) the essence of everyday things, showing the shapes and colours within them rather than strict representations of the objects as such. The geometric abstraction of Mondrian has had an influence on modern design and architecture.

Is music the oldest art?

Music is almost certainly older than painting, sculpture or poetry – the art forms devised for expressing thoughts and feelings. Possibly only dance is older among the arts. But far less is known about the music of early civilizations than about their art, literature or religion. A few examples of a kind of musical notation, or written music, used by the Egyptians have been discovered as well as Egyptian wall paintings which depict people playing various instruments. However, although some of the architecture, sculpture and paintings of ancient Egypt can actually be seen, and writing of the period can be deciphered and read, their music cannot be easily reproduced. It is known what their instruments may have sounded like, but not how the peoples of the ancient world organized these different sounds into music.

Below: A page from a medieval book of plainsong

Right: A fifteenth-century miniature showing two musicians entertaining an audience

Facing page, left: A grand piano showing the strings which make sounds when struck by hammers. The hammers are activated by the keys.

What was medieval music like?

In the Middle Ages, music, in common with most forms of art and knowledge, developed within the church. Particularly important was the form of chanting known as Gregorian, which is still used in services today.

The first secular music (that is, music which was not composed for religious ceremonies) grew up in the Middle Ages with the "minstrels". These wandering vagabonds earned their living by singing and playing for the amusement of anyone who would give them a supper in return for a song. After the minstrels came the "troubadours", who usually sang songs of love and courtship. They were often men of noble birth and were treated with honour and respect.

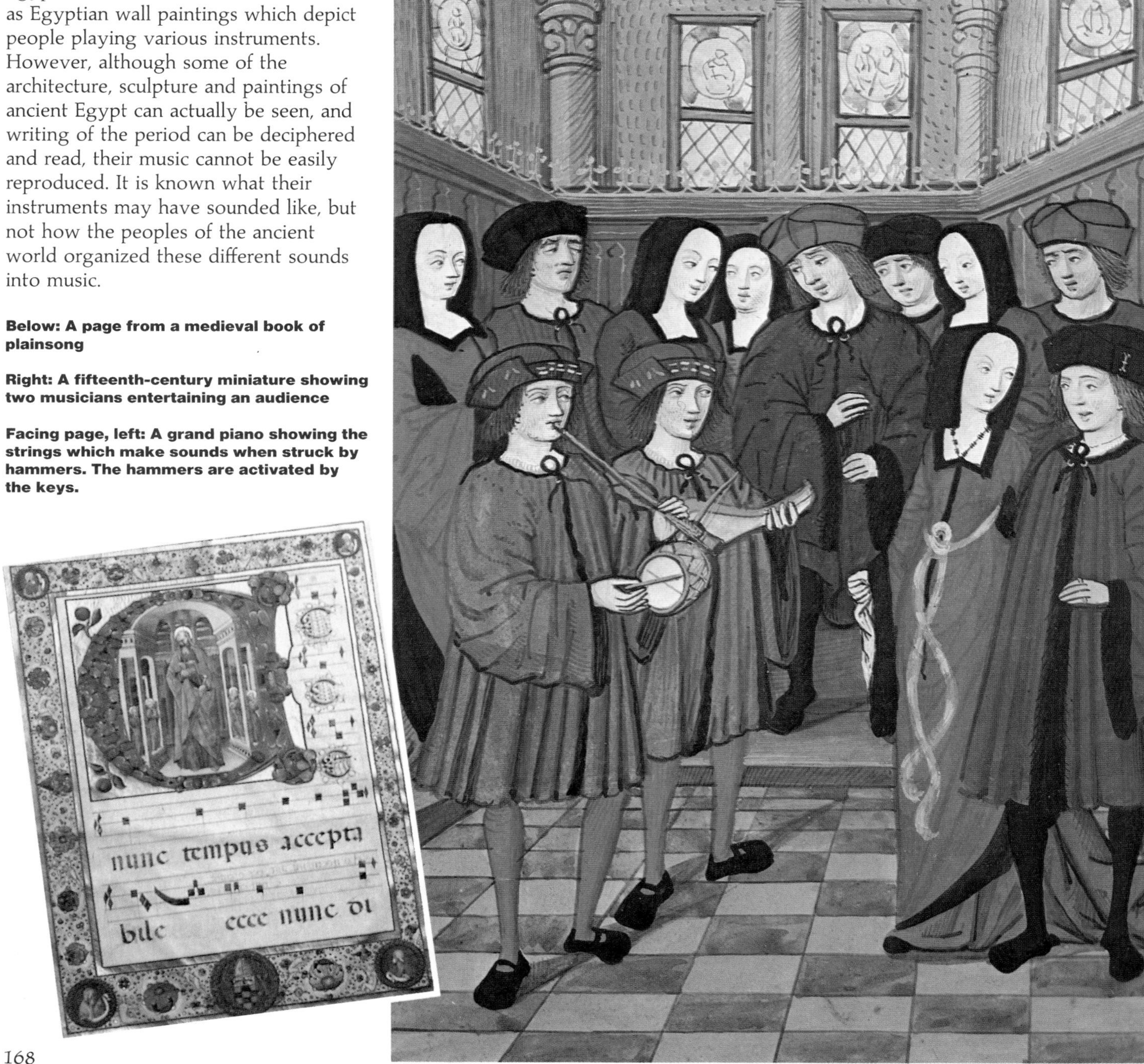

When was the greatest classical music written?

The person who did most to establish the shape of the modern orchestra and to develop the symphony was the Austrian composer Josef Haydn (1732–1809). He lived in Vienna in the eighteenth century when that city was the centre of the musical world. Mozart, Beethoven and Schubert all lived in Vienna during a period from about 1780 to 1830 when the greatest classical music was written. The nineteenth-century romantic music of Brahms, Schumann and Chopin, and the operas of Wagner and Verdi, led to the new sounds of the twentieth century.

Haydn

Mozart

Schubert

Who invented the piano?

By the seventeenth century there was a wide variety of keyboard instruments, including the virginals, clavichord, harpsichord and spinet. They were called keyboard instruments because of a series of balanced levers called "keys" which, when depressed by the fingers of the hand, operated a mechanism which plucked a set of strings. Bartolommeo Cristofori (1655-1731) invented a mechanism whereby a hammer struck the string instead of plucking it, and then immediately bounced back into its original position, leaving the string to vibrate. He called his invention the "piano forte" – literally, in Italian, the "soft loud" – because of the great range of tone it produced. In reality, it was some years before his pianofortes sounded very different from harpsichords, but he had achieved a technical breakthrough in keyboard instruments.

Where was jazz born?

The word "jazz" was first noted at the end of the nineteenth and beginning of the twentieth centuries in the poorer districts of New Orleans, Louisiana, USA. It was a form of music born among black slaves, whose roots were in Africa. The original African form of their music gradually faded away when it came into contact with music of European origin. The blacks sang in Methodist and evangelical churches and assimilated new musical styles from their new country. They came into contact with others – Italians, Scots and Spaniards – who had their own native folklore. The religious gospel songs and spirituals were heard and their theme was introduced into work songs. These are the basis of the "blues".

Blues have played an extremely important role in the history of jazz. Their very simple, melodious backgrounds have always been used as a basis for improvisations.

Among the other forerunners of jazz is "ragtime" – a dance music of West Indian origin which was very popular among white people, who transposed the skipping and syncopated rhythms, playing it in the saloons on pianos or mechanical pianolas.

When did people first sing in harmony?

For hundreds of years the only European music of which there is any definite record was religious chanting known as "plainsong". It was exactly what its name suggests – a song or melody which everybody sang together, without any kind of accompaniment. It can still be heard in some monasteries and churches today.

Harmony is the playing or singing of two or more different notes at once. It first appeared in western music in about the ninth century. Instead of everyone in the choir singing the melody on the same note, the lower and higher voices were divided so that the melody was doubled, sometimes an octave (eight notes) apart, and sometimes only four or five notes apart. This made singing easier, because the basses did not have to struggle to reach very high notes or the tenors to reach very low ones.

Why is the human voice so musical?

The musical instruments which people have made for themselves down the ages have produced sounds of an amazing variety and range. However, it should be remembered that the most flexible and expressive instrument of all is the human voice. Here the sound waves are produced by air passing between the vocal cords. These are two bands of elastic-like tissue, contained in a space called the "glottis", which in turn is found in that part of the throat called the "larynx". Muscles attaching the vocal cords to the glottis can stretch them, bend them, bring them close together or hold them apart. No other instrument can match the range of pitch and tone which these actions produce.

Above: Elvis Presley, the "King" of rock and roll, who was renowned for his strong voice

Left: A classical ballet being performed at the Scala Theatre in Milan

Why did dance begin?

Music and dance are arts which grew up together. Dance is perhaps the older of the two, as from the earliest times people have expressed in movement their feelings of joy, anger or hatred of an enemy. Dance was often led by a magic-maker as part of a religious ceremony. He would lead war and hunt dances, dances to bring rain and to celebrate the return of spring.

The oldest dances known today are probably the religious temple dances of the East. In the West, folk dances among country people grew from earlier dances such as the Morris. From folk dancing developed the ballroom and disco dancing of today.

Below: Dance is one of the oldest arts and every society has its own forms. Here, young Zulu men show their skill at a traditional dance.

Who was the first ballerina?

Marie Taglioni (1804–1884) was the first ballerina in the modern sense of the word, that is the female dancer who plays the chief classical roles in a company. Her Italian father, Filippo, taught her and although nearly all the ballets he devised for her were worthless and long forgotten, the influence of her style remains – even down to such small details as the traditional arrangement of the ballerina's hair, with centre parting and a bun at the back. Taglioni could take a few steps on her points, although ballet shoes were not yet stiffened enough for real point work. The male dancer, who today rivals the ballerina as a "star," was still very much in the background and existed only to display the ballerina to an adoring public.

Taglioni's most celebrated performance was in *La Sylphide* in 1832. Her pioneering talent helped create the modern ballet.

Who was Sergei Diaghilev?

The American Isadora Duncan (1878–1927), who first danced in Russia in 1905, brought new ideas and freer movement into dance. She was seen by Michael Fokine (1880–1942), a brilliant dancer who was to become the greatest choreographer in the history of dance.

Fortunately, a Russian impresario (organizer of entertainments) of genius, Sergei Diaghilev (1872–1929), was at hand to give Fokine the chance to realize his dreams. In 1909 came possibly the most exciting moment in ballet history – together with an opera company, Diaghilev brought part of the Russian ballet to Paris. Fokine was the ballet master, and among the dancers were such stars as Anna Pavlova (1881–1931) and Vaslav Nijinsky (1890–1950).

Who created Don Quixote?

The Spanish writer Miguel de Cervantes (1547-1616) wrote the famous novel *Don Quixote*. It recounts the adventures of a foolish but charming knight.

One episode from the book describes how the hero is about to engage in a fight with some windmills, imagining them to be giants. Don Quixote has read so many tales of deeds by knights of old that he wants to be like them. He therefore rides out in rusty armour with his faithful servant, Sancho Panza, to do battle with the world. All kinds of everyday things are seen by him as exciting but his adventures always end in a beating and disillusion. Cervantes' book was written as a satire, making fun of the old ideas of knightly chivalry.

Top right: Don Quixote and Sancho Panza in a painting by Salvador Dali. The scene shown is the prelude to the famous episode in which the two characters 'tilt' at windmills with their lances.

Bottom right: The great nineteenth-century Russian novelist Leo Tolstoy (1828–1910)

When was the greatest age of novel-writing?

The nineteenth century was the greatest age of novel-writing. One of the major novelists of the period was Charles Dickens. His *Pickwick Papers* was published in 1836 and was a great success. Dickens' other books include *David Copperfield* and *Oliver Twist*. There were many other novelists in England at that time. William Makepeace Thackeray's books include *Vanity Fair*, while Anthony Trollope wrote the famous *Barchester Towers*. Charlotte Brontë wrote *Jane Eyre* and her sister Emily, *Wuthering Heights*. George Eliot (Mary Ann Evans) wrote *Middlemarch*. Thomas Hardy wrote novels set in Dorset, such as *Tess of the D'Urbervilles*.

There were equally great writers in Europe during the same period. The first major Russian novelist was Nikolai Gogol who wrote *Dead Souls*. Leo Tolstoy's great work was *War and Peace* while Fyodor Dostoevsky wrote the impressive *Crime and Punishment*.

In France in the nineteenth century, Honoré de Balzac wrote ninety works in twenty years. *The Human Comedy* is a series of novels giving a complete picture of life at that time. Three other important French writers active at the same time were Stendhal (Marie Henri Beyle), Emile Zola, and Gustave Flaubert.

Who was the first English novelist?

The eighteenth century saw the rise and development of a new and major literary form – the novel. There had been earlier works which were true novels, like *Don Quixote*, and there had been works which were close to the novel in form, such as *Gulliver's Travels* by Jonathan Swift (1667-1745). Swift intended this work as a social and political satire, but it is also an excellent tale of fantasy–adventure in its own right and is more often read in this way today than as Swift intended it to be.

Daniel Defoe (1660-1731) was the first true English novelist, however. His *Robinson Crusoe*, the story of a castaway on an island, based on a real-life character, has never lost its popularity and is still much read today.

What was the Romantic movement?

The Romantic movement in literature borrowed from all sources, but its central beliefs were in the power of the creative imagination, the necessity for genius to overthrow rules, and in Nature as a source of inspiration. It began with the publication of the *Lyrical Ballad* by William Wordsworth (1770-1850) and Samuel Taylor Coleridge (1772-1834) in 1798. The aims of these poets were simplicity of form and the use of ordinary everyday speech for their poetry.

Later, George Gordon, Lord Byron, (1788-1824) enjoyed European fame as a romantic poet and satirist. The other two romantic poets of the age were Percy Bysshe Shelley (1792-1822) and John Keats (1795-1821). Keats was not really interested in literary fashions. For him the essential doctrine both for poetry and life was "What the imagination seizes as beauty must be truth" - in other words "Beauty is truth, truth beauty". His odes are among the greatest in English poetry.

Right: An illustration by Arthur Rackham of an episode from *Alice's Adventures in Wonderland*

Below: George Gordon, Lord Byron (1788–1824)

Was there a real Alice in Wonderland?

One hot summer afternoon Alice chased the White Rabbit down a rabbit hole and began her strange *Adventures in Wonderland*. This story by Lewis Carroll is one of the most famous children's books ever written but it appeals to people of all ages. Carroll's real name was Rev. Charles Dodgson (1832–1898) and he was a lecturer in mathematics at Oxford. The real Alice was Alice Liddell, who with her sisters went on river expeditions with Rev. Dodgson, during which he told them the story, piece by piece. Alice's adventures also appeared in *Through the Looking Glass.*

How did drama begin?

Drama grew out of religious festivals and dances. The Greeks of nearly 3,000 years ago were the first to make these dramatic and the first to write plays and build theatres in which to act them. At first, dances were performed on a dance floor on a hillside, so that people could see. Then the Greeks built amphitheatres with seats cut into the hill in a semicircle. Gradually, theatres developed from this.

Eventually Sophocles, one of the three great Greek writers of tragedies, introduced stage scenery. He wrote at least 120 plays but only seven of them are performed today. His three plays about King Oedipus are probably the best known. The other two famous writers of tragedies were Aeschylus and Euripides. Another Greek playwright, Aristophanes, is famous for writing comedies – plays with happy endings. These four playwrights lived around the fourth and fifth centuries BC.

How did theatre design develop?

During the Middle Ages, theatre stages were of timber and could usually be dismantled. They were raised up, with a curtained area beneath as a room for the actors who reached the stage by climbing up a small ladder. There were often several stages, each representing a different setting, and during the performance the actors moved from "heaven" to "hell" or from "home" to the "tavern". The audience stood around the raised stages, leaving space for the actors to perform on the ground if necessary.

From the sixteenth century onwards, two types of stage were used. In England, during the late 1500s, the stage consisted of a platform which projected out into the audience and of a small structure at the back, the "tiring house" (or "house of the actors"), which was used by the actors when they were not performing and by musicians who played during the performances.

The other type of stage was found in Italy where temporary stages were erected in the courtyards and halls of palaces – it was only later that buildings were specifically designed as theatres. The greatest Italian theatre designer was Andrea Palladio (1508–1580).

Left: The Greek amphitheatre at Taormina, which was built in the third century BC

Below: A modern stage. It is designed to revolve so that scene changes can take place rapidly.

How many plays did Shakespeare write?

William Shakespeare (1564–1616) is probably the world's greatest playwright, yet little is known about his early life except that he was born in Stratford-upon-Avon, Warwickshire and was married in 1582 to Anne Hathaway. He went to London about 1585, became an actor and began to write his plays and poems.

In 1592 the London theatres were closed because of the Plague and did not reopen for two years. But when they did, Shakespeare was writing a new kind of romantic comedy, in which characters were more important than story. To this group belong *The Merchant of Venice*, *As You Like It* and *Twelfth Night*.

By 1600 he had become interested in tragedy, and to this period belong perhaps the most famous of all his plays – *Hamlet*, *Macbeth*, *Othello* and *King Lear*. His later plays, sometimes seeming close to tragedy, are *Cymbeline*, *The Winter's Tale* and *The Tempest*. After this, Shakespeare returned to Stratford-upon-Avon, where he lived until his death.

Shakespeare's range is enormous and expresses every emotion known to humankind. Thirty-seven plays are attributed to him although there is doubt about whether he wrote all of them.

Below: William Shakespeare (1564–1616)

Above: A *commedia dell'arte* presentation

When did the commedia dell'arte start?

It is not known exactly when the unwritten comedies of the Italian *commedia dell'arte all' improviso* (meaning professional improvised comedy) were first performed. Certainly by the end of the sixteenth century they were acted all over Europe. Leading figures from the *commedia dell'arte* were popular as toy theatre characters. They included Arlecchino, (Harlequin), and Pulcinella – the pierrot who became Mr Punch in England. Wearing masks, the actors in *commedia dell'arte* plays were expected to dance, sing, play the fool and perform acrobatics as well as act.

How did opera start?

During the sixteenth century, Count Giovanni Bardi (1534–1612), who lived in Florence, had the idea of setting some of the plays and legends of ancient Greece to music. The idea appealed to other Italian poets and musicians of the time, and they formed themselves into a group called the *camerata*. Vincenzo Galilei (1520–1591), father of the astronomer and scientist, Galileo Galilei, was one of them.

This was how opera started. Opera is a combination of drama and music, requiring both a stage and an orchestra for its performance. Some of the first operas were written by Jacopo Peri (1561–1633). In them the dramatic action on stage was still much more important than the music. But with Claudio Monteverdi (1567–1643), music became the chief ingredient of opera.

What does a theatre director do?

A theatre director shapes and interprets a play in the way a conductor shapes and interprets a symphony – to the greater glory of the playwright or composer. At least, that is the aim of the good director, although it is possible for a director to distort plays much more disastrously than actors ever can. One of the first and most influential directors of modern times was the Russian, Constantin Stanislavsky (1865–1938), who produced many of Chekov's plays and inspired actors to "live" their parts on the stage. He tried to produce the "complete illusion of reality" in actors and productions. Not everyone accepts his methods but nevertheless perhaps his greatest achievement was to make actors *think* more about their work.

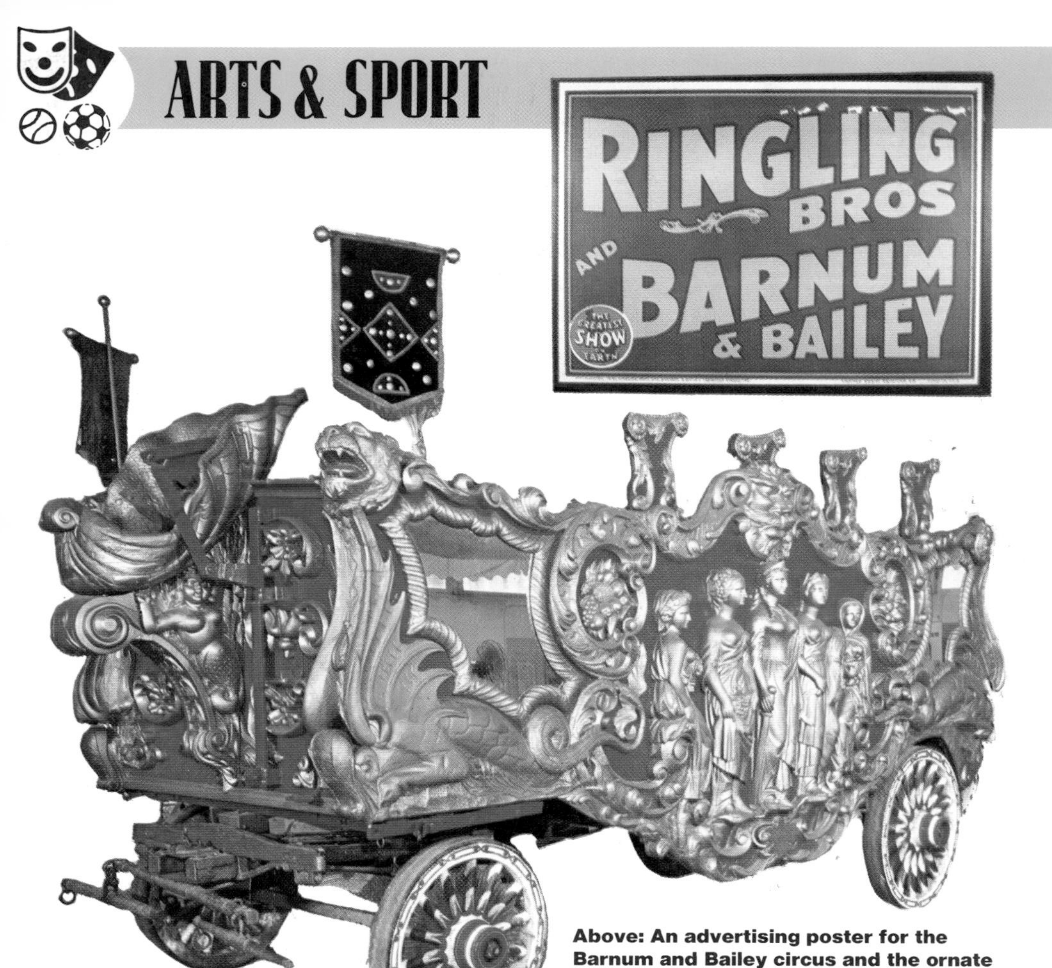

Above: An advertising poster for the Barnum and Bailey circus and the ornate parade carriage used in the shows

Below: Charlie Chaplin (1889–1977)

What was "The Greatest Show on Earth"?

In the past, fairground entertainers travelled the country to give their shows. From these shows grew the "circus". One of the first European circuses was staged by Philip Astley in England in the late 1700s. At first horses were the only performing animals but later lions, elephants, bears, sea lions and other animals became part of the circus.

The circus took place inside a huge tent called the Big Top. The sawdust-strewn arena inside was the "ring", and the man who introduced the circus acts was the "ring master". As well as animals, there were clowns, jugglers, horseback riders, strong men, trapeze artists and tightrope walkers. The world's largest circus was Barnum and Bailey's, in the USA. It was proudly called "The Greatest Show on Earth". Today, the Moscow State Circus of the USSR is one of the best circuses.

How did Hollywood become famous?

The first, silent films were shown in the 1890s, usually as part of a music-hall show. An early film of railway trains entering a station alarmed its audiences who thought the trains were coming straight at them.

By 1901 a Frenchman, Georges Méliès, was making story films. America's first story film was *The Great Train Robbery* in 1903. Two of the first film stars were Mary Pickford and Charlie Chaplin. American film-making developed and Hollywood, near Los Angeles in California, was established as a film centre.

During the 1930s and 1940s, vast sections of the world's population went to the cinema, usually twice a week. These were the golden years of Hollywood – the world's film capital.

Which are the most popular horror film monsters?

Since time immemorial people have made representations of their fears by creating terrifying monsters. Among those remembered from the days of ancient Greece are: Argus with the hundred eyes, who slew Echidna, half beautiful woman and half serpent; the Harpies, grossly deformed birds; Polyphemus and the Cyclops, giants each with a single eye; the terrible Medusa, whose head was covered with wriggling snakes in place of hair; and the Minotaur, with the head of a bull and the body of a man.

In modern times, monsters and vampires have become popular subjects for the cinema. The most popular film monster is perhaps Dracula, portrayed by Bela Lugosi in 1931, closely followed by the monster created by Boris Karloff in *Frankenstein* (1931). In 1933, Merian C. Cooper and Ernest B. Schoedsack filmed *King Kong* with a gigantic gorilla as the main character. Science fiction has created an entirely new breed of monsters to delight (and scare) audiences.

How has entertainment changed?

)nce, almost all entertainment was 'live''. People made their own music at ome, or went to the theatre, concert all or music hall (vaudeville). But this hanged with the invention of radio by ;uglielmo Marconi in the 1890s, the rrival of the cinema, and, in the 1930s, f television. Soon after the First World Var (1914–1918), radio stations began o broadcast programmes of talks, plays nd music. People bought "wireless sets" o listen and enjoy a new experience – ome entertainment over the radio vaves.

Films were invented at about the same ime as radio and millions of people 'isited the cinema every week during he 1930s and 1940s. At first there was o sound and the films were in black and vhite only. Talking pictures arrived in 927, soon followed by colour. In the 930s, Hollywood became the "movie apital of the world", and audiences in very country watched westerns, ;angster films and musicals. Walt Disney rought a new cinematic art – the nimated cartoon – to a huge film (and ater television) audience.

light: A scene from *Pinocchio*, one of Walt isney's most popular films
nset: Mickey Mouse, the most famous of isney's characters

elow: Boris Karloff playing Frankenstein in he 1931 film of that name

When did television broadcasting start?

With the radio and the gramophone, people could enjoy sound entertainment at home. On television, they could see pictures too. Television was invented in the 1920s and the first regular TV broadcasts were begun in Britain in 1936. It rapidly took over from radio as the most popular form of home entertainment, and as a result fewer people went to the cinema.

In some countries, all broadcasting is controlled by the government. In others, there are many small independent radio and TV stations, which transmit programmes paid for by advertising. Satellites in orbit around the Earth can now relay TV signals around the world, so a viewer in the USA can watch a live programme from Europe, India, or Australia. With a dish aerial, a viewer can pick up hundreds of programmes in different languages from different countries – a wonder undreamed of 100 years ago.

Below: An early television receiver with a circular screen

When did sport begin?

People have played games of various kinds since our early ancestors lived in caves during the Stone Age. The oldest of all sports is probably hunting. Prehistoric people had to hunt animals for food, but they would also have been proud to show off their skill with the spear or bow.

The ancient Egyptians enjoyed hunting and chariot racing 4,000 years ago. Centuries later, during the ancient Olympic Games, the Greeks exhibited their physical strength and skill in sporting contests. In Roman times, people flocked to the arenas to watch races and contests between gladiators. In Rome itself, the Circus Maximus, a huge arena used for horse races, was even bigger than the sports stadiums of today, holding 250,000 people.

It was in the nineteenth century that enthusiasm for most modern sports grew. At this time, increasing numbers of people began to play games for both exercise and recreation.

Above: The opening ceremony of the first of the modern Olympic Games held in Athens in 1896

Below: Basketball was one of the first sports to have formal rules. They were written down by James Naismith in 1891.

When were sports given modern rules?

The ancient Greeks knew that sport was good exercise for the body. They also believed that it helped to develop the mind and character. They thought of sport as being just as important as science or the arts. During the nineteenth century, people in Europe and the USA began to think in the same way and as a result organized sport began.

The early nineteenth century was the time of the Industrial Revolution. More and more people were moving from the countryside to work in factories in towns. Schools and universities were the first to take many sports seriously enough to formulate rules. The first football rules, for example, were drawn up by representatives of public schools in 1846, while basketball was formalized in 1891 by James Naismith at a YMCA training school in the USA. Town workers soon followed the students' example and formed their own sports clubs. The modern rules of many sports were drawn up at this time, although boxing had written rules as early as 1743 and cricket as early as 1744. In time, many sports that had originated as purely amateur opened their doors to professionalism.

How old are the Olympic Games?

The Olympic Games are the greatest international festival of sport. They are a revival of the ancient games of Olympia in Greece, records of which exist from 776 BC, although games had been held there for hundreds of years before then. The ancient games were in honour of the god Zeus and, like today's, were held every four years, the last being in AD 393, after which they were banned by the Roman emperor, Theodosius. Olympia then declined rapidly.

The revival of the Olympics was the inspiration of Baron Pierre de Coubertin, a Frenchman, and the first of the modern games was held in Athens in 1896. The first separate Winter Olympics were held at Chamonix in 1924.

When were Olympic gold medals first awarded?

Nowadays, an Olympic gold medal is one of the most coveted prizes in all sport. When the modern games began in 1896, the winners of each event won a silver medal, and those who came second a bronze. Gold medals were first awarded in 1908, with the silver going to the person who came second and the bronze to the one who came third.

The current design of the medals was the work of an Italian, Professor Giuseppe Cassioli, and it depicts victory, fraternity and universality. All medals now bear the name of the appropriate sport, and are attached to a removable chain or ribbon. The names of all winners are inscribed upon the walls of the stadium.

What is the purpose of sport?

The main purpose of sport is enjoyment. It brings a sense of achievement as skill and performance improve. But it also brings other things. If people train and play hard, they become fitter and their bodies become suppler and stronger.

There is a Latin phrase, *mens sana in corpore sano* (a sound mind in a sound body), which expresses the fact that if the body is fit then the mind will be too.

Which are the most popular winter sports?

The most popular winter sports are skiing, skating and tobogganing. These sports were originally enjoyed by people living in cold climates who had to travel over snow and ice on skates, skis or sleds. Today, many more people can travel to enjoy a winter sports holiday at a tourist resort. Here beginners on ice skates can admire the speed and grace of expert skaters. Skiers race downhill over the snow slopes and ski-jumpers launch themselves into the air from the tops of high ski-ramps. Toboggan and bobsled racers hurtle down twisting courses such as the famous Cresta Run in Switzerland. Every four years the best winter sports athletes meet in the Winter Olympics, first held in 1924.

Above: Many people now participate in walks and marathons in some of the world's major cities. Here hundreds of people are engaged in a 20 km walk in Milan, Italy.

Below left: Winners of the bronze, silver and gold medals for the 200 metres at the 1980 Moscow Olympics

Below: Skiing is one of the most popular winter sports.

3M Office
EUROSYSTEM
3M Office
EUROSYSTEM
58
3M Office
EUROSYSTEM
51
42
71

Which football games use an oval ball?

Soccer is played with a round ball. Other major football games, including American football and rugby football, are played with an oval ball. According to legend, rugby football began in 1823 when a boy at Rugby School in England picked up the ball and ran with it. Britain is, therefore, the home of rugby, which is also played in France, Australia, New Zealand, South Africa, Argentina, Romania, Fiji and now Japan and the USSR. American "gridiron" football dates from 1873 when college students agreed on rules. It is very popular in the USA and has spread to other countries. Australia and Canada also have their own football games, and use an oval ball.

Who played in most soccer World Cups?

The only player to play in five World Cup final tournaments is Antonio Carbajal of Mexico, who kept goal on eleven occasions in the finals of 1950, 1954, 1958, 1962 and 1966. The most appearances in World Cup finals were made by Uwe Seeler, of West Germany, who played twenty-one times in 1958, 1962, 1966 and 1970. Pelé of Brazil played fourteen times in the same four final tournaments, and on three occasions was in the World Cup winning squad (although he did not play in the 1962 final because of injury).

Who is Brazil's most famous soccer star?

Pelé (1940–), perhaps the most famous footballer of all, was born Edson Arantes do Nascimento in Tres Coracoes, Brazil. A complete attacking player, he was first noticed by the world when he scored a brilliant goal in the 1958 World Cup Final, when only seventeen. He played in the World Cup finals of 1962 and 1966, and had another brilliant tournament when Brazil won in 1970. He won numerous medals with his club, Santos, played at the end of his career for New York Cosmos, and, in all, scored over 1,200 goals, 97 in 110 matches for Brazil.

Which are the two main forms of competition in golf?

Golf is played throughout the world, and a universal handicapping system allows players of unequal skill to compete satisfactorily. The origins of the game are obscure, but Scottish claims to its invention are as strong as any.

There are two main forms of competition. Stroke-play (or medal play) is used for almost all major championships, in which golfers count their total strokes for the round or rounds – the golfer with the lowest total wins. Match-play is when two sides play on a hole-by-hole basis, the winner being the side that wins most holes. Most major professional championships consist of four rounds of stroke-play. Every two years a team representing Britain and Europe plays against the USA for the Ryder Cup.

Facing page.
Top: A rugby scrum
Bottom: American football, which is derived from rugby, was first played in 1873. The characteristic "armour" of the players protects them from injury.

Left: Pelé (1940–), one of the most brilliant footballers of all time

Below left: A game of ice hockey in progress

Which country invented ice hockey?

Ice hockey is played on an ice rink between two teams of six men wearing ice skates and protective clothing, using sticks to play a circular rubber disc called a "puck" into the opponents' goal. Up to eleven substitutes are allowed. The game originated in Canada in about 1860. Canada remains a strong nation in this sport, but has been overtaken in the amateur game by the USSR. Sweden, Czechoslovakia, the USA and Finland are also strong. There are good professional leagues in the USA and Canada, where the Stanley Cup is the chief prize.

What are the origins of tennis?

The first tennis tournament was held at Wimbledon, England, in 1877, and was a men's singles event. The success of this event meant that the popularity of tennis spread to the rest of the world, and major competitions both within and between countries have now been established, with the professionals earning vast amounts of prize money. Major tournaments are: Wimbledon (England), Roland-Garros (France), Flushing Meadow (USA) and a variety of venues in Australia. This game can be enjoyed by amateurs and professionals.

What is the origin of polo?

A number of traditional sports originated in ancient times when they were helpful in training warriors for battle. In Europe during the Middle Ages there were tournaments at which armoured knights fought mock battles called "jousts". Warriors on horseback loved to show off their skill. The ancient Persians and Indians played polo, a game a little like hockey on horseback that was invented by the skilful warrior-horsemen of the Central Asian plains. Playing polo was excellent riding practice for these expert cavalry soldiers.

How is the score kept in archery?

A championship target in archery, often made of basketwork, has concentric rings, and the scoring is one for an arrow in the white, three for black, five for blue, seven for red and nine for gold.

Archery has its own terminology and the parts of a bow and arrow have their special names. The tip of an arrow is called the "pile"; the notched end that fits into the bowstring is the "nock". The positions of the hands, and the techniques of sighting and drawing the bow are best learned by instruction from an expert.

Below: Archery targets with their concentric rings of different colours clearly visible

Below left: A game of polo in progress. The ball is made of wood.

What is dragster racing?

A "dragster" is a specially adapted car o motorbike, "hotted up" to achieve maximum acceleration in a short time. Dragster (or drag) races are held on a straight track only 400 m long and each race lasts only a very few seconds. The winner is the competitor with the fastest getaway.

When did sport on wheels begin?

Motor car racing started soon after the invention of the motor car in the 1880s. Today, there are Grand Prix races for high-speed motor cars, rallies across country roads, drag races and stockcar races for specially adapted vehicles. Motorcycles too are raced, on road circuits and over muddy "scramble" courses. Speedway races for motorcycles are held on special dirt tracks.

Cycle racing also began in the nineteenth century. Modern racing bikes incorporate the latest technology, but the rider must still be a highly trained athlete. Huge crowds follow the progress of the cyclists in important road races such as the *Tour de France*.

When were board games invented?

Board and table games are among the oldest games known. Chess, for example, was first played some 1,500 years ago, probably in India or China. A similar but simpler board game is draughts (called checkers in the USA). It is fascinating to think that people have been playing board games like "snakes and ladders" for thousands of years. In prehistoric times, the players probably used animal bones or stones as dice and counters.

Playing cards were first used in the ancient Far East and arrived in Europe during the fourteenth century, possibly introduced by returning Crusaders. Some games, such as bridge, require considerable skill.

Left: A painting from the second century BC apparently showing an ancient Egyptian playing chess

Above: The renowned Italian racing cyclist Francesco Moser

INDEX

Bold page numbers refer to illustrations.

Acknowledgements

Colour Library International p.111 (right); National Aeronautics and Space Administration, Washington p.39 (right); North West Thames Regional Health Authority, London p.77